WHAT
MURDER
LEAVES
BEHIND
The Victim's Family

Also by Doug Magee

SLOW COMING DARK:
Interviews on Death Row

WHAT
MURDER
LEAVES
BEHIND
The Victim's Family

By Doug Magee

ILLUSTRATED WITH PHOTOGRAPHS

DODD, MEAD & COMPANY · NEW YORK

1   2   3   4   5   6   7   8   9   10

Library of Congress Cataloging in Publication Data

Magee, Doug, 1947–
What murder leaves behind.

1.Victims of crimes—United States—Family
relationships—Case studies. 1. Title.
HV6250.3.U5M29   1983   362.8'8   83–5181
ISBN 0–396–08153–3

This book is for my son, Tim, who went along for the ride but who helped more than he'll ever know

Contents

Acknowledgments

THE FAMILIES who agreed to be interviewed for this book are its true authors. I have tried to put on the printed page both the letter and spirit of the stories they told me. To them I would like to give my heartfelt thanks and appreciation for their time, for the care they took with my questions, for their candor and good humor, and for their willingness to use their often painful thoughts, feelings, and experiences to educate us all.

Charlotte Hullinger of Parents of Murdered Children was enormously helpful in both the conception of this work and its execution.

I would like to thank the following people for their contributions to this book: Steve Levine, Connie Adelman, Scharlette Holdman, John Vodicka, Jeff Blum, Dan Miraflor, Laurie Etter, Susan Cary, Marie Deans, Rosemary Masters, Cecily O'Connor, Verdiacee Hampton-Gaston, Linda Esposito, Ruth Magee, Debby Ray, Margarette Karson, Ann Jonas, Stella Finley, Alice Cobb, Howard Zehr, John Genovese, Geoff Henning, Rick Homan, Richard Sanders, David Felton, and Harvey Chupp.

My special thanks to Larry Cox, who introduced me to the Hullingers and whose deep concern for victims' families has influenced me greatly, and to Roberta Tzavaras, who read the manuscript, who made many valuable corrections, and who tolerated a sometimes brooding writer in our house.

Lois Krieger championed this project from the first she heard of it and edited it with great care. Without her this book would not be.

Introduction

In the aftermath of murder we turn our attention to the murderer. That, of course, is where the action is. The chase, the arrest, and the trial are all served up to us as the story, and we rarely protest. The police make a frantic search and a sometimes dangerous arrest, and the cameras are right there, following the handcuffed suspect from the police station to the jail. The cameras are both inside and outside the courtroom, and now with the return of the death penalty, the cameras are even on the scene when the punishment of a few convicted murderers is carried out.

Occasionally, in all this, we will see the victim's family. In the time immediately after the murder we may catch a minute or two of a husband or a wife or a parent, squinting in the hot television lights, pausing to cry, and then trying to put words to some of the worst feelings imaginable. Or we may see a dramatic burial scene or an angry family charging out of a courtroom. But we usually only glimpse these families and we only do so when they fit in with the larger story; the families remain peripheral to the activity surrounding the murderer.

There are reasons for this. The person accused of a murder is alive, the victim is not. The victim's family usually can tell us nothing about the murder itself, whereas the police, the courts, and the suspect can. All the victim's family can tell us, we assume, is about their grief and their rage—things we would rather not hear.

We hope, of course, that they will be able to overcome their tragedy, and we assume that the people they come in contact with every day will take care of them.

This book looks at the aftermath of murder differently. The murderer no longer holds center stage, and the drama we normally associate with the aftermath of murder is not the one we see. Instead of our normal viewpoint, we see the days, months, and years after a murder through the eyes of the victim's family. And instead of focusing on the murder, we come to see something of what murder leaves behind.

My introduction to this viewpoint came in 1981, when I first met Bob and Charlotte Hullinger. The Hullingers are the founders of a self-help organization called Parents of Murdered Children. In 1978 Lisa Hullinger, then nineteen, was killed by an ex-boyfriend while the two of them were exchange students in Germany. Several months later Bob and Charlotte, who had encountered what Charlotte calls "a conspiracy of silence" from people around them who could not talk about the murder, began to meet with a few other couples whose children had been murdered. In 1981 Parents of Murdered Children had grown from that Cincinnati group to a national organization with chapters in fifteen states. Charlotte had by that time spent thousands of hours on the phone with members of victims' families.

During our first conversation I began to see a picture of victims' families quite different from the commonly held one. I expected to find that law enforcement agencies, prosecuting attorneys, and courts made every effort to be helpful and protective of the survivors; I saw instead, through Charlotte's eyes, that in the criminal justice system victims' families are "not in anybody's job description." I expected to find that neighbors and relatives gave support of all kinds to the families; I found instead that the survivors are often flung from normal society, even from the company of kin and, as Charlotte had been, faced with a "conspiracy of silence" from those around them, especially when it comes to the subject of murder; I found that members of the helping professions often do not know how to deal with victims' families and, in the case of religious counselors, frequently add to a family's grief by using inappropriate theology to explain a murder ("it was God's will") or by suggesting that in some indirect way the family was to blame for the murder; and I found that the normal grief process families go through in the aftermath of the death of a family member—even sudden, early, or accidental death—a process that has certain definite stages and can be charted on a fairly reliable timetable, often doesn't apply to victims' families, whose healing is frequently disrupted by everything from community response, trials, and parole hearings to lingering images of the horror of the killing itself.

All this seemed to amount to a second victimization. Charlotte agreed, mentioning several things she thought were part of the victims' families' experiences that did not need to be a part of the aftermath of a murder: marital problems and a high divorce rate among survivors, a sense of being abnormal and freakish, profound guilt in some families about having somehow caused the murder, a sense of injustice engendered as much by being excluded from the criminal justice system as by any sentence given the offender, feelings of meaninglessness and powerlessness, as well as a continuing rage and bitterness that can eventually become debilitating.

Charlotte went on to say that victims' families need to be understood as normal, ordinary people who have been forced to live through a horrible, extraordinary experience. Their stories, told from their own viewpoint, need to see the light of day.

The sample of victims' families in this book is small when you consider that from 1973 to 1981, roughly the period covered by these stories, there were approximately two hundred thousand murders in the United States. Even as a cross section of victims' families this selection does not conform to the statistics on murder victims. If it did, nearly half of the murders would have been committed in the South, over 40 percent of the victims would have been black, and over half of the victims would have been killed by an acquaintance or a friend or relative.

But this is not a book of statistics; it is a book of stories. I am not a social scientist, and this is not *the* cross section of victims' families;

but it is certainly *a* cross section. There is in these accounts a full range of families' experiences in the aftermath of murder.

This is not, strictly speaking, balanced journalism, either. I have tried to tell these stories in the manner and sometimes in the language in which they were told to me. The point of view here is almost exclusively that of the families. I have tried to make reading this book something like attending a Parents of Murdered Children meeting in which people talk to each other about their children, about the murders, and about the things that have happened to them since the murders.

The accounts in this book have as much to do with the way our society reacts to murder and the survivors of murder victims as it does with the victims' families themselves. Feelings of isolation, whether they are caused by a police officer who is not sensitive to the victim's family, a court system that wants nothing to do with the family of the murder victim, or friends and relatives who, by refusing to talk about the murder, make the family feel like outsiders—all are probably at the core of the most devastating aspects of the families' experiences. Grief, shock, anger, revenge, loss, rage, and horror are certainly normal reactions to the murder of a loved one. But all of these are intensified and prolonged by a family's feeling alone, cut off from normal society. Conversely, families who experience only minimal isolation or are immediately given close support by their communities are in a better position to heal and to try to come to terms with the murder.

Victims' families remind us of our own vulnerability: if a murder can take the life of someone in the family down the street, the brother of a co-worker or a distant relative, what's to prevent us from losing someone in our family to murder? Such a reminder can easily lead us to fear victims' families and through our fear to isolate them in one way or another. Pity for the families can isolate them just as much as avoidance.

In the aftermath of murder, which is perhaps the most profound injustice, families need some sense of counterbalancing justice. Exactly what that justice might entail differs from family to family, but the community usually plays as big a role in delivering that justice as any sentence given the offender. This paragraph from the first report of the Families of Homicide Victims Project of New York City's Victim Services Agency speaks to the point:

> We have learned . . . that families expect from the criminal justice system something more subtle and more complex than just punishment of the offender. These families have experienced the failure of what is perhaps the most fundamental task of society—to preserve their physical safety. They feel vulnerable, helpless, and set apart. They look to the police and courts to give them formal acknowledgement of the wrongs against them. They expect from the courts a ritualistic expression of regret and concern.

To some degree the failure of society to respond to victims' families is being addressed by the current interest in victims' rights. Legislation to assure victims and victims' families certain rights has passed or is being considered in the U.S. Congress (the Heinz-Laxalt Omnibus Victim's Protection Bill was enacted in 1982) and in a number of state legislatures. Often these bills are proposed as a way to balance the legislation and court decisions of the last few decades that expanded the rights of the accused and of convicted offenders. The thrust of most of the legislation is to protect victims who are also witnesses and to give victims and victims' families access to the judicial process that they have in the past been denied. Under some of the proposed legislation victims' families would be kept informed of the disposition of their case, would be allowed to make a statement to the court on behalf of the murder victim, and would be advised of upcoming appeals and parole hearings.

Thirty-six states have already enacted legislation to compensate victims and survivors. Usually, for the families, victims' compensation means money for burial and funeral expenses. In some states, such as New York, counseling and facilitated groups are available to the families, although not yet mandated by law. Most of those I interviewed were unaware of such compensation or did not know how or simply did not want to apply for it. Some victims' rights legislation, such as the Heinz-Laxalt bill, has stipulated that there be restitution paid to victims' families by the convicted murderer, and where the murderer is unable to pay, the government will pay restitution. New Jersey's supreme court has upheld a law that requires payments to victims' families as a condition for the parole of murderers. And recently there have been several instances in which courts have, in civil suits, awarded substantial damages to be paid by murderers to their victims' families.

Although many of the reforms now being proposed under the broad banner of victims' rights are welcomed by victims' families, these legislative efforts and the bureaucratic programs that will follow them will not go to the heart of the problems faced by survivors. The government and the criminal justice system certainly need to improve their efforts on behalf of victims' families, but the people closest to the survivors—friends, relatives, neighbors, religious counselors, and the helping professionals—are going to be more important to the well-being of victims' families than any legislation or judicial rule changes. If we continue to treat victims' families as outsiders, as people who are in some way tainted by the murder of a loved one, then we will both increase their misery and decrease our ability to be of help and to begin to understand their experience.

Many of the subjects of this book became active in some organization, such as Parents of Murdered Children, or a political action group, after the murder of their family member. Several became spokespersons for the groups they joined: Betty Jane Spencer for Protect the Innocent, Pat Burke for Concerned Citizens for Correctional Officers, and Camille Bell for the Committee to Stop Children's Murders. The reasons for such activity are varied: it is a way to help others who are suffering alone, it is a way out of one's own suffering, and it is a way to let other people learn from one's experience.

The reason we are willing to listen to members of victims' families who testify before legislative committees and speak out publicly is that they have been through an experience, which, as horrible as it is, has given them an authority, an insight, and a wisdom that few of us can or would want to claim. Yet though we need very much to listen to the things victims' families can tell us, we cannot afford to think of them as people above debate and criticism. To do so would be one more way of not treating them as human beings who are an integral part of our society. The less we isolate victims' families, the more we talk to them and the more we include them in our discussions without giving them undue deference, the more we will see them as full people and the better prepared we will be to learn from their experiences.

My first book, *Slow Coming Dark*, was a book of interviews with people on death row; in it I firmly stated my opposition to capital punishment. My feelings haven't changed since then. There are those who would like us to believe that opposition to the death penalty indicates either a direct or indirect lack of concern for victims' families. Victims' families want the death penalty, this argument runs, and so to oppose capital punishment is to oppose the families. Of course a substantial majority of victims' families would like to see the death penalty used, at least in their cases, but there is by no means unanimity on the issue. The first victims' families I met were through my work against the death penalty, and thus very concerned about the use of the death penalty and upset that, because they were members of a victim's family, they would be assumed to be in favor of capital punishment.

I am always bothered when, talking about the death penalty to a college audience, I am asked, "What about the victim and what about the victim's family?" The question is usually stated as an accusation. Nothing about opposition to the death penalty necessarily precludes concern for victims' families. The death penalty, in fact, focuses inordinate attention on the criminal to the detriment of the victims' families. We all know Gary Gilmore's name, but few of us know the names of, much less anything about, his victims.

The death penalty does not play a big part in the profiles in this book. I have not avoided the issue, and I have tried to report the families' feelings accurately. But the subject came up infrequently in the interviews, and when it did come up the families usually discussed it as some faraway punishment that had little real bearing on their lives. The people I spoke with who sincerely wanted revenge were most anxious to take it themselves and not rely on the criminal justice system.

Many of the problems I have mentioned here have to do with cases in which a suspect is caught and tried. In three of the cases in this book, though, the murder is as yet unsolved. Such a situation, as you will see, presents the families with a whole subset of problems. These families may not have to go through the agony of a trial, but often they feel they would prefer to endure one simply to know who killed their loved one and why. They want desperately to clear up the mystery.

In many ways families who do know the name of the murderer have the same problem. They have a name and perhaps a motive, there is a trial and a conviction, but after it is all over there is still a mystery at the core of the whole thing: Why did this all have to happen? Each family in this book has dealt with that question in its own way; some have found satisfactory answers, some never expect to, and still others are plagued daily by the question.

The act of murder makes no sense, and it is those closest to the victim who, in murder's aftermath, bear the brunt of the absurdity. The utter senselessness of one human being killing another scares us all and it is probably only normal that we go to unusual lengths to avoid hearing directly from victims' families. But such avoidance only prolongs our state of ignorance and increases our fear. The families in this book and the hundreds of thousands of families across the country who have had similar experiences deserve better.

I

Bob Hart

In june of 1978 Bob Hart, an electrical engineer with the Veeder-Root Company in Hartford, Connecticut, took three weeks off work so that he and his wife, Liz, could have a long, relaxed vacation. Bob felt they needed it. For seven months they had been trying to start a family, and there had been tensions caused by their lack of success. Bob thought that all the tears, temperature-taking, and doctor's visits of the last half year were unnecessary and that he and Liz just needed to get away and forget about the whole thing.

As it turned out, not long into their trip, Liz realized that she was pregnant. A few weeks before they had left their home in Glastonbury for a week on Cape Cod and two weeks in Colorado, Liz had quit a job she had struggled with for a year. That must have helped, since by the time they were out on the Cape, Liz started having morning sickness. She was ecstatic.

Bob was happy too, but his was a qualified happiness. He was happy for Liz, he was glad the difficulties of the past half year were behind them, and he was glad that he was about to become a father. But he wasn't certain how having a baby would affect the carefree life he and Liz had led since they had met ten years before in college. Bob didn't know all that much about children, but he knew that having an infant was going to make it hard to do the backpacking, cross-country skiing, and sailing that he and Liz were fond of.

The nine months of pregnancy gave Bob time to prepare. When

he and Liz started taking Lamaze classes, watching birthing films, getting down on the floor and practicing the breathing techniques they would use in labor, Bob started to catch the excitement Liz had felt from the beginning. He wasn't about to sit around the waiting room while the birth took place. Not only was he going to be there and coach Liz, at the last minute he decided to tape-record as much of the birth as he could.

Tommy Hart was born on March 30, 1979, after Liz had been in labor for twelve hours. He came into the world in a soft-lit birthing room that looked more like somebody's living room than a hospital. At the end of the long labor, Liz had to be given an anesthetic and Tommy had to be brought out with a suction cup device that is the modern equivalent of forceps. During her pregnancy Liz had hoped for a girl, but once Tommy was in the world, she couldn't have been happier with her first child.

Liz's attachment to Tommy was immediate. Bob took his time. He was willing to wait and see what being a father was all about.

Tommy cried a lot the first three months, and Bob spent hours at night holding him and walking with him in a circle from the living room to the kitchen and back out to the living room. He didn't have to help out with a lot of the other tasks because Liz devoted herself to them. She was very much in her element. Early on they got carrying slings and backpacks and were able to take Tommy on hikes, show him off to people in the neighborhood, and take him with them when they ate out.

Bob had expected some disruption, but he gradually came to see Tommy as an addition. He and Liz rarely got on each other's nerves now as they had during the half year preceding the pregnancy. Indeed, they were as much in love as ever. And now, on top of that, they had another person to love.

On June 17, 1980, when Tommy was fourteen months old, Bob drove home from work, dropped a fellow worker up the road, and headed back to his house. It was a Tuesday, a warm, summery day, the last day of classes in the local schools. It was the kind of day that made Bob look forward to vacation, some sailing on the Cape, maybe, some time to spend with Liz and Tommy.

Their house sat back in a wooded area down off a road that led out of Glastonbury. From their front windows they could see a couple of houses across the road, but they were in some ways out of view, below road level. That arrangement was perfect for Bob, who was a bit shy, anxious about people watching him, afraid to speak in front of others unless he knew exactly what he was going to say. A circular dirt driveway dipped off the road and passed in front of the carport and the house.

Because the new Caprice stayed in the carport, Bob pulled into the driveway and parked in front of the house. As he did so, he noticed an object in the driveway. As he got out of the car, he realized it was Tommy. He was lying on his side in front of the empty carport. He wasn't moving. He was dressed in a diaper and T-shirt with no shoes. Liz would never have let him out like that.

Bob approached him and turned him over on his back. There were red marks up one side of him. He seemed lifeless. Bob's heart raced, but his mind began an immediate search for solutions, reasons, resolutions. He wanted to get Tommy breathing again. He pushed down on Tommy's chest. The rib cage gave way and blood oozed from Tommy's mouth. Tommy was dead.

Bob's mind began to catalogue all that was around him. Tommy was warm, there were some erratic tire tracks in the soft dirt of the driveway, Liz and the Caprice were gone. He had no way to begin to put all those things together.

Suddenly Bob felt embarrassed. He couldn't bear the thought of people driving by on the road looking down and seeing his dead baby lying in the driveway. He went into the house, got a towel out of the bathroom, and returned to the driveway. There was blood all around Tommy, so Bob covered him with the towel, picked him up and took him back into the carport. He laid him down in a small utility trailer stored there and went inside to call the police.

Though the newspaper would later report that he was incoherent when he called, he was not. It was the police who were flustered. Bob had to repeat information several times. While waiting for the police to arrive, Bob called his parents, who lived in nearby Meriden, and his sister Nancy, who lived just down the road. Nancy at first thought he was kidding. He convinced her he was not.

The shock had not numbed Bob. His mind was open and clear and running. But an explanation would not come. He noticed, while he was calling the police, that the stove was on. He didn't even consider the possibility of violence or foul play. Some accident had happened: the car had backed out of the driveway on its own, or Liz had backed over Tommy by mistake and then left in a grief-stricken frenzy. He began to think of Liz, to wonder how this was going to be for her, what she must be going through, perhaps even that she would kill herself over it. He knew that he and Liz would have to find some way to work through Tommy's death, to start over again.

Realizing that he would have a long night ahead of him, he changed into jeans, a T-shirt, and running shoes. Two cruisers were there almost immediately, but they had to wait a while for the medical examiner to pronounce Tommy dead. The police were suspicious of Bob, but not overly so. He told them what he knew. Nancy arrived, and then Bob's parents. Bob's father was teary-eyed and wouldn't look at the body. He said he wanted to remember Tommy the way he had last seen him.

When the medical examiner got there, Bob went out to watch over them. He felt that the police and the medical examiner had no right to look at his dead son. He was embarrassed for Tommy; he wanted to protect him from all these eyes. Throughout the days and months ahead, Bob would feel compelled to see and know all he could, but he would always feel that he was the only one really entitled to know and see.

Instead of crying or going to pieces, Bob struggled to be in control and to stay rational. He couldn't give in to his churning nervous system. He had too much to do: he had to figure out what was going on, what had happened.

That night, after he had talked with the police, called Liz's family, and tried, without success, to eat something, he lay on the couch while his parents sat in the living room chairs. Toward morning, his mother dozed and, while she dozed, something crept into Bob's consciousness. Perhaps someone else was involved in this whole thing. Even when the police had asked fairly pointed questions about the way he and Liz got along—did they fight?, etc.—Bob hadn't gotten the gist of the line of questioning. Tommy was dead, Liz wasn't there: there must have been an accident. But as early light began to give shape to the woods around the house, he began to imagine other possibilities.

At 9:30 A.M. on Wednesday, Bob got a call from his bank saying that someone had turned in Liz's checkbook, which had been found in the nearby town of Andover. In an instant, Bob realized that Tommy's death and Liz's disappearance were not the results of an accident.

Bob's thoughts moved from how he and Liz were going to get over the accident to what Liz must have gone through now that he was almost certain she had been killed. He began to be haunted by the ordeal she must have suffered, the ordeal that included Tommy's death. He tried to bring all these things up with his father, but his father would hear none of it. Bob's father still had hope, he wanted to believe that Liz was not dead.

Later that morning, the major crimes squad of the state police asked Bob to move out of his house so that they could look for evidence. Bob and his parents moved down to Nancy's house. Soon Liz's family, the Cushwas, and Bob's brother arrived in Glastonbury. Nancy's house was filled with people. Bob found support in Liz's family as well as in his own. The Cushwas, who had come from South Hadley, Massachusetts, Boston, and New York, were close to Bob in temperament. They had gone through the death of Liz's mother when Liz was seven, and their way of getting through such emotionally difficult times as this Wednesday gathering was to be light about some matters. This helped Bob in his anxious, nervous state.

During the day on Wednesday, the police would call or come to the house occasionally to ask for photographs of Liz, for pieces of clothing for the search dogs to sniff, and to ask more questions. About 2:00 in the afternoon, they called to say that they had found the Caprice in a field near a baseball diamond close to Bob's house. They said little about the condition of the car.

At 10:30 Wednesday night, a cruiser pulled up to Nancy's house. A state policeman came to the door and asked Bob to come outside. They said they thought they had found Liz's body. Had the policemen been five minutes later Bob would have gotten the information through the news. While he was outside talking to them, the rest of his family was watching a television newscast in which the broadcaster reported that a Connecticut Power and Light lineman had found Liz's body early that afternoon.

The two policemen and Bob moved inside to the dining room table to talk, and the family gathered in the kitchen. The officers affected a detached, objective voice in asking what Liz's wedding ring looked like and what the inscription was. When the identification seemed certain, Bob started to ask questions. The policemen's answers were sketchy. Bob wanted to know more. Had she been raped? One of the policemen answered that it appeared she had had intercourse. The implication that there had been some sort of voluntary sex made Bob angry, even though he could see that the policeman was only trying to be professional. He was able to find out that Liz had been shot, and then the policemen left.

On Thursday morning Bob and Nancy's husband, Bill, went to the morgue in Farmington to identify the bodies. Members of both families were surprised at the way Bob was controlling his emotions. He wasn't surprised, though. He felt that what was required of him in the situation was to be strong, and he knew that he could be. He was certain that he would be admired for being strong, for not being controlled by his emotions. But he was afraid to view Liz's body. Since he had learned of her death, really since he had learned of her checkbook being found and had realized that she had been killed, he had conjured up all sorts of images of her death. But he was not sure how she would actually look or how he would feel and react.

When they pulled the curtain, he could only see Liz's head behind the plate glass window. Her right eye was swollen and bruised. It was clear that she had been beaten severely. He heard them ask whether he could identify the body, but all he could say was "Poor Liz." Bob realized that he would not see her again, so he took his time. After a few minutes he turned away and said, "That's Liz."

6

He was surprised when they asked him to identify Tommy, too. Hadn't they taken him from his house, hadn't that been enough? He saw Tommy's swollen face. They had done an autopsy, but it didn't show.

Later that day Chuck Blacknay, the Cushwas' family minister from the Congregational church in South Hadley, came to Glastonbury and talked to Bob about some of the things he might expect to feel and experience in the months ahead. Bob liked the man, had known him for several years, and listened. He understood what he was going to have to go through and felt up to it, that he could control himself. But he could not stop thinking about what Liz and Tommy had been through in the last moments of their lives. He wanted to know as much about those last moments as possible.

He knew Liz had been beaten, raped, and shot, and that Tommy had been run over by the Caprice. The police had taken some rope from a garbage can at his house, so he assumed that Liz had been tied up. The police were vague about details, but Bob didn't want to be spared. Months later he would go to the state attorney's office and read through the file on the case. Wading through the technicalities of the autopsy report, he managed to get the gist of that afternoon's events. He learned that she had been beaten, tied up, and thrown into the back seat of the car, that Tommy's car seat had been ripped from its place and Tommy run over and crushed, that Liz had been driven to a deserted area near Andover, twenty minutes away, and her clothes torn, that she had been raped, shot three times at close range, and then dumped from the car.

Bob felt he had a right to know these things, more of a right than anyone else. And, as he came to know the details of the abduction and murders, he felt such sorrow for Liz, for the horror of those minutes that she had had to endure. He realized that there was nothing he could have done to prevent the murders, but he could not shake the anguish of seeing Liz and Tommy the target of such violence.

On Friday it became apparent that the police weren't about to let Bob back into his house. He had thought they were only going to keep it for a few hours, but he learned that they wouldn't give up anything without a fight. He had to demand that they let him back in. When they did it was a shambles, full of smudge marks from the fingerprinting. He had to make another fuss in order to get them to clean up; and then, a little later, he had to put up a fight to get back Liz's wedding ring. His car was impounded; they never did return it. He had to write the chairman of the board of his insurance company before he was reimbursed. On Friday he began to feel that, on top of having lost his wife and son, the police were persecuting him. Besides keeping him from his house, they gave out only scanty information about their search for the killer or killers. When Bob heard something about the case from a neighbor and went to ask the police about it, they confirmed or denied the rumor, but offered nothing more.

On Saturday both families went to South Hadley for a memorial service at the Congregational church. Bob knew that his emotions would be very close to the surface, so he went into the service with his mother after everyone was seated and left immediately after it was over. The church was packed. Chuck Blacknay gave a brief speech. Bob thought the service was a good one, appropriate to Liz's and Tommy's lives.

Afterwards, those who had attended the service gathered at the Cushwas' house. But Bob couldn't face them. Instead, he and his brother Ron, who had come from Ann Arbor, Michigan, where he was doing graduate work, and two college friends, Seg and Pam Williams, went next door. Bob had decided sometime during the last few days that he was going to have to pamper himself in the months to come. On Thursday and Friday he had found that a Beefeater gin and tonic at night smoothed out his tangled nerves. He wasn't exactly sure how he got on to Beefeater gin and tonics, but in the first year after the murders there were times when they proved very useful. One such time was after the memorial service. Bob and Ron and Seg and Pam talked and drank and it made Bob feel safe. Ron became a confidant of sorts. He told Bob that their mother, with all good intentions, had sent out an edict that they were not to discuss the particulars of the murders with Bob; she didn't want him to be upset. Nonetheless, the four talked about what they knew. Bob was able to talk about the violence and the way Liz and Tommy had looked. And he could cry.

Bob never really tried to control the crying after the first time because it made him feel better. But it would take a while, several weeks to a month, for the grief and the loss and the feelings of anguish over Liz's and Tommy's ordeal to peak, and only then would he cry. After the tears, the hurt would subside for a while.

Bob didn't have any trouble talking with others about the murders. In fact he welcomed opportunities to do so. It was easy to discuss his feelings with Ron and with Nancy, but for the most part he sensed that his family and close friends didn't want to talk much about what had happened; they were uncomfortable when the subject came up. So Bob adopted a policy of answering all questions, telling anything he knew, but not initiating discussion of the murders. When Liz's younger sister Charlotte came down a few times during the summer after the murders they talked about Liz and Tommy, but they stayed away from the subject of the violence.

In one of his interviews with the police, Bob had suggested that they talk to Larry Gates's friends for possible leads. The Gates family lived across the street—theirs was one of the houses visible from the Harts' front window—and Larry Gates, who was nineteen at the time and had just finished the eleventh grade, had a group of rowdy friends the Harts used to see tearing up and down the road in cars and trucks. When the police asked about people who might commit such violence, Bob could think of very few. Then he remembered all the commotion Larry Gates's friends caused and threw out the suggestion of talking to them.

Several days after the murders, Bob heard from neighbors that the police were talking to Larry Gates himself and that they were searching the Gates house. Bob called the police and had this information confirmed. The police followed Larry for several days.

On June 26, Larry Gates was arrested and charged with the murders. One of his palm prints had been found on the Caprice, the gun used to kill Liz had been found in a closet in the Gates house, the gun had blood on it similar to Liz's blood type, and rope found in the Gates house was of the same type as that taken from the Harts' garbage can. Larry Gates admitted to owning and having used the gun before, but denied having anything to do with Liz's or Tommy's murder. Liz had withdrawn a hundred dollars from the bank a half an hour before she had been abducted, but the money was never recovered. Larry Gates, who the police said had been having trouble scraping together money for a drug purchase, was allegedly able to buy cocaine the night of the murder. He had been seen driving around downtown while Liz was making a withdrawal from the drive-in teller the afternoon of the murders. Larry Gates was a big teenager, big enough to have committed the kidnapping, rape, and murder.

Bob didn't know much about Larry or his family, but some of the things he did know were troubling. Once, when he and Liz had taken a vacation, they had asked Larry to look after their cats and water their plants. He had done so, but when Liz asked for the key back sometime later, someone at the Gates house, Bob wasn't sure who, said that the key had been lost. And then about a year before the murders, one of the Harts' cats was missing for a long while. Finally a neighbor told Liz that he had helped Larry bury the cat after Larry said he had found it dead in the road. Larry knew the cat to be Liz and Bob's, but neither he nor the neighbor had ever said anything about the burial. Bob and Liz thought that was strange, and after Liz's murder and Larry's arrest Bob couldn't help imagining that Larry had somehow caused the cat's death as well. When Liz, who was a home economics teacher, had substituted at the local high school and had had so much trouble with the boys in her class, Larry had been one of the troublemakers. Nancy remembered seeing Larry Gates in the crowd of people that had gathered in front of the Hart house when the police had come to investigate Tommy's death.

As it became clear to Bob both who had killed Liz and Tommy and what the circumstances of the murders had been, Bob's rage surfaced. He believed the police had found the right person, and he surmised the motive to be a very general one: in the festive mood of the last day of classes, Larry had needed money for drugs, and in the process of getting it he had slaughtered Bob's family. That was the way Bob thought of it. The senselessness of the murders overwhelmed him. To his way of thinking, Larry Gates's joy ride had wiped out his own reason for existing.

Shortly after Larry Gates was arrested, he was let out on bail. His family had hired Max Heiman, a prominent defense lawyer with a reputation of being very aggressive and who was also a leader in the state bar association. Heiman had succeeded in getting the bond lowered and having the judge accept real estate for part of it. Heiman advised the family that Larry should voluntarily commit himself to a local mental institution. Gates followed his lawyer's advice, and for the next nine months, while out on bail, he was in the mental institution during the week and at home on the weekends.

Bob went back to work a week after the murder. He needed something to fill up the long days, and he felt comfortable in his work and workplace. On his first day back he went to his supervisor and told him what he expected he would be able to do and what he wanted from people at work. (His supervisor and the other engineers he worked with had come to the memorial service in South Hadley. Bob knew they were well aware of his situation.) He said that he wanted to be treated as normally as possible, that he might have problems and would perhaps need time off. His supervisor understood and said that he should feel free to take as much time off as he needed.

Bob didn't want to be seen as different, didn't want people looking at him as a victim. He felt like one, certainly; he would always feel that way. But the combination of his usual shyness and the murders made him acutely aware of stares and glances. He knew he couldn't work as well as he used to, but he wanted his colleagues to treat him as they always had. They obliged.

After Larry Gates was let out on bail, the pressure built in Bob. He could see the Gates house from his kitchen window. His brother had gone back to Michigan and he was alone in the house. He had lived with Liz so long that he was at a complete loss as to how to fill up the empty space and time. In July he took time off work and

Bob Hart

spent a couple of weeks at Liz's aunt's house in a beautiful, expensive part of the Cape. He found that his nerves were helped by the distance from Glastonbury. He realized that not only would he have to pamper himself, not only would he have to use a crutch like Beefeater gin and tonics now and then, but also he would have to escape.

Once Bob knew that Liz and Tommy's murderer lived across the street, the notion of revenge began to preoccupy him. Bob had never been an angry, vengeful sort, but his rage and the images of the killings would not go away. It seemed as if he himself had been grossly violated, and he wanted to *do* something instead of just sitting there and staring out his kitchen window. Larry Gates had taken everything from him. Bob was nothing now without his family. Revenge was the only thing that made any sense to him. Such a feeling was hard for Bob to accept, but it was there; and when he heard others express similar feelings, he took more stock in his own.

The first time that happened was after he got back from the Cape. Bob's neighbors invited him over for a barbecue one night. They had two children, one born about the same time as Tommy, and they could identify with Bob's rage. In the course of the evening, after some heavy drinking, the subject came up: What would they like to do to Gates? The man didn't hold back. He said right out that he'd like to go over and kill Larry Gates. He was drunk, but he was serious. Bob could feel both of them thinking the unthinkable in a serious way. Somewhere outside the buzz of the drinking Bob knew the man would never do it; but the surface had been cracked, and the raw feelings were right there on the table.

Later a college friend of Bob's would make a serious suggestion that they work out a way to kill Larry Gates without getting caught. This was a much more logical approach than the first, but Bob was just as certain that they would never do it.

Bob's own thoughts about revenge became increasingly determined. He fantasized about explosives, about blowing Larry and his family sky-high. He didn't care whether Larry was there or not. He was beginning to hear in the neighborhood that Larry's parents were taking their son's word, were seeing him as persecuted, and were blaming Bob for his arrest. He fantasized setting the house ablaze. When Larry was first let out, Bob bought a .22 rifle with a scope, in part for defense and in part because he thought he might use it for revenge. He had never owned or used guns, and somewhere in his mind he realized that he could not carry out the revenge he imagined. But so much had been taken from him by somebody living so close to him that he felt he had to make a serious effort to do something in return. During the year after the murders, his thoughts of wild revenge would be tempered, but he would never lose the sense of wanting to do something in response to the ordeal Liz and Tommy had had to go through. To this day he would like Gates to get the electric chair, and he fantasizes prefacing the execution by personally beating Gates and shooting him in the balls.

*   *   *

13

Early in August the president of Bob's company, who had been away during the time of the murder and had just returned, sat down with Bob in the cafeteria and told him he was sorry to hear about the killings and that if Bob wanted to take time off, the company would cover him. Bob booked a flight to Los Angeles the next day.

He spent two weeks there visiting a friend from high school, Mark Deniham. Bob and Mark thought so much alike at times it was eerie. Mark and his girl friend, Julie, had known Liz almost as long as Bob had. The four of them had partied together, sailed together, and come to be very fond of each other. Mark and Julie were perfect people for Bob to see. They would talk about Liz and indulge such common passions as Mexican food, sailing, and hiking. Bob couldn't forget Liz and Tommy, but at least he was away from Glastonbury.

He rented a twenty-six-foot Catalina sailboat and took Julie and a friend of hers, a television writer named Elizabeth, on a jaunt to Marina del Ray. The women got seasick, but Bob lapped up Beefeater gin and tonics and loved being out in the sun on the ocean. He and Mark and Julie sailed out to Santa Catalina Island one weekend; the next week they hiked up Mount Whitney and slid down a snow chute cut into the snow fields. He was living again, taking in deep breaths and getting away from Larry Gates.

A week after returning from Los Angeles, Bob went to the Cape for a weekend. On the way out he picked up Joan Murphy in Boston. Joan and Liz had been friends in college and had kept up the friendship after graduating. Joan had come down from Boston for the memorial service. During the summer Bob had dated a couple of times, and after coming back from California, he realized how much he needed to be with someone. He and Liz had been together ten years, and he was lost living alone. Joan and Bob hit it off and saw each other frequently during the next few months. Joan seemed to understand Bob's loneliness; late in November she moved to Glastonbury to live with him.

In October Bob had found a conference on analog circuitry to go to in San Francisco, and after the conference he went to Los Angeles to visit Mark. This time they went out to Joshua Tree Monument.

It was hot out in the desert, and Bob was introduced to Coors beer. His trips to Los Angeles kept him sane.

After his October trip, Bob stayed in Glastonbury until April. It was a difficult winter. He never saw Larry Gates across the road, but that wasn't necessary. Every time he swung out of his driveway he had to look in the direction of the Gates house. That was enough to remind him. In increments, the tension built. Bob and Joan planned a month-long trip that would keep them out of Glastonbury during April, when the grand jury was to meet to consider indictments against Larry.

Three months after the murders Bob had talked to several lawyers about a civil suit against Larry Gates and his family. A civil suit, Bob thought, was a way to perhaps gain some sense of justice, a way to focus his anger. He wanted the Gateses to pay for what Larry had done to Liz and Tommy. The lawyers he eventually retained for the suit began work on the case but advised not pressing the civil action until there had been indictments in the case. When Bob and Joan were away the grand jury met, indicted Larry Gates for the murders, and raised the bond under which he was out on bail. After Bob and Joan returned, it looked like the Gates family might be able to meet the raised bond. Bob's lawyers then pressed the civil suit, attaching the Gates property and thereby denying them collateral for the bond. Larry Gates was forced to wait in jail for his trial.

The month-long trip took Bob and Joan through the South and out to Canyonlands National Park in southeastern Utah. They stayed with friends and some of Liz's relatives along the way. In New Orleans, they visited Rich Birdsey and his fiancée. Rich was another high school friend of Bob's. When they got back to Connecticut, they were going to go to a reception in honor of Rich's wedding. Joan and Bob backpacked for a week through Canyonlands. They had a good time out on the road, and Bob found it difficult to go back. They arrived in Glastonbury two days before the reception.

Rich Birdsey and his wife had been married in Texas, and the reception in Meriden, where both Rich and Bob had gone to high school, was a follow-up to the wedding. It was the first time Bob had seen a lot of his high school classmates since the murders. Bob drank a lot during the reception and so did the wife of one of his high school friends. She was familiar with his situation and, after a while, began to talk about it. She didn't mince words. In emotional language she began to say things that Bob had often repeated to himself. She and Bob spent a good part of the reception walking around out on the lawn getting angrier and angrier about the murders, about Larry Gates. How, she wondered out loud, could anybody do what he had done to such a likeable person as Liz? Rage and revenge bubbled to the surface. That asshole kid messed up your entire life, Bob, she said. He slaughtered your family. Bob was not in the least disturbed by her attitude. The trip back to Connecticut had been hard, the tensions had built, and the booze kicked inhibitions out the window. The woman set Bob off. Right. Larry Gates slaughtered my whole reason for living just for an afternoon of kicks. Fuck him.

There had been so much he had wanted to say all these months, and things he hadn't allowed himself to say. He was certain that others didn't want to hear his rage. Talking about the murders recently, he had been so polite and proper. And then, having to return to Glastonbury, having to look out his kitchen window again, the dark feelings had returned. But there had been no outlet. This sloppy drunk raving was just what he needed.

He came near violence and really scared Joan. She was not afraid for herself, but for Bob. She had not seen these raw feelings before. In the car on the way home Bob cried and cried. It was scary to see someone give vent to such anger and rage and to come so clean.

When Bob woke up in the morning it was if a barrier had been broken. He was hung over and embarrassed about his behavior of the night before, but he was a different person now. From the moment he opened his eyes he could feel that he was in a new lifetime. The feelings of revenge were different, the anguish over the ordeal Tommy and Liz had gone through was different, and the grief was different. These feelings had not gone away, but Bob felt they would never threaten him the way they had in the past.

*   *   *

What did threaten Bob, though, was the prospect of having to go through Larry Gates's trial. There were two things about the trial that made him anxious. He knew that he would have to take the stand and testify, and he knew that he would have to go through cross-examination by Max Heiman. He had gone to a pretrial motion and had seen Heiman tear into an impeccable expert witness as if the man were an idiot. Bob imagined all sorts of things that Heiman might try to do to him in cross-examination. The second thing that made Bob anxious was the possibility that the state would lose its case and Gates would get either a drastically reduced sentence or go free. Robert Myers, the district attorney assigned to the case, was a competent man, Bob thought, and he told Bob that with the evidence they had they should not lose the case. But he would not predict victory. He respected Max Heiman and said that if there were a way to get his client off on a technicality, Max Heiman would find it.

Larry Gates was initially charged on five counts, including two first-degree murder charges that could have carried the death penalty. But by the time the case came to trial, capital punishment had been struck down in Connecticut. Bob wanted Larry Gates to die in the electric chair. But if that wasn't possible, he hoped that the state would get a conviction on both murder charges, insuring that Gates would stay in prison for the rest of his life.

Two years after Liz and Tommy had been murdered Larry Gates's case still hadn't come to trial. In those two years Bob had become cynical about the criminal justice system and the courts in particular. He knew that he and Liz and Tommy were not in any way culpable, yet he suspected that the system was such that he would go into court on the defensive. One slip and Heiman would be down his or someone else's throat and the case would be lost and there would be no chance for Gates to get the punishment he deserved.

Bob felt too as if the Gates family, not just Larry, was against him. He couldn't see why they had never made any show of remorse, why they apparently supported Larry without any censure of his behavior whatsoever. Things reported to Bob by friends as to what the Gates family was saying and doing about their son's case, whether they were true or not, fueled Bob's feeling that they were trying to make him seem like the bad guy who was persecuting their son.

In the spring of 1982, Bob began to think about selling his house. He had thought of doing that from the beginning, but the market and interest rates at the time would have forced him to take a big loss on the sale. Early in 1982 he decided that interest rates were falling enough that he could begin to think about selling the house. He figured he would finish some improvements in the basement and, after the summer, sell.

He simply couldn't take Glastonbury any longer. In the summer he and Joan left the house and rented another on a lake a half hour from Glastonbury. There Bob could get away from his kitchen window view of the Gates house. There he could practice the wind surfing he had taken up the summer before.

After the summer, Bob and Joan moved back to the house in Glastonbury knowing that the trial was just around the corner. The district attorney wasn't saying exactly when the case would begin, but he assumed it would be sometime in the fall. Bob tried to divert himself by wind surfing on the weekends and doing carpentry on the basement of his house. But being back in Glastonbury and knowing that he would soon have to go through the trial, he simply couldn't keep his mind off the combination of grief and revenge that hung over him.

On the first day of jury selection in September Bob and his father went to the courtroom, but Bob was asked to leave because he was to be a witness. Before he left he saw Larry Gates. He had seen Larry once before since the murders, at the pretrial motion. Bob thought he had something of a crude, insolent look about him. Larry didn't pay any attention to Bob.

The day before Bob was to testify, at the end of September, the district attorney and his assistant took him into the empty court-room and gave him a mock examination and cross-examination. Bob thought that their attempts to "grill" him were a bit silly, but he was glad to get the feel of the courtroom.

The first day Bob testified, the district attorney asked him about discovering the body and his identification of Liz and Tommy. Bob was nervous, but he was also certain that Robert Myers wasn't out to get him. His sister Nancy, his mother and father, and Joan were in the courtroom. There weren't many seats for spectators. The Gates family sat behind Larry on one side of the room, and Bob's family sat in back on the other side. Even though press cameras were allowed by law in courtrooms, Max Heiman had succeeded in getting them eliminated from this trial.

On the second day Bob testified, he was cross-examined by Heiman. Bob was very nervous. He had to walk past Larry Gates when he went into the room and over to the witness stand, but he didn't look at him. Liz's father and brother were in the courtroom as well that day.

Max Heiman's style of questioning might be classified as Perry Mason with a dash of disgust. It seemed that nothing about the proceedings pleased the man. Bob was trying very hard to see where Heiman was going with his line of questioning and how he was trying to trip him up. Bob studied each question and took a long time to answer. His delaying, of course, made Heiman even more impatient.

After several perfunctory questions about the discovery of the body, Heiman changed the subject and asked about Joan's moving in with Bob in November of 1980. He seemed to be leading up to something. He asked if it was true that the woman who moved in with Bob was a co-worker. Bob said she was not, that she was someone whom he had known for years, a friend of his wife's. The implication in Heiman's question was that Bob had not been all that bothered by the loss of Liz. Bob wanted to explain why he and Joan had decided to live together, to say that he missed Liz and Tommy terribly, that his life now was so hollow compared to when they were alive. But there was no place for him to do so. He had to sit there and answer Heiman's questions.

The lawyer stood in the back of the courtroom, in front of the spectators, and would frequently turn his back or look away from Bob as Bob answered questions. He was putting on a show and Bob, even though he was intent on answering the questions properly, could see that the posturing was somewhat transparent. He hoped the jury could see the same thing.

Heiman asked Bob about the civil suit he had initiated against the Gates family and made certain that the jury knew that Bob was asking for money damages. Bob could not tell the jury that one reason he had done so was to put Larry Gates back in jail. Heiman tried to make it seem as if Bob were trying to cash in on Liz's death.

In the civil suit, Bob had signed an affidavit concerning things that had happened on the day of the murders. There was a slight discrepancy between some of the details of the story Bob had told the court and what he had sworn to in the affidavit, because at the time of the civil suit Bob was not certain of some of the facts in the case. Heiman tried to make it seem as if Bob, somewhere along the way, had changed his story.

In summation, Max Heiman told Bob with mock pleasantness that he just wanted to make certain that he had everything "in perspective." "Three months after your wife died you went to a lawyer to inquire about a suit for money, and six months after your wife died you moved a lady into your house. Isn't that right?" The implications were there, but rather than try to explain himself and be ruled out of order, Bob just said yes.

Bob went up to the district attorney's office after he testified, and while he was standing in the hall outside the office, he stepped aside for some people who were passing in the narrow corridor. He looked up to see Larry Gates several feet from him. Larry looked away. When he had seen Larry in the courtroom and when he saw him again now, Bob did not think of revenge. Seeing him face to face was different from being at home and imagining Liz's and Tommy's murderer. The anger that could rise quickly at times when Bob was home thinking about the murders did not come.

Bob had refused to talk to the press throughout the two years since the murders. He didn't feel comfortable talking to them, and he knew that one Hartford paper would sensationalize anything he said. He had enough trouble with the exposure his private life was getting because of the murders, and he didn't want to have to see a sensational story printed about him.

During the trial, the local papers and newscasts picked out the most lurid details of each day's testimony and reported on those. On the first day Bob testified, the reporters bore down on the way in which Bob had discovered Tommy, the blood. Watching the evening news after that first day had disgusted Bob. But he finally did agree to give an interview to the local Glastonbury paper. He thought that people in Glastonbury should know his side of the story.

When, eventually, after the trial, the article was written and printed, Bob greeted it with mixed emotions. He was glad that the reporter had done a good job on the story, but he was worried that people who had read the article were now thinking of him as "that man whose wife and son were killed." He didn't know many people well in Glastonbury, and when he walked into a restaurant after the article with his picture appeared, he felt that people were staring at him. It could have been just his imagination, which was normally overactive when it came to people looking at him, but it was an uncomfortable feeling.

The trial came to an abrupt end. Bob was at work one morning several weeks after he had testified when he got a call from Robert Myers. Myers said that they had been negotiating with Heiman as the trial had progressed and that they had come to an agreement. Larry Gates would plead *nolo contendere* to two counts of first-degree murder in exchange for all other counts against him being dropped. Bob started shaking when he heard the news. He had not been aware of the negotiations, and the news came as a shock to him. At first he was annoyed at not having been kept abreast of the plea bargaining, but when he thought about it he was glad they hadn't told him. He felt that he would have been very bitter if he had known that they were bargaining, haggling about Liz's death.

Bob called Joan at the clothing store she operated near Hartford and told her. She too started shaking. Bob was having trouble talking. The plea change was to happen in court that afternoon, and Joan agreed to meet Bob there.

Bob was still nervous when he first got to the courthouse, though in Robert Myers's office, before the afternoon session, he calmed down. He was pleased that they got two counts of murder and that Gates would probably have to do a lot of time. His sister Linda, who had had trouble talking about the murders, would say a week later that she thought Gates should get more than life, that he should get life in the electric chair, and Bob would agree with her. But torture wasn't on Bob's mind in the courtroom. He could see and hear the case come to a close, but there was no feeling of resolution, no relief, and not the revenge that he had thought might be a part of the finish of the trial. In effect, Larry Gates, through his lawyer, had used a legal loophole to say he committed the murders without actually saying that he committed the murders.

In accepting the plea change, the judge asked Larry to stand and answer some questions. He wanted to make certain that Larry knew what he was doing. The questioning went on for fifteen minutes. Max Heiman had to interrupt his client several times to keep him from directly admitting his guilt. That infuriated Bob. He listened to Gates and felt that Gates didn't sound in the least bit sorry for anything he had done.

The trial was over, and sentencing was to be on the first of December. Over Thanksgiving Bob took a trip to Martha's Vineyard to get away from the whole business. He felt neither a sense of release nor satisfaction, and he wasn't sure the sentencing would provide either of these. He fantasized taking a gun into the courtroom. It would be the last time he would have a shot at Gates. But he knew that he would never do that. The trial had depressed him, and he didn't know how he was going to pull out of it. While he had been waiting for the trial, he had kept thinking that with its conclusion there would come an end to some of the grief and frustrating desire for revenge. But now he wasn't certain there would ever be a release. He filled his life up with work and recreational activities, but he felt that these were nothing compared to the family he had had. He could wind surf all he wanted but that could never hold a candle to the love he had felt for Liz and Tommy. He couldn't see himself ever having another family.

He felt that he had had his chance, that it was gone, and that his life was over.

Larry Gates was sentenced on January 28, 1983. He was given twenty-five years to life in Liz's murder and fifteen years to life for Tommy's. A psychiatrist at the sentencing testified that Larry Gates had a very low I.Q. and that early in his life his father had encouraged him to learn to use firearms.

Gates would be eligible for parole in fourteen to seventeen years and Bob would have preferred a sentence that made the minimum sentence much longer than that, but he was not displeased with the sentence. He was puzzled as to why Liz's murder brought one sentence and Tommy's another. Both were first-degree murders. Perhaps the jury felt a fourteen-month-old life was different from an adult life.

With the trial over, Bob could see only two things that he could do to improve his situation. He could press the civil suit against Larry Gates and his family. He didn't expect any more of a sense of satisfaction from the civil trial than he had gotten from the criminal trial, but he did feel there was an important principle involved in the civil suit.

The second thing he could do was to leave Glastonbury. After the summer he had bought land near where he and Joan had rented, on the lake, and he hoped soon to build a new house on the property. He finished work on the basement of his house and put it on the market two weeks before Larry Gates was sentenced. The Gates family had already moved out of their house. The Hart house, with its newly finished basement and wooded setting, should have been a quick sell, but very few prospective buyers visited. When Bob inquired he was told that agents did not want to come to the house because of "what had happened there." Bob's anger rose when he heard that. He knew that there were buyers who would not be as fearful of the history of the house as the agents seemed to be. He hoped one would show up soon. More than anything he wanted to leave Glastonbury, to live in a house with a different view from the kitchen window.

2

The McCulloughs

THE GRAYS FERRY section of South Philadelphia is a racially mixed yet segregated neighborhood of lower-middle-class to poor families. Blacks live in a city-run housing project and whites, for the most part, live in small, single-family row houses. Thirty-first Street roughly divides the two areas and is known to all as the DMZ of the neighborhood.

Blacks and whites have always coexisted uneasily in the Grays Ferry section. In the early seventies there was rioting and open street violence in the neighborhood, but mostly the tensions have been expressed in small daily skirmishes. These incidents, caused by one group or the other crossing Thirty-first Street, have included everything from harassment to rock- and bottle-throwing battles. The teenagers of the neighborhood, who have lived with this fear of the other group all their lives, are the main combatants in these skirmishes.

Jim and Jane McCullough live in the white part of Grays Ferry, but if you ask them about their neighborhood they're more likely to say they live in St. Gabriel's Parish. To the Catholic families of Grays Ferry, at least to the McCulloughs, parish concerns come before political boundaries.

St. Gabriel's Parish extends to the black part of Grays Ferry, but few blacks attend mass. The McCulloughs, who in 1974 were one of the cornerstone families of the parish, raised their six children to be respectful yet apprehensive, if not downright fearful, of blacks. Instead of having the children take the integrated city bus, Jim and Jane drove the kids to school until their oldest daughter, Jane, got her driving license. When the three kids after Jane—Jim Jr. (whom everyone called Earl), Danny, and Beth—got a paper route, only Beth would go near the several black homes on the route, and Jim Sr. would get home from work early to escort the kids as they delivered papers close to Thirty-first Street.

In 1974 Danny McCullough, a big fifteen-year-old and a sophomore at Bishop Neuman High School, looked to outsiders like a teen who might easily join in the racial battles that went on in the schoolyards on summer evenings; but the family knew better. He was a mild-mannered, sensitive kid who didn't even like the tame violence of Pop Warner football. Around the McCullough house he was known as the "I-wouldn't-know kid," because whenever he was asked to report on an incident in the neighborhood he had witnessed he would reply, "I wouldn't know."

On the night of March 29, 1974, a group of white teenagers harassed a black nineteen-year-old, Alphonso Geiger, and his cousin, both of whom had wandered across the DMZ. Geiger was chased back into the housing project, but he vowed to return. He went home, picked up a handgun, bought and drank some wine, and went back across Thirty-first Street.

It was dark by the time he got to Twenty-ninth Street, where the bottles had been thrown at him, and an early spring rain had emptied the normally busy corner of Twenty-ninth and Tasker streets. Danny McCullough, who had come out of a candy store near the corner and was shielding himself from the rain under the eaves of the roof of Dean's Bar, had just said good-bye to a friend of his. The friend walked past Geiger. In the dark, under the roof's overhang, Geiger couldn't see Danny all that well. He mistook him for one of the teenagers who had harassed him earlier. Geiger raised the handgun and fired twice. One of the bullets hit Danny's right temple.

When the news of the shooting reached her, Jane McCullough was in the living room watching TV and Jim was in the kitchen doing a neighbor's taxes. Joe Fulton, Danny's godfather, who was next in line to have his taxes done, was talking to Jane. Four of the six McCullough children were in the house.

The front door opened and Jane's nephew, Paul Haggerty, stepped into the living room with his mother, Jane's sister, and another of Jane's sisters. Paul didn't need to say a thing; his face said it all. The way he moved, the way he came awkwardly through the doorway—he was a walking alarm.

The world just stopped for a small second, and Jane understood. Something had slipped, something had gone wrong; a seam had ripped, a hole had opened; and there would be no way to control it. The words forming in Paul's throat were already pumping in her ears. There was no question, no uncertainty. She knew, and she knew that she was not prepared.

In one motion Jane flung herself to the sofa, knees to the seat, and slammed her hands over her ears. At the top of her voice she screamed, "I don't want to hear it! I don't want to hear it!" But the words came. Soft and even though they were, they cut through the room and worked in around Jane's screaming. "Danny's been shot."

Jim's voice filled Jane's ears next. He had come out of the kitchen when he heard her scream, and he was trying to find out what was wrong. He was calm. He questioned Paul. Jane didn't need questions, she knew and kept screaming. Beth and young Jane, along with Bobby, who was eleven, and Christine, who was ten, were downstairs almost instantly and started screaming and crying with their mother. The house was all noise now, and Jim was trying his best to put a cap on it, to get some order, to find out details.

His nephew couldn't tell him much. Paul had come over because he had thought Danny's parents would already know about the shooting. He had brought his mother over to help Jane. He hadn't realized until he had gotten inside the door that he was the messenger, and now he didn't know what to say. He had come out of a bar across from Dean's Bar with some others after they had heard the gunshot. When he had seen that it was his cousin Danny who had been shot, he had headed for home. He didn't know much and couldn't be much help.

Jim remembered the man in the kitchen sitting in front of his tax forms and went to tell him that he wouldn't be able to finish. On his way to the kitchen, he said that they ought to call Father Ambrogi. But before Jim made it to the kitchen, there were two priests at the front door.

Father Ambrogi and Father McKee had been at the scene of the shooting. Jim pounced: "Is it true that Danny got shot?" Yes. "How bad?" They didn't know. It might just be a graze.

A graze. There's the answer. Bullets don't always penetrate. Some miss. A graze.

"They took Danny over to Philadelphia General, and we've come to take you there," one of the priests said. That was just what Jim wanted to hear. He wanted to get out of the screaming house, go with Jane to the hospital and see Danny, see that graze, look into Danny's bright blue eyes, do something for him.

The trip through the rain in the priest's car was a blur. When they got to the hospital, Jim went on ahead. Jane didn't know if she could stand to see Danny wounded. Jim found a woman who had information. She said the wound was hard to diagnose. They would have to clean him up, do some X-rays.

A few minutes later when they wheeled Danny out of the emergency room and headed for the X-ray room, Jim was in the hall waiting. Danny looked whole; he recognized Jim and said, "Hi, Dad. I'm all right. Don't worry." He wasn't a mess. He was still Danny. Jim thought it had to be a graze. Maybe it was just a bottle; maybe he wasn't shot at all. Then Danny was rolled away.

Gabber Dean, the bartender who owned Dean's Bar and who had cradled Danny's head in the ambulance, met Jim in the hall and told him that it wasn't a bottle, Danny had definitely been shot. But he also told Jim that Danny had been conscious during the drive to the hospital. Gabber Dean, a friend of the family, had tried to stop the blood by cupping his hand over the wound. He had said the act of contrition with Danny. He said that when he had come out of his bar to see what the noise was all about, he had seen a young black man running down Twenty-ninth Street.

Father McKee began to talk about the neighborhood. If word got

27

around that Danny McCullough had been shot by a black man there could be a lot of trouble, retaliation, maybe even riots like those of a couple of years before. Things had been quiet, especially during the winter, but this shooting could change that quickly. The priests and the McCulloughs could imagine the pressure building in the neighborhood. A black had crossed no-man's-land and shot a young white kid. The streets must be buzzing with the news. What if there were some retaliation and it turned out that Danny wasn't seriously injured? The community, they felt, needed to be kept informed, so Father McKee went back to tell the network of corner hangouts and bars that it might only be a graze. Jim phoned home to give the children the same message.

Back at the house, family had already started to gather. Jim and Jane had twenty-three brothers and sisters between them, most of whom lived in the parish or the adjacent parish, St. Anthony's. Jim's parents were no longer alive, but Jane's were, and they came to the house as soon as they heard. So did brothers, sisters, aunts, and uncles. The small rooms of the house were soon packed with people. There were those who cried and those who stared. When Jim called to say that it might be a graze, the family hung onto that word; it was the best word they had.

Danny was in the X-ray room a long time, too long for Father Ambrogi. He left Jim and Jane for a while and, without telling them, went to hear Danny's confession while the doctors read the X-rays.

Jane was prepared to see Danny by now. After all, Jim had said he looked normal. Jane wanted to make sure for herself. What was taking so long? Suddenly the X-ray room door opened and he was there, on a gurney, being wheeled quickly down the hall, doctors and nurses at his side. They had to catch him on the fly.

Danny saw Jim first and once again tried a light "Hi, Dad." But this time it was different. The words slurred and bubbled. Jim could see that something was wrong. Danny turned, saw Jane, and said to her, "When you find out who did this to me let me know."

The request was pure Danny. There was no vengeful edge to it, no rancor. It was all curiosity. The look on his face and the slurring words he directed at his mother said only, "Why me?" He had been standing next to Dean's Bar and before he knew it he was shot and bleeding, in the hospital, and feeling worse all the time. He just wanted to find out why.

As they watched him being rolled away, Jim and Jane saw him try to vomit. They knew what that meant, but they didn't want to acknowledge it.

The doctor remained with them after Danny was gone. Jim asked if Danny was sedated, if that was why he was slurring his speech. No sedation, the doctor said. That's the pressure from a bullet that went deep. The doctor wanted to hurry. "We're going into surgery," he said. "I'm not going after the bullet; I'm going to try to tie off the bleeders." Jim asked how long it would take. The doctor looked at his watch and said, "It's nine now, come back around midnight." And then he was gone.

Jim and Jane needed no schooling on pressure and slurred words and fluids pumping into the skull. Earl, their oldest son, is a hydrocephalic. During his sixteen years he had been taken into surgery some twenty times because of pressure and fluids, water on the brain. The McCulloughs had learned to be ready at any time to whisk Earl off to the hospital if they heard the warning signs in his speech. When the pressure was really bad they knew to expect vomiting as well. Danny, they understood, was hurt very badly.

Danny, a year younger than Earl, had taught Earl all the basics. For the first year of his life Earl had been very sick and had learned virtually nothing. By the time Danny came along, Earl wasn't sitting up, or moving around as if he were ready to get up and walk, or crawling even. But when Danny had started to move around like a normal baby, Earl had caught on by watching. Danny had showed him the way. Danny would roll over and Earl would imitate. Danny would sit up and Earl would give that one a try. He was a year behind kids his age, but if Danny hadn't come along when he did Earl might have been even farther behind. Just by living, Danny had brought Earl along. Danny, the family came to see, was a godsend for Earl. But on this rainy night things were different; it was Danny who was in the hospital now, with slurred speech and a swelling head.

Father Ambrogi drove them back home to wait there for the surgery to be over. Jim and Jane had to tell the family that it was more serious than just a graze, but that they didn't know how serious. Nobody in the family knew what to say or do. Father McKee came back to the house very upset. He was a newly ordained priest who had worked closely with the teenagers of the parish trying to bring about some change in the racial tensions in the neighborhood. He was an emotional man who took responsibility for things that happened in Grays Ferry even if they were beyond his control. He looked at the large, crying, staring family and suggested that, instead of just sitting for hours, they say the rosary. The house calmed as it filled with the words of the prayer.

Though the first floor was bulging with family, Jim and Jane would not have thought things complete unless there was a priest in the house. They had both grown up in the church, in the adjacent St. Anthony's Parish, and had been so much a part of parish life that each of them had been asked several times by priests and nuns whether they thought they might have a "vocation." Their children used to hear Jim described by some in the neighborhood as a "holy-roller type" who was probably religious and strict at home. That made the kids angry, because Jim and Jane's religion wasn't like that. They were devout Catholics, but they were not pious. They truly liked the company of nuns and priests in the parish, many of whom they knew as close friends. They worked on parish projects and helped organize social events because the church was the center of their social life. Now, with a tragedy darkening the door by the second, Jim and Jane felt the priests were as much of a necessity in their house as brothers, sisters, aunts, and uncles.

Twenty-three brothers and sisters are a lot for any two people, but Jim and Jane aren't all that much of an oddity in their neighborhood. Veins of families run through so much of St. Gabriel's Parish that, no matter where you are, at least in the white part of the neighborhood, you have a relative close by. It was no startling coincidence that Danny was cradled in the ambulance by a man who knew his family, that his cousin was in a bar across the street from the corner where Danny was shot, or that two of Jane's sisters were working in the kitchen at Bingo not more than a block away.

At midnight the priests drove Jim and Jane back to the hospital. After a while a doctor came out to talk with them. "I don't know what to say," he began. "The damage was monstrous. It was much worse than I ever expected. There's very little hope for him now." The doctor explained that the bullet had torn through Danny's brain and that they really had done nothing in the surgery other than contain the brain inside the skull. Jim asked if Danny was going to make it, and the doctor repeated that he had very little hope. Jim asked how long he had to live and the doctor said he didn't know. "It's all in God's hands now. I've done all I can for him. I doubt he'll live through the night."

"God's hands." God had a hand in this. God's will. That made some sense. That was something Jim could accept. Danny came from God and it was God's will that Danny go now, though way too soon. Jim and Jane held each other and cried.

Father Ambrogi and Father McKee stayed the night with Jim and Jane. Jim called home and told the family that Danny was probably not going to make it and that they should come and say good-bye. The hospital would let people visit. Jim and Jane stayed in Danny's room all night. His head was wrapped in white gauze and his eyes were closed. Jane thought he looked like an angel. His complexion was smooth, and the white, turbanlike bandage gave him a halo of sorts. She noticed how clean his feet, sticking out of the sheet, were. She wouldn't forget those feet with their smooth soles, because they reminded her of the pride Danny had always had in his appearance and his cleanliness.

His brothers and sisters came to visit. They touched Danny and stood with their parents for a while. Some aunts and uncles came and said what they could to Danny. It was odd. This was not like a wake or a viewing. It was a one-sided good-bye.

After the operation, Danny had been given tests that had indicated there was no brain activity. As Jim stood in Danny's room watching the family say good-bye, he worried that Danny might live and remain completely crippled, a vegetable. He had accepted Danny's having been shot as God's will, but he was frightened that his faith would not stand the test of seeing Danny comatose for years and years.

After Jim and Jane visited Danny on Saturday night, Jim made up his mind that he was not going back to the hospital. He told Jane and the family that, as far as he was concerned, Danny died Friday night, and there was no reason now to keep going back to the hospital.

Jane, who had not been hysterical after the initial shock of the shooting, had trouble understanding Jim's feelings. She had mouthed the words, told people there was no hope, and tried to appear as if she and Jim thought alike; but they really didn't. Danny may have looked like an angel lying in his bed, but she hadn't really let him go yet. During one visit she went to the end of the bed, to where those immaculate feet were just barely covered by the sheet, and she ran a fingernail along the sole of one of them. It curled! The toes flexed and bent toward the sole! He was alive!

But the doctor said that these were just reflexes, and that there was no hope. Jane accepted this, but she still would not go as far as Jim did. When Jim said that he couldn't bear going back to the hospital, Jane decided she'd stay away too; but her heart wasn't really in it. Danny *was* still alive in some small way, and to her God's will seemed like some distant cipher, not the reality it was for Jim.

On Sunday morning Jane awoke at 4:00 A.M. and then woke Jim. She felt Danny was waiting for her, that he wanted to see her one more time before he left. It was more than a feeling, more than intuition. It was a certainty. She didn't feel she could wait until after mass. She and Jim went to the hospital to be with Danny. But nothing changed, and a second day began.

On Saturday morning a priest the family didn't know had come to the house. His name was Ted Nabuurs, and he was a community worker. He said that he had come to see what the family's feelings were, what response the family would like from the community. He indicated that people in the neighborhood, meaning the white part of the parish, were prepared for anything, all the way to a riot if necessary. Jim told him that the family wanted no retaliation of any sort in Danny's name. Jim was firm. He told the priest to inform the neighborhood that Danny had been hurt as an innocent bystander, and that to retaliate and possibly hurt another innocent bystander would not be the answer. The priest said, "You make my job easy."

Somebody from the Grays Ferry Community Council, an organization used mainly by white families, came to the house and asked the same question the priest had asked: What would the McCulloughs like done? Jim gave the same answer, and soon there were people walking through the neighborhood, knocking on doors and passing on the word: no retaliation.

Saturday's paper carried a small article on the shooting picked up from the police blotter, but that was all the press the shooting got. The family was relieved not to be besieged, but they wondered why there was so little press coverage. They assumed that the news editors at the papers and the television stations knew how tense the situation was in Grays Ferry and didn't want to exacerbate it.

A policeman came to the door on Saturday to say that there would be a guard in front of the house, but that was all they heard from the legal authorities. They assumed the police were trying to find the man who had been seen running from the scene, but no one even called to brief them.

On Sunday Jim and Jane began to get a sense of their powerlessness. They inquired about donating Danny's eyes and kidneys, and they were told that they couldn't. A detective at the door to Danny's room said that if Danny died he would be a ward of the coroner during a murder investigation. And besides, the detective said, if you donate kidneys they have to be taken out just before actual death; the murderer could then get off by claiming that it was the kidney removal that had killed Danny. In dying Danny might have been able to pass on life to others, but red tape and legal loopholes prevented it. Jim began to realize that his son's body was going to be in somebody else's possession. He couldn't quite accept that, but he had no choice in the matter.

On Sunday afternoon the police took nineteen-year-old Alphonso Geiger from a hiding place at his sister's house and charged him with the shooting. He confessed to having committed the assault, saying that he had gotten the wrong boy, but that he was just trying to get the first white he could find.

The McCulloughs had to hear about the arrest through people at the Community Council and through neighborhood hearsay. The police never called to inform them. On Sunday night, when Jim and Jane went back to the hospital, Jim asked the detective stationed in front of Danny's room about the arrest. The detective told him it was none of his business. Jim blew up. His anger for the past forty-eight hours had been minimal; he had tried to let everyone see that this tragedy need not lead to vengeance. But this was different. The police were supposed to be on his side, weren't they? Jim was starting to feel like the criminal. He let the detective have it full force. The detective, taken aback, relented and confirmed the arrest. Jim calmed down.

Danny was still alive on Monday morning, April first. Jane urged the children to get out of the house, to get away from the crying and shock of the weekend. Earl went to school. Beth couldn't manage that, but she did go out into the neighborhood and hung out for a while at Bill's Variety, the candy store down the street from where Danny had been shot.

Around mid-morning, Jim and Jane went back to the hospital. They had a mission of sorts. They wanted to tell the doctor that they did not want Danny kept alive by machines. But when they got to the hospital, a friend who had just visited Danny met them in the hall and told Jim that he ought not let Jane see Danny just yet. Jim went into the room and saw that the bandage had been removed. Danny's face looked gray. He guessed that they had done tests and had not replaced the "halo" that had been such a comfort to Jane. He found a nurse, had the bandage replaced, and at about 11:00 A.M. he and Jane went into the room.

Close to 1:00 that afternoon, Jim and Jane were asked to leave the room, and several doctors went in. There was a flurry of activity, then quiet. Soon after, a doctor came out of the room and told Jim and Jane that Danny had died.

The rest of the family gathered in a conference room at the

34

hospital and were given the news. Some cried, some were determined not to. They all went, in small groups, to say a final good-bye. For those who had held out hope that he would live, this trip into Danny's room was much different from the one during the weekend. Danny still looked peaceful, but now there was no chance he would be back on the street again, no chance he would be walking down a school corridor again. He was gone.

The five days between Danny's death and his funeral were busy ones that nevertheless passed slowly. There were things to do, plans to make, but each task seemed both surreal and insurmountable. On Tuesday, Jim had to see to one of the worst of those tasks: he had to go to the morgue to identify Danny's body.

Jim's brother went with him. Neither of them were prepared for what they were to go through. Jim had seen Danny in a coma, and he had seen him in death; he figured he would have one more look at his son's peacefully dead body at the identification. But that was not to be.

The tiled room looked like a hospital and was fitted with a television monitor. Jim and his brother were shown into the room and then asked to look at the monitor. A black and white, grainy image flashed on the screen. The morgue had said they would make it as easy as possible, but this was anything but easy. The combination of the camera angle and the high contrast of the image made Danny look ghastly. His bald head was deeply scarred and his eyebrows, normally heavy like his father's, now looked like black bars across his forehead. And he was so remote. The question that came from the attendant—"Do you know that person?"—seemed to come from far away.

Jim, still trying to make sense of the image on the screen, said that it was Danny. As the monitor was flicked off, though, he turned to his brother and asked if that distorted image really was his son. The attendant asked if he had some doubt, and Jim snapped out of it enough to make the identification seem believable. But Jim walked out of the morgue shattered, imprinted with the mangled image of something he had been forced to say was his son but which bore no resemblance to the flesh-and-blood boy he could remember. If he had dreamed that horrible scene, he would have awakened relieved, would have walked to Danny's room and assured himself that his son was still alive and not a dead body on a television screen. Instead he returned to a house full of people who were making plans for Danny's funeral.

With their family close by, Jim and Jane expected the wake and funeral to be big; but they had no idea of the number of people who would turn out. A mass for Danny on Monday night had been packed, and people were either calling or coming to the house throughout the week. But when the line at the wake spilled out of Shea's Funeral Home and backed up for two and a half blocks, the McCulloughs could see that Danny's life had touched many more than just his cousins and aunts and uncles.

The funeral director sent a car around for the family and the police escorted the car. The funeral home itself had been cordoned off because the police feared that there might be racial incidents. Nothing like that happened, though. Blacks, even those like a friend of Jane's from work who wanted to express sympathy, stayed away. During the week, Jim had been quoted in the *Philadelphia Daily News* as saying that the family held no malice toward the person who had shot Danny; but it was still possible that the murder would be seen as having been racially motivated. A columnist in the same paper had tried to downplay the racial tensions in the neighborhood. He had claimed that drugs, not racial strife, scrambled the lives of Grays Ferry teenagers. The thrust of his column, however, had been that an innocent white boy who took his religion seriously (he erroneously reported that Danny had just come out of mass a half hour before he was shot) had been killed by a young black man. And a black newspaper, the *Tribune,* had painted a picture of Jim McCullough as a white bigot. Jim didn't know why they had printed the article. No one from the paper had interviewed him. Lacking any significant amount of information due to scant press coverage, perhaps the *Tribune* had simply assumed that Jim fit the stereotype of a Grays Ferry white man. Jim wrote a letter in reply, but it was never published.

Standing in the funeral home greeting the long line of people who came to view the body, the older children and Jim and Jane began to see just what Danny meant to other people. Those who came did so not out of curiosity, not to gawk, but out of real affection for Danny and his family. There was crying here and there, but for the most part the family surprised the people they greeted by being open and tearless. It had been that way during the week as well. Friends would come to the house not really wanting to face the family's grief, but would leave uplifted by the spirit of the McCulloughs.

For Jim the wake was a twofold relief. He was relieved that Danny would not have to live out the rest of his life as a cripple. And he was relieved that he was Danny's father, not Alphonso Geiger's. From the first time he had heard of Geiger, he had felt some small connection to the boy's parents. He knew it would be impossible, but he had wanted to go over and tell them that he held no animosity toward them. He had made that clear in the small article in the *Philadelphia Daily News*. Now, as he stood in the funeral home and saw the tribute being paid to his son, he couldn't help but think of how horrible it would have been to have wound up on the other end of the stick, to have had Danny under arrest and an innocent boy dead because of his son. Something about the people coming through the funeral parlor and that sense of relief lent further credence to his initial, immediate belief that Danny's passing had been God's will.

St. Gabriel's Church was full for the funeral mass. Danny's friends, many of whom had come around during the week to ask if they could be pallbearers, formed an honor guard that lined the center aisle of the church, went through the foyer and down the steps to the street. Twenty-three priests, some of whom traveled hundreds of miles to be there, concelebrated the mass and made an unusual sight filling the first two pews. Father McKee began his sermon by noting the turnout. "Jim McCullough mentioned last week that he would hope that his son Danny was as good outside as he was inside his home. Today, I think Jim has his answer." He went on to speak of the McCulloughs' faith. "God, in taking Danny to Himself, has fulfilled his life and has left us something in return. For God has given tremendous faith to the McCullough family, and in doing so has permitted them to share that faith with us. A faith that trusts in God's will even without understanding why. . . . A faith that would rather love than hate. A faith that seeks peace with one another, not strife."

For Jim and Jane and the kids, the funeral was as much about them as it was about Danny. Their reaction to the killing, their reliance on their faith, and their lack of rancor was, as Father McKee noted, a light of sorts to the people of the parish. As they were about to ride away from the church, one of the priests who had concelebrated the mass stuck his head in the window of the family's car and said, "You are one beautiful family. I hope you stay that way the rest of your lives."

In the months after the funeral Jim made an effort to show that he held no malice toward Geiger, Geiger's family, or blacks in general. He had experienced one of the most feared things in the parish. A black had come out of the Tasker Homes housing project and killed his son without provocation. But he was determined to demonstrate to the rest of the people in the neighborhood and to his own family his faith in God and his own lack of racial hatred. Jim insisted—to the columnist who came to interview the family a month after the murder, to family, and to friends—that Danny's fate had been ordained by God and maintained that perhaps Danny's work on earth had been finished. Jim sincerely believed that it might have been part of God's design for his family that Danny had followed Earl to help him with his illness. Just before Danny died, Earl had become much more independent of his younger brother. Jim could understand God taking Danny because his task on earth had been completed.

Jane endorsed Jim's belief that Danny's death was part of God's will. She wrote a letter to the *Philadelphia Daily News* in which she replied to a letter a black mother had written. Jane seconded the woman's plea for racial harmony. In her letter Jane also mentioned that her family was glad to have their faith intact after their tragedy. In saying so she was alluding to her own belief that God had some purpose in Danny's death.

Jane also talked, in the letter, about her grief and sense of loss. "The loss of Danny," she wrote, "left such an ache in our hearts that we know it will be a long time before these wounds begin to heal." It was in the area of that "ache" that Jane felt she and Jim differed.

Jim thought that his faith required a stolid, no-cry approach, an outward sign of a deep inner acceptance of God's will. Jane and the children might cry over Danny, but he would hold it in. Jane was deeply hurt by Jim's not showing his emotion. Certainly she could understand his reliance on faith; they had both been so close to the church in such a genuine way. But she could not understand why this man, who since they were children had been a synonym for life and love in her world, seemed to be turning cold and callous, not crying once after the funeral of their son.

Jim and Jane began to clash in small ways. Jim was offended by her hints that his lack of outward emotion was somehow inhuman. He was beginning to see that Jane was like others in his family who looked askance when he began to talk of his faith in relation to Danny's death. He was in a bind. As far as he was concerned, his religion had, throughout his life, prepared him to understand a situation such as Danny's death. Now here were people he loved, even his own wife, challenging his beliefs at the time he needed those beliefs the most. Just what did they expect him to do?

It took the family doctor to bring the problem to a head. Several months after the funeral, during a routine checkup, Dr. Sciubba confronted Jim. He said that he was worried about Jim's lack of emotion, worried that Jim was holding too much in and that there would be unpleasant results later on. Jim listened and then left the doctor's office. He and Jane drove home and on the freeway Jim suddenly burst into tears. He had to pull over and cry it out. The hurt, the deep sense of loss could not be held back. The sudden and extreme pain seemed to crack him open. Months of feelings came up in wave after wave.

In crying about Danny, Jim acknowledged feelings that were

nearly intolerable. He had learned to cry, but he had also learned the real price of his love for Danny. In seeing him cry, Jane could see that Jim was suffering as much as she was, she could see that he was not inhuman. In that regard Jim's breakthrough brought them much closer together. But there was a side effect that, for the next year, put distance between Jim and Jane, between Jim and the kids. He did not want to pay the price again.

Jim decided, almost consciously, that if he did not get close to his family, losing one of them would not be as excruciatingly painful as it had been with Danny. He started to build a wall between himself and his family. Uncharacteristically, he began to leave the house at night. At times he found himself in the car driving with no destination. He would go places where there was activity, people moving about, stores open at night, and simply watch others. His house and his family, once the locus of most of his pleasure in life, now only reminded him of the deep pain he had come in contact with driving home from the doctor's office. The house had been where all that pain had started, and he could not stand to be there. He would not make himself vulnerable again. If Jane or one of the kids were to die, he could at least make the hurt less powerful, the challenge to his faith less agonizing, by keeping his distance. Though Jim was somewhat conscious of what he was doing, the rest of the family was not really aware of the wall Jim was building. They were dealing with their grief in their own ways. And they were doing that by trying to keep Danny and their relationship to him alive.

Christine remembered her brother as a big clown who used to try to make her laugh. He'd poke his head around the door between the living room and the kitchen, call her, and then, when she was looking, grab his hair with his own hand and make it look like someone was yanking him from the door. Christine could make herself laugh just by imagining that hand coming out, remembering how Danny had made his face look funny.

Bobby wouldn't talk at all about Danny or the murder. He would leave the room if the family started to bring up the subject. In that, he was like his grandfather, Jane's father. Jane had realized from the first night that her father's way of dealing with Danny's death was going to be to say absolutely nothing about it. She knew her father well enough to know that on some level he was assuming that, if he said nothing about it, it would go away. He maintained his silence to his death in 1977.

Young Jane was getting ready to graduate from high school and to marry. She looked to her boyfriend, who had just joined the police force and who had been something of a role model for Danny, for support, for someone to cry with. She wore Danny's St. Daniel medal.

Before Danny was murdered, Earl, who was sixteen, had begun preparing himself for the day when Danny would not be with him all the time. He and Danny had been feeling, without ever saying so, that the closeness of their childhood was not going to be possible once they got past their teens. But Earl was not prepared to be on his own so soon. Danny had asked him, the night he was killed, if he wanted to go out with him, and Earl had said he'd catch up with him later. In the months after the murder Earl couldn't stop wondering what he might have been able to do if he had gone with Danny.

Beth's love for Danny was fierce. He was, by a year, her older brother, he made her laugh, and she looked up to him; but he was a soft person and he needed her protection. In a reversal of the stereotypical roles of big brothers and little sisters, Beth was always ready to stand up for Danny. When he was murdered and her father reacted by eschewing anger or retaliation, she was forced to follow his lead publicly; but privately that wasn't her way. As far as she was concerned, a black, a nigger, had killed her brother. The hell with racial harmony. Give me a gun and put Alphonso Geiger in front of me and I'll do the same thing to him he did to Danny.

Beth's chance to express this anger came the summer after the murder. She was at the playground one evening when a fight broke out between white and black teenagers after a basketball game. The whites had cornered the blacks in the fenced-in yard. Beth watched as one big black youth snuck out of the melee and, seeing an open gate behind where Beth was standing, headed for it. As he approached, Beth fantasized about grabbing the guy's beltloop and holding him until some of the boys could get to him. She was in the middle of this fantasy when he came near her and something automatic in her took over. Her left arm swung in a big arc and she punched him in the face. He fell back, more shocked than hurt, and then ran off. Beth's whole body trembled with satisfaction. Months of pent-up anger had gone into that split second.

The McCulloughs knew almost nothing about Alphonso Geiger and had little curiosity. Jane hated the word *murder*—none of them used it in relation to Danny's death. Jane felt that talking about Danny's "murder" linked her son to his murderer, Geiger. To her, Danny was an innocent boy who had been killed, who had suffered an accident. She told people at work that she was going to the trial of the boy who had killed Danny. She couldn't say "murder."

For Jim, justice would have meant a life behind bars for Geiger. He did not believe in the death penalty, but he thought it would be fair for Geiger to spend the rest of his life in prison. Beth and Earl thought Geiger should get the chair.

Had it not been for someone at the Community Council, the McCulloughs would have had no warning of the upcoming trial. In the eight months since the shooting they had had no official contact with anyone investigating the killing, neither the police nor the district attorney's office. There had been no news coverage of the investigation and no profile of Geiger. When they were informed of the trial date by the Community Council and they realized that they were going to receive no official notice of the trial, that the trial was not to be the *McCulloughs v. Alphonso Geiger* but the *Commonwealth of Pennsylvania v. Alphonso Geiger*, their hopes for justice began to fade and their anger to grow.

Their first contact with the district attorney's office did nothing to diminish those feelings. During jury selection, the D.A. prosecuting the case took Jim aside and told him he would be called to the stand to testify, to verify his identification of Danny's body. The D.A. went on to say that, because Jim would be a witness, he would have to be out of the courtroom for the remainder of the trial. Jim refused. He had not been subpoenaed and he insisted on staying in the courtroom. The D.A. said he would see what could be done, and eventually he was able to get a special ruling allowing Jim to testify and then remain in the courtroom. The incident, though, showed Jim and Jane where they stood in the whole affair. They were to be bystanders.

The trial lasted five days, and the mechanics of each day were similar. The Geiger family would sit on one side of the gallery and the McCullough family on the other. Shortly before the judge would take his seat, Alphonso Geiger would be brought into the room. His route to the defense table led directly in front of Jim and Jane, and he and Jim would stare at each other before Geiger sat down. To the McCulloughs he appeared arrogant and completely without remorse. The stares that he and Jim exchanged were matched by stares between members of the two families. Jim's and Jane's increasing anger at the court system found expression in the looks they directed at the Geiger family.

During the trial, it was never a question of whether or not Geiger was guilty of the killing. He admitted it. His defense seemed to be based on his contention that he had not been looking for Danny McCullough specifically, that he had been hassled by white kids earlier in the evening of the killing and that he had gotten a gun and returned to the neighborhood looking for a white to shoot, any white.

To the McCulloughs that didn't seem to be much of a defense. The D.A. was asking for a first-degree murder conviction, and Geiger's confession included clearcut premeditation. He had intended to kill someone. As the trial progressed, Jim and Jane felt more and more like outsiders, but they also felt certain that the jury had no choice but to bring back a guilty verdict on the first-degree murder charge.

Jim did have doubts about the jury—not the people themselves, but the system they were forced to operate within. For instance, they had been instructed not to take notes. Jim didn't understand the reasoning behind this. The judge, the prosecutors, and the defense attorneys—people trained in the law, people who had practiced law for years and who were clearly better versed in the various intricacies of the proceedings than were the members of the jury— were allowed to make notes, to keep records of the goings-on. How were the jurors expected to remember all they were hearing? There were a lot of technical points being discussed, and they were being asked to keep track of them as well as to balance all the arguments in making their decision. This did little to increase Jim's faith in the court system.

Out of this growing apprehension that the court might not hand out justice, as well as his feelings of anger toward Alphonso Geiger and his desire to be more than a passive observer of the proceedings, came a fantasy wherein Jim saw Geiger standing alone in the hallway next to the courtroom somehow out of the reach of the court personnel. As Geiger makes a dash for freedom, Jim realizes that he is the only one who can prevent him from escaping. Jim runs him down, gives him a good beating, and foils his escape forever. Now and then during the last few days of the trial Jim would reenact this fantasy, drifting away from the proceedings before him.

In his charge to the jury, the judge told them that they could bring back verdicts of guilty of first- or third-degree murder, or not guilty. Third-degree murder, like manslaughter in some states, would be the verdict if the jury decided there had been no premeditation, if they thought the killing had been more accidental than anything else. At least that was the way Jim and Jane saw it. Since they knew from Geiger's confession that there had been nothing accidental about his action, they were confident that the jury could bring back but one verdict: guilty of first-degree murder.

Tensions on the last day of the trial ran high. The stares and looks had continued throughout the five days and had become stronger; now there were glares and dirty looks. Shortly before the jury began its deliberations, during a recess, Jane felt she was being stared at by one of the members of the Geiger family. Jane couldn't help herself. She yelled across the fifteen feet of hallway between her and the other woman, "What are you staring at!" That was all. The incident was over quickly. But it was indicative of the way in which the trial had transformed Jane and the whole family. After the five days in court, they didn't care whether they showed ill will or not. They simply wanted justice to be done and the trial to be over with.

The jury's verdict—third-degree murder—was a blow. When Geiger left the courtroom, instead of the usual staredown with Jim, he gave the McCulloughs a quick smile. He had won. The sentence would be ten to twenty years; with good behavior he could be out in five. But more than that, he had somehow managed to come out of the whole thing appearing not to have been really responsible for Danny's murder.

The judge asked the stunned McCulloughs into his chamber after the verdict had been read. He said that he had seen their family during the trial and he knew that they were good people. He said that in his opinion the verdict should have been first-degree murder, but under the law his hands were tied. He promised that he would not let Alphonso Geiger leave jail until he was certain he was no longer a danger to society.

Jim thought it was decent of the judge to talk to them, but the meeting changed nothing. His prejudices and opinions about the court system had been confirmed, and his anger now had a clear focus. He would, over the next few years, grow to hate the very idea of a murder trial. Even though there had been tensions and bad feelings between the families, even though he would forever carry the ugly picture of a remorseless Alphonso Geiger, all of this would take a back seat to the verdict of that courtroom. He had said all along, and sincerely, that he held no malice and wanted no vengeance taken in Danny's name. But now he knew that the justice he felt was due him and his family, even society, was not to be had. Shortly after the trial, Jim had a nightmare in which he was charged with murder himself and was about to be taken to court. He refused. There was no way he would ever go before any jury. He let his animosity toward the court show outside of his nightmare as well. He vowed never to sit on a jury. He told all who would listen that the trial had been one big waste of time. Because there had been no press coverage of the trial, there was no outlet for the McCulloughs' anger. Soon they realized that they would simply have to chalk the whole mess up to experience and move on.

45

The way they moved on was to keep Danny with them as much as they could. Because Danny had made them laugh so often and had loved a good joke, they tried to keep their memories of him in that spirit. They began to label events either B.D. or A.D., before Danny's death or after Danny's death. The paper route Earl, Beth, and Danny had was, of course, B.D. Jane Jr.'s high school graduation was A.D.

For the most part, the kids and Jim and Jane had little trouble talking with people outside the family about Danny; but there were some things they kept to themselves. They weren't sure outsiders would understand such things as the house fly they were certain was Danny.

The first time the fly showed up was after Jane's graduation. They were sitting around the kitchen table talking about Danny and how he would have been proud of his sister. A large fly buzzed around the table, and somebody jokingly said that Danny had made it to the party after all. Then somebody else remembered that there had been a large fly in the car that had taken the family from St. Gabriel's Church to the cemetery. They thought it a little out of character for Danny to return as a quick little fly; a snail would have been more like it. But the fly was not to be denied. In January, after the trial, one of the priests at St. Gabriel's was wearing for the first time vestments donated in Danny's memory. Beth almost fell off the pew when she noticed that a fly kept landing on the priest's shoulder. A fly in church in the middle of the winter? The joke was beginning to take on the character of a family legend.

Then, five years after Danny died, the children had their picture taken as a twenty-fifth anniversary gift for their parents. They debated inserting an old photo of Danny but decided, once they saw the proofs, that it wouldn't be appropriate. They were photographed out in the park, and an insert would spoil the mood. They chose one of the shots, had it enlarged, and without having seen the enlargement first, gave it to Jim and Jane. As everyone was sitting around admiring the photograph, Jim noticed a suspicious speck on Beth's bare arm in the photograph. Sure enough it turned out to be a fly. Danny, they guessed, had made it into the photograph after all.

46

The McCulloughs. Standing from left to right: Jim; Jane; Beth's husband, Jack; Beth; Christine; Jane's husband, Ray; Jane; Colleen. Kneeling: Earl and Bobby. Seven hours after this photograph was taken, Jane gave birth to Ray, Jr.

The wall Jim had built to protect himself from the possibility of further pain came down about a year after the murder. Jim and Earl were at a church retreat, and suddenly Jim saw that he was going to have to let the pain come again, cry again, be close to Jane and his children again in order to get on with his life. He came home from the retreat and began to talk to the family about what he had been doing over the past year and what he was going to do in the future. The kids understood but were a bit embarrassed by their father's confession.

Jim followed through. The distance decreased, he stayed home at night, and he learned to cry. Once he and Jane were served at a restaurant by a waiter who looked a lot like Danny. Jim cried and didn't feel the need to choke off the hurt and sense of loss that prompted the crying. He and Jane decided after a while to attend mass at the church they had been raised in, St. Anthony's, the neighboring parish. Sitting in the pews of his childhood, he remembered the priests he had known growing up, he remembered the ways in which St. Anthony's Parish had formed his faith, and he cried. He cried for the son he had lost and for the faith that had brought him through. He knew there would be more tears to come, but he suspected, hoped, he'd seen the last of the wall.

After the first, wrenching year, things improved for Jim and Jane. Once again they were able to lean on each other, to enjoy the kids together. Jane, who worked for the city Redevelopment Authority, told Jim about a job opening. People at the community council recommended him for the job, partly because of the way he had reacted to Danny's murder. In March of 1975, he was hired as a community worker for the Authority in Grays Ferry. Though he had spent twenty years in the lithography business, he would later say that his work with the Redevelopment Authority had been the best job he had ever had.

Eight years after Danny's murder Jim and Jane, by looking at their other children, could get a rough idea of how Danny might have turned out. Jane and Beth had graduated from high school, and both were happily married. Jane had given her parents their first grandchild. Earl, whom the doctors had once predicted would never live, was a good-natured young man who worked in a shoe store. Bobby had graduated from high school and gone on to Kutztown State College. Christine, who had grown to look so much like Danny, was about to graduate from high school.

As the kids left the neighborhood for college or work downtown, their fears of blacks decreased. The biases of their childhood in Grays Ferry didn't suddenly disappear, but no one in the family was bothered when Bobby brought a black friend home from college for a weekend.

Imagining what Danny would have become, trying to keep him alive through stories and jokes, had its limits, of course. Jane had spoken and written about Danny as an angel to whom the family could now pray. She remembered how his bandage had looked like a halo. But that image and her belief that Danny now rested in heaven were little consolation when the feelings of loss and absence hit her. The word she used—*void*—didn't even begin to express the way she felt at times. When Paul Haggerty had come through her front door eight years ago and she had seen almost immediately what had happened, she had tried to fight it. But Danny had been pulled from her and was gone now. No matter how they tried to keep Danny's memory with them, no matter how good-natured they were about their loss, that sinking sense of someone forever gone would return time and again and would never leave for good. It would come at expected times like her birthday (Jane and Danny shared a birthday), and it would come at unexpected times. It was something she was going to take to her grave.

Jim doesn't make predictions about an afterlife. He speaks about living his religion, and he believes Danny's death was part of a divine purpose; that faith has made some aspects of the tragedy more meaningful than they might have been otherwise. But an afterlife, another existence, even the reappearing house fly—who knows? Jim will go as far as to say that Danny's murder was God's will, but beyond that he knows only that the "I-wouldn't-know kid" is gone.

3

The Spencers

IF YOU HAD asked Betty Jane Spencer whether or not she felt safe on Valentine's Day in 1977 she would have said, "Certainly." She lived on a country road in Hollandsburg, Indiana, in a county that had not seen a murder in fifty years, at least not a real murder. Even if the improbable happened and some sort of violence came to her door, Betty Jane would have told you that she felt safe. Keith, her husband of ten months, his three teenage sons, and her own twenty-two-year-old son all surrounded her like the walls of a fortress. She was so certain of her security that day that she didn't even bother to lock her front door after her husband left, just before midnight, for the television station where he worked as a broadcast engineer.

Shortly after he left, Betty Jane was standing in her kitchen and she looked out into the living room. She had a clear view of the front door. As she looked, a strange thing happened. The front door burst open and a young man with long, unkempt hair crashed into the house carrying a shotgun. He pointed it at Betty Jane's son, Greg, who was sitting on the living room couch, out of Betty Jane's line of vision, and yelled, "On the floor, buddy. Hands behind your back."

For a full thirty seconds Betty Jane could not move a muscle. She could neither scream nor walk nor think. She had seen something that looked no more real than television. What was happening? A shotgun? There was something terribly wrong going on in the

50

living room, but none of it made much sense.

Then the back door flew open and two more young men with shotguns burst into the kitchen. One of them told her to go into the living room. As she was doing so a fourth one, a bit older than the rest, came in the front door and acted as if he were in charge. He was yelling something at her about who was at home and the number of cars in the driveway. Greg was already down on the floor with his hands behind his back. Reeve, Keith's sixteen-year-old son, and his fourteen-year-old brother, Ralph, were being hauled out from their bedroom.

Betty Jane looked at Reeve for some sign. Reeve was the quick thinker in the family. Betty Jane hadn't the slightest idea of what to do, but if there was a way out of this, Reeve had already thought of it. Reeve returned her glance with a shrug of resignation.

Betty Jane was extremely alert now. Something told her that, no matter how crazy this whole thing was, she had to see everything very clearly, especially the intruders' eyes. They could change their hair when they left her house, but they couldn't change their eyes. She was going to remember them.

When Betty Jane, Reeve, and Ralph had joined Greg on the living room floor, the four intruders began to ransack the house. The leader kept telling the others to "disable that clock, disable that radio." They asked where the money was and said that if they didn't get it all they would kill them. Betty Jane and the boys told them about all the money and valuables they could think of.

The leader asked whether or not everybody was home, and he asked again about the number of cars in the driveway. Betty Jane knew that Raymond, Keith's eighteen-year-old son, was due back from work any minute, but she lied and said that everybody was there except Keith. She hoped Raymond would get wind of the intrusion and go for help. The leader looked at her and said, "Anybody who drives up the driveway is dead." Greg reacted: he asked Betty Jane out loud if Raymond was home. He wanted to save him. Betty Jane could see what Greg was thinking and said no, Raymond wasn't home yet.

No one heard Raymond's car come up the driveway. The lights

were off in the living room. Only the kitchen light and an outside security light filtering in through the living room window illuminated the house. Raymond walked into the house suspecting nothing. He was soon on the floor with the others.

They had not killed Raymond as they had threatened, and Betty Jane took this as a sign that they wouldn't kill any of them. They kept saying "if" all the time. She felt all the things in the house fall away like dust. They meant nothing to her. Take everything, tie us up, and go. Keith will be home in the morning. We'll be alive. That's what counts. We'll laugh about this someday.

Betty Jane's senses were so sharp that time stretched and she packed hours of impressions into minutes. The crack of wood, the voices, the shoes the intruders wore, the sound of the phones being ripped from the wall. She was working like a camera. She had to get it all down.

"Okay. Let's get this cleaned up and get out of here," the leader said to the others. Betty Jane and the boys were told to lie face down, shoulder to shoulder, on the rug in front of the coffee table. Betty Jane assumed this would be the part where they tied them up. At one point she saw that she could probably have tripped the leader, who wasn't carrying a shotgun. But at the same time she saw a shotgun barrel inches from Ralph's head. She didn't want to do anything to set them off. There was no way to make any kind of move. She lay down next to Greg, with the other boys to her left.

Suddenly there was a thudding boom and Greg screamed. Betty Jane looked at him. Their shoulders touched, and he was about to yell again. He half turned over and pleaded, "Please, don't shoot again. Oh, God, I'm flying. I'm flying."

Betty Jane knew at once they were all going to be killed. But there was no time to think and there was no time to be afraid. She couldn't scream. She was going to die. It was very close now. A strange peacefulness filled her.

The leader seemed disgusted. He grabbed a shotgun from one of the others, mumbled something about showing them how to do it, and stepped toward Greg. He yanked Greg's head back by the hair, put the barrel of the gun inches from his head, and fired.

Betty Jane saw her son's head explode.

Then there was firing from everywhere. The room cracked open with sound. The boys screamed. Betty Jane felt the force of two shots hit her square in the back and thought it was all over.

But she didn't die. The firing and the noise stopped and she was still thinking, still alive. The wig she had been wearing was askew, and her back was numb. The men were behind her now, checking the bodies.

"That one's still alive," she heard the leader say.

"Which one?"

"The second one, the woman."

Betty Jane rolled her eyes to the right and saw the shotgun barrel. Another boom and she felt the pellets rip across the back of her head and shoulder. In the dark they had mistaken her wig for her head. She didn't move.

When she heard them leave, she raised herself up on her knees. The room was dark, smoky, and still echoing with the blasts of the shotguns. Through the side window she could see the four men piling into their car and backing down the driveway.

Betty Jane spoke into the silent room: "Is anybody alive?" There was no answer. Her ears began to clear and she heard what sounded like running water. The noise came from the floor beside her. She realized it was blood gushing from the boys.

Betty Jane's arm and shoulder were numb and she could feel blood on the back of her head and her neck. She went into the bathroom, got a towel, and wrapped it around her head. Then she put on a coat and boots and walked out into the snowy night.

She went to an elderly neighbor's house fifty yards down the road and knocked on his door. The man opened the door to her, but he had trouble understanding what she was saying. She tried to explain that she had been shot and she needed a phone. As the towel hid Betty Jane's blood, the man couldn't believe she had really been shot. But he showed her to the phone.

After calling the sheriff's office, she tried to reach Keith, but he hadn't gotten to work yet. She left a message that there had been an accident and that he should come to the hospital. She didn't want him driving all the way from Indianapolis knowing that the boys were . . . She couldn't finish the thought. She called her sister and brother-in-law, who lived nearby. Then the sheriff's deputy arrived.

She was in severe shock now and was gripped by fear. Those men with the shotguns were still out there somewhere. She heard the elderly man ask the deputy whether or not she had really been shot.

The deputy sent his partner up to the house and called an ambulance for Betty Jane. By the time the ambulance came, she was barely in touch with reality. For the next hour it seemed that she was in a glass bubble, moving from the house to the ambulance and from the ambulance to the emergency room in the hospital. People kept staring at her. Then she had to get back in the ambulance and go to another hospital. Nurses were staring at her. What had happened? She was having trouble making sense of it all. She didn't want to think about the boys and what had happened to them. She was alive. Maybe they were too.

Her sister and brother-in-law were at the hospital and seemed to know what had happened. She just wanted to be safe. Her mind was jumping all over the place. She could hold on to some thoughts, but others were too much for her.

She was going from one hospital to another. All the time people were looking at her; all the time she felt so distant. Her sister kept saying things that didn't make much sense. She said that Greg was at peace. Betty Jane asked why he needed to be at peace. And she heard something about the boys and an autopsy. All these thoughts of death. If she could just get rid of them, everything would be all right. She heard a nurse in the hallway say, "One survivor in critical condition." One survivor. Which one of the boys was it? Which one would I want it to be? She didn't realize that she was the survivor they were referring to.

She was being X-rayed when Keith came in the door. He just stared at her the way the others had. He didn't know anything yet. Thinking that somehow he too had been shot, Betty Jane blurted, "You're alive!" "Of course I'm alive," Keith said. "What happened to you?" Betty Jane's sister took Keith out into the hall.

When they finished the X-rays, she was taken to a private room.

There were police all around. Someone said that there were even police up on the roof. The shades were closed and it looked like a dungeon. But it was safe. The fear did not go away, but something about this room made her feel a little better.

A nice-looking man came and asked Betty Jane's brother-in-law to leave. He was Barney Thrasher, a detective. He spoke softly, asked how Betty Jane was feeling and whether she was up to a few questions. He didn't seem to stand back like the others, and he wasn't staring. He handled her very gently, but he pressed forward. He said that she was going to have to remember as much as she could so they could catch the men who had done this to her. Betty Jane liked him and the way he was treating her. She desperately wanted someone to be close to her and to talk the way he did. She told him some of what happened. She was forgetting so much already. Some pictures flashed into her head, but she couldn't talk about them. She would just be quiet and they would go away.

Barney listened and stayed with her for a while. Then Keith came into the room. He was different from the man she had dated back in high school in the forties, different from the man she had married ten months before, different from the man who had come into the X-ray room minutes before. He came over to the bed but stopped short of touching her. They looked at each other and Keith said, "I'm sorry."

The words hung there while Betty Jane tried to make some sense of them. Other words like *dead* and *autopsy* floated through. Maybe she could do something to stop them. She didn't want them around. But all she could say was, "Don't tell me how many are dead." Then they were both silent.

Barney broke the silence to say that the doctor would be in with some medication in a minute and that would help her sleep. He asked Keith to go with him, and they both left. Betty Jane's sister and brother-in-law stayed until the doctor had given her medication, and then they left also. She was alone in that dungeon of a room.

*   *   *

55

Keith had gone to the first hospital thinking for sure that Raymond had been in an accident on his way home from work. When he got to the nurses' station, though, they said that *she* had been moved to Union Hospital. Something must have happened to Betty Jane. He identified himself at the second hospital and was taken to her, but nobody said anything to him about what had happened. It wasn't until Betty Jane's sister had taken him out into the hall that he knew.

Several men had gotten into the house, had torn up the place, and had killed the boys. Betty Jane was in a severe state of shock and no one in the hospital knew what might happen to her. She was on the edge, and they were handling her with extreme caution. When he went back in to see Betty Jane, all he could think to say was that he was sorry.

Riding out to the house with Barney Thrasher, he didn't find out much more. The detective said that Betty Jane was the only witness, probably the only one who could help them find the murderers. The doctors were certain that she would pull through, but no one could predict how her mind would go. They would have to go slowly with her, not push her on the details.

Keith's head was crammed to the breaking point. There was much to think about, all of it painful. The boys were gone and they had died terrible deaths. He had not been there to protect them, he had not been there to protect Betty Jane. He couldn't bear to think what they had suffered. He didn't want to know. It was hard to believe that any of this had happened. He had lived his whole life in Parke County and had always felt safe. This was rural Indiana, not New York.

And there were all the things he was going to have to do—the details of the funerals, the people he would have to call: the boys' mother, who lived in Indianapolis; and his first-born, Diane, who was at Purdue.

When they got to the house, the driveway was alive with whirling lights, blasting two-way radios, and cars. The sheriff's deputy asked Keith if he would go in to identify the bodies. They needed to know which was which. From the driveway Keith could see lights on in the house and people moving around in the living room. He told them he couldn't do it. His ex-brother-in-law, the boys' uncle, was there and he went in to make the identifications.

When Betty Jane awoke the next morning, Barney was there almost immediately. He told her that the doctor thought she was going to be fine after a while, that the three shots had miraculously not hit any vital organs. He told her that the people who had shot her were still loose and that she was the only one who could help find them. He made her feel as if she had no choice. The boys were gone and, if she couldn't remember, if she didn't tell them what had happened, some other family might have to look at those guns.

They started slowly. He was gentle. He let her talk and hardly ever stopped her. She stopped herself a lot, though. She would see things that she couldn't talk about, and she would hear screams and that gushing sound. She couldn't go near all that again. So much of what had happened was not clear, just a blank. And her arm and back hurt terribly. The medicine they were giving her was doing something strange. She didn't make sense. She couldn't finish sentences.

Barney said she was doing fine and that an artist would be in later to do a composite drawing.

When Keith came, Diane was with him. They did not talk much. She and Diane hardly knew each other. Betty Jane couldn't tell what Keith was thinking. He talked a lot about the funeral and the twenty-four pallbearers. He said that Greg's stepfather, Betty Jane's second husband, was on his way from California. Then he left. They were like strangers.

The police artist came, and Betty Jane tried hard to remember those four sets of eyes. She got a fix on one of them, and the drawing the artist did looked familiar. But she didn't think she could capture the leader. She tried and they made a drawing, but she wasn't sure. When she began to describe the third man, the artist pulled a drawing out of her portfolio. It was the face Betty Jane was trying to describe. The artist said she had done it after a robbery in the county a week or so ago.

Later in the day Fred Stewart, the minister at the Marshall Federated Church Betty Jane attended, came to see her. She and Fred didn't know each other very well, but after a few minutes she found herself talking to him as she had talked to Barney. He didn't try to tell her anything or read her Bible passages. He listened and seemed very distraught himself. Betty Jane asked him why all this had happened. He said that he had no idea why it had happened. There was no answer; things were not okay and he could not pretend they were.

He asked Betty Jane what she would like done or said at the funeral. She had trouble focusing on the word *funeral*. She said she didn't want any singing. Her mind wandered, looking for some words she might like to hear.

"God doesn't make mistakes," she blurted out loud. Where had that come from? She couldn't say, she felt so sleepy. Reverend Stewart asked if that was what she wanted him to say. She nodded and fell asleep.

By the time of the funeral on Thursday, three days after the murders, Parke County had changed radically. Before the murders, there was hardly a door in the county you couldn't knock on without expecting a warm welcome, help with your stalled car, or directions to your destination. But when it became known that the murderers were still loose, there wasn't an unlocked door or one you dared approach after dark. There wasn't a gun or a box of ammunition available in any store in the county. Even the state trooper guarding Betty Jane said that if he were stalled on a farm road he would wait until daylight to go to a farmhouse for assistance. Parke County was scared.

Though people in the county armed themselves and locked their doors, it was hard for them to believe that the Spencers had been the targets of random violence. Parke County had been so secure for so many years that people didn't even want to begin to doubt their own security. If the Spencers had just been the first house the murderers happened on, then that meant everyone in the county was equally vulnerable. That just couldn't be. A year ago a man had

had his wife and child killed for the insurance money. It had been a shock to the county, but as soon as it became known that it wasn't random violence, Parke County residents could rest assured that they were still safe. There had to be a reason why the boys had been killed.

The weather those days was harsh and made it hard for people to get out and around, but the rumors managed to circulate over the telephone wires. They were attempts to fight back the fear that was building in the county. Most of the rumors were centered on Betty Jane. She had been born and raised in Waveland, five miles from where the murders took place. She had known Keith in high school and they had dated right up to their graduation in 1951. Betty Jane had moved to Arizona during her first marriage and to California during her second. In 1975 she and Greg moved back to Waveland and she and Keith, who had also been married twice, got back together. They were married in 1976. To the people of Parke County, Keith was a local and Betty Jane was that gal from California. She must have brought some wild ideas with her. The rumors generally had Betty Jane or Keith or both of them carrying out some ghoulish money-making scheme akin to the murders of a year ago. A typical rumor had it that Keith had lined up the kids and Betty Jane, shot them all, trying only to wound his wife, so that he and she could collect the insurance money they must have had on the boys. The rumors were far-fetched and slanderous, but that was how people convinced themselves that what had happened to the Spencers could never happen to them.

Eight hundred people attended the funeral. The national press as well as state and local media were there in great numbers. Their presence annoyed many of the Spencers' friends and family members, but Betty Jane and Keith hardly noticed. They came into the church after everyone had already been seated. Betty Jane was heavily medicated and leaned on Keith as they walked down the center aisle to their pew. A doctor friend from Huntington accompanied them in case Betty Jane needed help.

Betty Jane hardly knew what was going on. The church was full, and there were four closed caskets on the altar. They seemed to swim in front of her eyes. She sensed, though, in the pit of her stomach, that Greg's casket was out there and that Greg was in it alone. She was starting to feel that she had failed to do the one basic thing a mother is supposed to do: protect her son. He was out there alone. She was still in so much shock, so medicated, that her thinking and reactions were primitive and childlike. She wanted to be protected herself, and she wanted Greg to be protected.

Reverend Stewart spoke first. "God doesn't make mistakes," he began. "Only man does. Oh, the evilness of man."

The service was short and ended with the twenty-four pallbearers carrying the four coffins out of the church. Betty Jane watched as her brother Dale walked to Greg's casket and gripped the handle. She was relieved. Her older brother, the one who had always kept his sisters safe, was taking care of Greg now. Her boy was not alone.

The security at the funeral, and then at the gravesite in the small cemetery in Hollandsburg, was heavy. The press as well as the mourners were kept well away from Betty Jane and Keith. There were state police everywhere. Though the detectives on the case had received a number of tips, not one had panned out, and the four men who had killed the boys were still at large.

Several days after the funeral, Betty Jane was let out of the hospital. Her shotgun wounds were such that the pellets couldn't be removed without ruining muscle tissue. When she went to stay at Keith's mother's house, she had eighty pellets in her back and twenty-nine in her shoulder and right arm. The arm was paralyzed, but the doctors assured her she would regain at least partial use of it. And her body would in time bring the lead balls to the surface and work them out. She was given an ample supply of antibiotics and Valium.

After the funeral, Betty Jane's life had but one purpose: she had to do all she could to remember every detail of the murders and to help identify the killers. For three weeks she did little else but this, talking to Barney Thrasher for long hours at a time. He would bring books of mug shots to the house and she would spend hours poring over the pictures.

It wasn't easy to uncover the specifics of that night. She could say out loud that she had seen Greg killed, but she didn't dare tell anyone the graphic details. Keith didn't want to talk about any of it. He could be protective and comforting at the funeral, but he couldn't bear to hear about the murders. When he had gone back to the house he had seen the destruction and the blood, where the police had put blankets over the place on the rug where the boys and Betty Jane had been shot. Keith's mother didn't want to talk about the details either. Betty Jane had come through something so ghastly that most of the people around her did not dare come close. But her grief was enormous and she needed affection. Keith's grief was the equal of hers, but all he wanted was to be left alone.

After weeks of looking through books of mug shots, Betty Jane came across a face that was so close to the one she had seen first come through her front door that she stopped and could not go on. She was certain. Barney knew how hard she had pushed herself to remember, how many internal defenses she had circumvented in order to help him, and he could see immediately that she really had made a find.

The man's name was Michael Wright. He was from Montgomery County, Indiana, which was adjacent to Parke County. Betty Jane was on the phone to Barney often while the police searched for him. Within days they had tracked him down and had made him talk. Betty Jane felt a small amount of relief. At least one was out of commission. Michael Wright named the three other men he had been with that night. The police picked up Daniel Stonebraker soon after Michael Wright confessed. He confessed as well. It took the police another three weeks to capture the other two. Roger Drollinger, the leader of the group, was out on bail at the time of the murders and about to go to trial on a drug charge. David Smith was only seventeen years old.

It had been almost two months from that Valentine's Day night to the day all four suspects were in custody. Betty Jane had spent that time almost entirely consumed by the search. When it was over, when she and Barney no longer had to meet every day, the bottom of her life dropped away and the fullness of the tragedy came rushing up at her. She no longer could see a purpose to her life, her life without the boys.

For weeks she had hung onto God as one would a life raft. Now she despised God. The boys were dead and she was alive; she hated God for that. She couldn't admit it to anyone, though. Her Bible Belt neighbors would not have understood. Reverend Stewart understood, though. When she found the courage to tell him her feelings, he said that he got mad at God too.

Her anger didn't stop at God or at the murderers. She hated everything and everyone. It was a raw, ugly, destructive feeling that could rise in her and control her for days on end.

She became suicidal. Driving along main roads in the county, she would have a strong impulse to swerve in front of oncoming trucks. But she knew that first she had to convict the four men she had helped capture. She had to do that for the boys. She could almost hear Greg saying, "Mom, where's your guts?"

The severe depression that hit Betty Jane after the suspects were captured abated as she realized that her life once more had a point to it. She met with Clelland Hanner, the local prosecutor, a middle-aged county lawyer who had never worked on a murder trial before, and she began to see that the responsibility for putting Drollinger and the others away where they could kill no one else rested solely on her and her testimony. Barney Thrasher convinced her that she should go back over the details of the murders as often as she could stand it. This was something concrete she could do for the boys, and for other boys as well. She had a mission again.

She became obsessed with remembering every detail of the night of the murders, and she made it almost an act of religion to recite as much of the horror as she could to herself every night before going to sleep. She was so afraid she would get on the witness stand and forget something. One by one, as she was going over the details, the fears and brutality of that night returned.

The details of the murders and the profiles of the suspects were not made public before the trial. Neither was the fact that two of the people in custody had made confessions. Both of them were officially pleading not guilty. Betty Jane could not tell anyone what she had been through for fear of ruining the case against her assailants. But people in the county were aware of the connection the suspects had to the drug world, and the rumor mill placed Betty Jane and Keith in that world. The rumors would have been bad enough on their own; but Betty Jane, relatively unknown in the Hollandsburg area, was able to get around and overheard some of them firsthand. She couldn't defend herself. At times, she could see that people in the county were just protecting themselves with such talk, trying to prove to themselves that they were not vulnerable. But usually it was hard to be charitable in the face of such rumors. They cut too deeply.

As the trial approached, Betty Jane's anxiety grew. She would have to do something that she knew was going to be very painful, perhaps impossible. The first test of her strength came when she had to give depositions to the defense lawyers. She and Barney had gone over what she was going to say, what details she had been able to remember. She had worked to keep the ones that were most difficult to hold onto, and Barney had said he would be there to protect her.

But when the time came to give the depositions, Barney was nowhere in sight and they had to start without him. She had never told the story to anyone but Barney and Clelland Hanner. The Parke County courthouse, where she was giving the depositions, was a cold, imposing place. The defense lawyers did not treat her the way Barney and Clelland did. Midway through the depositions, she went to pieces and ran out of the courtroom crying. The men who followed her didn't know what to do. Then she heard one of them say, "Here comes your friend," and she looked up to see Barney come bounding up the stairs two at a time. Someone had called him. He had forgotten the time of the deposition and had been out working on a case. He went right to Betty Jane's side and soothed her. Barney knew how to care for Betty Jane without being overly solicitous, and she felt it instantly.

He spoke softly, but firmly: "Now, Betty Jane. Let's go back in there. You're not doing this for yourself. You're doing it for those four boys and they're going to be disappointed if you don't get in there and do it right."

To an outsider, Barney might have sounded manipulative; but it was exactly what she needed to hear. She went back in and finished the depositions.

There were to be four trials; the first, Drollinger's, got under way in September. Security at the trial, which was moved to Hartford City, north of Indianapolis, was heavy. The courtroom was packed with people, some of whom had lined up at 5:00 A.M. for seats. Betty Jane was the star witness, the one people most wanted to see and hear.

There had been rumors that Drollinger's father was making threats against Betty Jane's life and so, the day before she was to testify, she and Keith drove in a circuitous route to a friend's house near the trial location. The next morning, Barney picked them up in an unmarked car and drove them to the courthouse. Betty Jane was to wait in a room adjacent to the courtroom. As she walked down the hall past the courtroom, she glimpsed the trial in session through an open door and had a full view of Drollinger seated at the defense table. It was the first time she had seen him since the murders. She went limp and hysterical and was taken to a room and calmed down.

She didn't testify that day. She was certain that Clelland Hanner had deliberately given her an early view of the courtroom and of Drollinger to prepare her for her actual appearance, which came the next day.

Hanner began by asking Betty Jane questions, but soon he just let her tell the story, interrupting only when he thought it necessary to divert her for a while and let her collect her thoughts. She testified for three and a half hours.

Betty Jane was in a trance during those hours, and in that trance she took herself back to the night of the murders. In her practice for the testimony she had never gone through the whole story from start to finish, but on the witness stand she was forced to. When her testimony was over, she was drained of all emotion. She had nothing left in her. She couldn't think or feel anything. She met Keith, who had not heard the testimony but had been in the next room in case she needed him, and together they walked out

64

past the spectators and the press.

Drollinger was convicted on four counts of first-degree murder and given four life sentences.

The editor of the *Parke County Sentinel,* the biweekly paper that served the county, attended the trial. He called Betty Jane and got her permission to print the details of the trial and her testimony. He and Betty Jane felt that people who did not want to read of the horror had only to close their newspapers. They both felt that the people of Parke County should know the full truth of what had happened.

Once people in the county read about Betty Jane's experience and understood the enormous courage involved in appearing in court, there was much head-hanging, especially among people who had convinced themselves that the Spencers had committed the murders or had somehow been involved. In an almost instantaneous reversal of public sentiment, the community that had seen Betty Jane as a suspect outsider now saw her as a saint. She was almost immediately aware of the change.

When she walked into a restaurant with Keith, conversation stopped completely. Standing in line at the supermarket, she would suddenly realize that two or three shoppers ahead of her had stepped aside to let her go first.

But deification meant nothing to her right after the trial. So much of her life from February 14 to September had been dedicated to reliving that one night of terror so that she could lay it before the court, that when she had done that she felt empty and once again in the very depths of depression.

There were three trials still to go, however. The second trial was that of seventeen-year-old David Smith, who was pleading not guilty by reason of insanity. There was a good chance that he might be sent to a hospital rather than to prison. Both Hanner and Betty Jane felt that he was as culpable as the rest and should end up in the same place as Drollinger. If they could get a conviction in Smith's case, Hanner felt certain they could do the same for the other two, Wright and Stonebraker. Betty Jane was once again on the spot.

In the second trial, Hanner led Betty Jane through her testimony.

He had seen what a nosedive Betty Jane had taken after the first one, and he was worried. He felt that to once again merely set her on the track and let her tap into the emotions of the night of the murders was to invite disaster. She went to the witness stand with a migraine headache. Smith had cut his shoulder-length hair and looked very boyish sitting there with his head bowed, his hands folded in his lap; when he cried it seemed to be with sincere emotion. Even Betty Jane, glimpsing him from the witness stand, felt that, in other circumstances, her heart might go out to him. She wondered how the women on the jury were seeing him.

The jury in Drollinger's trial had been out only fifty minutes when they returned with a guilty verdict. In the second trial the jury was out nearly three hours, but they too returned with a guilty verdict on all four counts of first-degree murder. After the conviction, Michael Wright and Daniel Stonebraker changed their pleas to guilty. Betty Jane did not have to testify again.

After the trials, Betty Jane was set adrift. She had lost twenty-three pounds and weighed only ninety-two. She had fought through an enormous amount of pain and appeared to others to be a paragon of strength. From Betty Jane's perspective, however, it was not a question of strength, but rather one of necessity. Her conscience had not allowed her to do otherwise. She was proud of her boys and she had wanted them to be proud of her. She knew that some people would have better understood withdrawal or hysteria, but the boys and what they would want her to do were always in front of her.

Yet all that drive and control left her after the four had been convicted. What earthly reason was there for her to be walking and breathing when those four boys were dead? She was consumed by guilt for just being alive. Then there were the waves and waves of anger: at the four murderers, at the various officials who had let Drollinger out on bail, at God, at the entire world. For two years after the trials, this guilt and anger came so often and stayed so long that Betty Jane, without wanting to or meaning to, drove friends and relatives away.

Betty Jane and Keith were invited to get-togethers and parties in the neighborhood, but after the first few Betty Jane found it hard to attend. The guests gawked at her and didn't include her in their conversations. She had the feeling that she was invited because of who she was; after all, she was a celebrity of a kind. Betty Jane longed for someone to invite her over for a cup of coffee and a morning of talking about the weather or the crops or anything ordinary.

Betty Jane and Keith could tell that their families did not want to see them all that much. Just their presence at family gatherings made everyone nervous. The family seemed to feel guilty at having live children; they couldn't understand the simmering anger Betty Jane and Keith carried around almost constantly. As soon as Betty Jane told her father the details of the night of the murders, he stopped seeing her. He would not come to their house; Betty Jane had to initiate all contact with him.

And then there were the times she would cry in front of people. It upset them because they were afraid they had caused it. It was hard to make them see that the tears were always there and just showed themselves at odd times. She couldn't hold them in, but she didn't want people to stop being close to her because of them.

Keith and Betty Jane had been married such a short time when the murders occurred that they had hardly gotten to know each other. Betty Jane had loved her role as mother to the four young men, and she and Keith had been quite content to center their social life on their new family. Almost everything had revolved around those boys.

With the boys gone, however, Keith and Betty Jane were lost. They sat night after night with little to talk about. For a while they shared the loss. They would talk about the boys, the things they had done, their involvements and idiosyncrasies. And they would tell each other how much they missed them. But Keith could not hear anything about their deaths, and the conversation would come to an abrupt end. Once, though, when Betty Jane was feeling certain that Keith was holding her responsible for the death of his boys, that he was thinking surely there was something she could have done to save them, she made him listen to one detail. She told him about the look she had given Reeve and the shrug of resignation he had made in return. Reeve, the quick thinker, the son most like his father, had been stumped for a solution to the problem. That seemed to help. Betty Jane felt Keith understood what an impossible situation she had been in.

For a year before the murders, Keith had been planning to build and operate his own FM radio station in nearby Rockville. The boys were all going to help out in the venture. Greg had gotten his broadcast license and was working as an engineer at Channel 38 in Terre Haute. The other boys were going to take up a lot of the work as soon as they got out of school. The final building permit for the station had come through nine days after the murders. Keith and Betty Jane had decided to go ahead with their plans. Had they not been so far along in the process, they never would have been able to do it; but they were all set and ready to go. Late in April 1977, Betty Jane and Keith moved from Keith's mother's house to a trailer on the site of the station building. They lived there all summer while the building went up.

When carpenters had finished repairing their own house, Keith and Betty Jane prepared to move back in. Many people who knew them, including Betty Jane's father and other members of their families, were aghast at their plans. They could not imagine ever setting foot in a house that had once been filled with such horror. Betty Jane looked at it differently, though. She knew that she could never escape the memory of the murders. The sounds and images of that night would be with her no matter where she lived. But she also knew that, even though she had lived in the house less than a year, there were many reminders of happy times with the boys that she could find nowhere else. There was the tree Greg had helped her plant and the bushes she and Ralph had put in next to the house. Keith, too, felt that those reminders were ones he wanted to live with despite what had happened.

Betty Jane spent weeks getting the house ready for them to move back into. Her arm was still mostly paralyzed, and her back gave her a lot of pain. She worked slowly. She was obsessed with washing everything that the murderers might have touched. Since they had had free reign, she washed the entire place. She didn't know what to do with the boys' things, so she spent weeks washing all their clothes and then packed them with their other belongings in boxes and stored them.

After she and Keith moved back in, Betty Jane found that she could not be alone in the house at night and that she didn't really want to be alone during the day. She had trouble even driving by herself. She was not afraid of dying, because she felt she had made her peace with death. She feared the fear, the terror of those horrible minutes before the shooting when she and the boys had been powerless and humiliated. She and Keith both bought handguns and learned how to use them. They each had one within reach at all times.

Keith tried to be with Betty Jane constantly at first, but it was difficult. He was trying to get the station off the ground and had a lot of running around to do. Not wanting to be alone was understandable, but it was very hard for Keith to handle.

In the spring of 1979, Betty Jane's frustration was unbearable. In the two years since the boys had been murdered, she had learned to live with some aspects of her new identity as both a victim and a bereaved parent; but there was still much of her life that continually confused and angered her. She needed someone to talk to, someone who might be able to help her sort out the issues, make some sense of it all, help her get on with her life.

She started seeing a psychiatrist. Her sessions went well in the beginning. There were many things that Betty Jane felt or remembered that she had declined to talk about with anyone, even while she had been on the witness stand. She had been afraid that something debilitating would happen to her if she brought them to the surface. But going over those things with a doctor, in her office, seemed like a safe way to do so. If those memories did unhinge her, she had a professional there to help, at least to get her to a hospital. After almost a year with the psychiatrist, she told about seeing

Greg's head shot at close range. It was the first time she had told anyone. She came out of the session in one piece.

At the time that she started seeing the psychiatrist she also began to attend meetings of Compassionate Friends, a national organization for bereaved parents. The people Betty Jane met there became very important to her. She liked the fact that she was not different there; she could talk about the boys and get responses, not silence. And she learned that the grief process she was going through was similar to what many parents went through, no matter how their children had died.

But she couldn't attend as many of these meetings as she would have liked because Keith had to drive her there (she still would not drive alone at night) and he didn't want to go to them. They confused and upset him. Talking things out was not his style. He dealt with his grief in other ways. After learning in Compassionate Friends that taking up a completely new skill was a good diversion, Keith decided to learn to fly. He took lessons and eventually bought his own plane. He wouldn't talk about his feelings, though. There were nights when Betty Jane wondered what he was going through, what he was thinking. He might stare at the living room wall for hours at a time. She knew from his periods of depression, from his sudden, occasional outbreaks of anger, that he was still aching inside. The grief process they both learned about in Compassionate Friends might have clearly identifiable stages, but two people don't necessarily experience those stages at the same time.

Though the psychiatrist and Compassionate Friends were able to relieve some pressures for Betty Jane, there was a part of her that had no outlet: she wanted to do something positive to help prevent other families from having to go through what she and Keith had. She saw things such as bail for dangerous criminals, parole procedures, and the plea of not guilty by reason of insanity as things she would like changed. Helping to make such changes might relieve some of her own guilt and be something she could do in memory of the boys.

But Betty Jane didn't have the vaguest idea about how to start. What do you do? Walk up and down in front of the statehouse

Betty Jane and Keith Spencer

carrying a sign? She felt certain that people would listen to her if she had a forum from which to speak, but none presented itself. She had never been one for causes or organizations, even clubs or women's groups, and activism was completely foreign to her. In May 1979, however, Ruth Ann Gordon, a local television news-woman who had interviewed Betty Jane several times, called with just the opportunity Betty Jane was looking for.

She said that a woman in Mooresville, near Indianapolis, was organizing a meeting of people interested in changing bail laws. Her name was Treva Richer, and she was calling the meeting because a young woman she had been acquainted with and her three young children had been killed by a man with a long record of mental disturbance and criminal behavior who had been out on bail at the time. The meeting, Ruth Ann said, was going to be held that evening in Mooresville. Betty Jane told the reporter immediately that she would be there. The reporter then called Treva Richer to tell her, and Treva in turn called Betty Jane and asked her if she would say something to the people at the meeting. Without hesitating, Betty Jane agreed to speak.

Treva and Betty Jane hit it off from the first. Their goals were similar and their styles seemed to mesh. Both wanted to do some sort of lobbying, and both were willing to do whatever public speaking was necessary in order to put pressure on the legislators. Neither had any experience in these areas, however.

The first meeting drew 350 people. Betty Jane realized that many of them had heard that she would speak and had come to see her. But it didn't bother her. This was different from those awkward parties where people just stared. This was for a cause she truly believed in. If she could use her celebrity status to good advantage, then so be it. She could see at the first meeting that her words would be listened to simply because of what she had gone through; and she could see that she, more than anyone else in the room, would be able to bring the reality of crime to a discussion of public policy issues. She didn't say a lot at that first meeting, but she did make the case for her own authority. "I think I know what it's like to be mur-dered," she said. "The only difference is I didn't die."

The organization that came from that first meeting was called Protect the Innocent. During the summer of 1979, it was an organization in name only. Treva sent out a questionnaire asking interested people to list things they felt needed to be changed in the criminal justice system and suggestions for ways to make changes. Some of the responses were outlandish, but a definite set of goals developed from the questionnaires. The main thrust of the group would be to correct what people saw as an imbalance between criminals' rights and victims' rights under the law. The scales of justice seemed to most in the group to be weighted in favor of those accused of a crime. No one wanted to take away rights given to the accused, but they did want victims to have equal rights. Once, before the trials, when Betty Jane had become frustrated with Clelland Hanner's constant worry that something might abridge the rights of the defendants and blow the prosecution's case, Betty Jane had pounded her fist on his desk and asked just where *her* rights were in all this, and where the boys' rights were. "Honey, I don't think you've got any rights until you kill somebody," he had replied.

In August, Ros Stovall, a young attorney in Mooresville who had done lobbying in Washington before moving back to Indiana, offered to school the group in lobbying protocol and to serve as counsel to the organization. When the state legislature met in January, Protect the Innocent was a definite presence—in the persons of Betty Jane, Treva, and Ros.

Over the next year and a half, the organization was successful in many of its lobbying efforts. Their biggest success was to effect a change in the law covering the insanity defense. Under the law that Protect the Innocent sponsored and saw passed, a defendant could plead guilty but mentally ill, or guilty, or not guilty. Defendants found guilty but mentally ill would serve their sentence in a hospital until they were deemed cured and then would move to a prison for the remainder of the sentence. The new law effectively did away with the plea of insanity. Treva and Betty Jane felt that truly mentally ill people, those who thought they were shooting snakes instead of people, for instance, would never be tried in the first place.

Betty Jane's role in the organization was to gain sympathy for their cause, to use her own story as an example, and to bring the reality of crime to the legislative proceedings. Legislators, expecting fanatics or emotional, unhelpful testimony, were surprised by Betty Jane and Treva. The two women had carefully researched the topics under discussion. Betty Jane, they found, delivered the most difficult of testimony with a great deal of dignity.

In going before the cameras and the committees, she had to draw on the same reserves of strength and the same reasons for exposing herself that she had at the time of the trials. She would tell legislators that she had nothing personal to gain from her appearance before them, that she could not save her boys, but that she hoped to save others by her actions. Though her testimony was often emotional in content, her outward demeanor was not. She thought it absolutely essential that she stick to the issue and make her points straightforwardly. She did this so well that many saw in her a woman of immense strength.

Soon, though, such admiration began to have a negative effect. Told that she was strong and courageous, Betty Jane felt she had to live up to that image, that she couldn't show any weakness in public. She might be nervous before a committee hearing and she might excuse herself after the hearing to cry or throw up in the ladies room, but she felt too much was at stake to make such weakness public. She longed to be able to be weak; but she was caught inside Betty Jane Spencer, courageous victim and crusader.

In January 1981, Keith and Betty Jane went through a particularly low period. Betty Jane felt that her feelings of freakishness could be eliminated if she dropped her appearances for Protect the Innocent. She did, but once again there was that sense of meaninglessness to her life. She felt suicidal and on the brink of a breakdown.

No one knew what to do with her. Her psychiatrist had been helpful at first, but she no longer seemed to know how to deal with her. And when Betty Jane went to her medical doctor with a physical ailment, he would say, "With what you've been through, you have to expect these things." Then he'd try to give her medication. Every professional she went to wanted to give her pills. Had she taken them all, she would have been in a drugged haze constantly.

Keith was the only one who treated Betty Jane as a normal human being, but in January 1981 he was struggling with his own grief.

Betty Jane decided to check herself into the county mental health center. She stayed there for twelve days. She knew that it was an escape, that she was dropping out, taking a vacation; but she didn't care. She just wanted all the pressures and the nightmares to go away.

In many ways, that's exactly what happened. Those twelve days were an enormous relief. No one in the hospital saw her as a freak. They had their own problems. Betty Jane didn't have to maintain that facade of strength. She could cry when she felt like it; she could be as weak as she wanted. In her work with Protect the Innocent, she had been tireless primarily because she felt her work was her justification for living, for surviving the boys. But in the hospital, she didn't have to cram her days with work. She didn't have to make one minute count so that she could draw a breath the next. All she had to do was live.

The stay in the hospital was not a miracle cure-all, however. She might be able to live for herself now, but she couldn't say what direction her marriage would take, how she and Keith would work through their grief. She had experienced the horror of the murders and he had not. Just how that would affect them in the long run she couldn't predict.

She knew that the horror would never go away. At night, if she was not completely ready to go to sleep when she went to bed, or if there were not a distraction like the television on in the bedroom, in that still time just before sleep, the screams or the sound of gushing blood would come to her and keep her awake for hours.

And she was still wrestling with God. In her work with Protect the Innocent, Betty Jane felt on several occasions that God was working through her. She did things that she didn't think she was capable of doing. She talked with God, asked his counsel, and felt often that her prayers were answered. But then her nephew in Kansas City, her sister's son, got quite ill, and Betty Jane prayed for his recovery and her prayer wasn't answered. She was there at his bedside when he died. She was furious with God. Was he going to wipe out her whole family? She and her sister came to understand each other on a much deeper level than they ever had before.

Betty Jane had just about worked out her anger at God when a teenage boy, who had started to work at the radio station a year after the boys died and who had been wonderful for Betty Jane, who remembered her on Mother's Day because she had no boys, committed suicide. She just couldn't see why God would give her little prayers consideration and would trip her up on the big ones. What was going on? Where was this God when she really needed him? She and Fred had many talks about the whole problem. On down days, she found that she could go to him and pour out her heart and things would be better even if there were no answers to her questions. Eventually she came to the conclusion that praying for specifics would not work and that she simply had to pray for the strength to meet whatever God had in store for her.

Betty Jane's relationship with Keith's daughter, Diane, had not been close after the murders. Diane had her own grief to work through. She spent much of her time with her boyfriend. She and Keith had a father-daughter relationship that did not include Betty Jane. Betty Jane couldn't help feeling jealous, Keith still had a child.

After finishing college Diane married and moved onto a farm near Keith and Betty Jane. In the fall of 1981 Diane had her first child, a daughter she named Sarah. After the baby came, Keith and Betty Jane began to see more of Diane and she and Betty Jane began to talk more. Having a child of her own gave Diane insights into Betty Jane's experience that she had not had before.

Sarah was a godsend. Betty Jane had taken a year off from Protect the Innocent activities and was about to go back into the fray, this time not as worried about being freakish, this time not feeling that her work was her justification for living. Sarah helped Betty Jane feel she had some normal connection with the world. She was a little person that Keith and Betty Jane could share in some ways. She was a grandchild Betty Jane could talk to other grandmothers about. She was not a replacement for the boys. She was Sarah, she was new life.

4

Pat Burke

In the late summer and early fall of 1980, Jim Burke was a forty-eight-year-old man living the life of a twenty-year-old college student. Every day he would pack his six-foot-two-inch, 230-pound frame into his Volkswagen and drive the forty miles from his home in Orange Park, Florida, a suburb of Jacksonville, to St. John's River Junior College for classes he was taking toward a degree in criminal justice and corrections work. When his classes were over in the afternoon, he would drive to the Florida State Prison in nearby Starke, Florida, and work the middle shift as a base-level correctional officer. After his shift ended at midnight, he would drive home to get some sleep and to study for the next day's classes.

Although the schedule was a grueling one, Jim was as happy as he had ever been. He saw himself in those months as at the beginning of a third life. His first life had been the twenty years he served in the navy. In those twenty years he had flown combat missions over Korea, taught aviation ordinance skills, and been part of the air wing stationed on the U.S.S. *America* when it was poised off the Israeli coast during the Six-Day War. He had retired as a chief petty officer in 1971. His second life had been the years after the navy, during which he tried several businesses and sales jobs before he decided he would go back to school to become a teacher. The stress of those years had nearly killed him. In 1977 he had three heart attacks, two of them almost fatal. After he earned his associates degree and started work on his bachelors, he began his third life. He started to work part-time for the Clay County Sheriff's Department as a correctional officer in the county jail, and he soon switched his major from education to criminal justice.

This third life was like a homecoming for Jim. He had always been enamored of anything related to law enforcement. When he had been a youngster growing up in Rome, New York, he had made friends with the motorcycle policeman who patrolled outside the junior high school. In the navy he had volunteered for shore patrol and, while stationed in California, would ride in patrol cars with the police in San Jose just for the pleasure of it. Working for the Clay County Sheriff's Department, he would often ride with the deputies on their rounds during his days off.

When a friend in the sheriff's office told him about openings at the state prison in Starke, he jumped at the chance to work in a maximum-security prison. He was hired in July 1980. At the time, he was only a few courses away from his degree, and the job, in combination with the degree, would be the start of a career he had dreamed of ever since he had gotten his first Dick Tracy fingerprinting kit.

Jim's first few months at the prison were not a disappointment. He had found his milieu. He had always been a gregarious sort who could walk into a room of strangers and walk out to good-byes from every corner. He was a good listener, as well as a good talker, and he loved to be around people. For him the worst part of his heart attacks had been the days he had had to sit home alone recuperating. The prison was full of people with little to do but tell stories, especially on his shift. He didn't see much of Pat, his wife of twenty years, or his daughters, Meg, seventeen, and Carolyn, fourteen, in those months, but when he did see them he was happy and full of stories from his new job.

Pat didn't know much about Jim's new job. She knew that the uniform they issued him was a shabby affair with a big bleach stain on the back of the brown shirt. And she once heard him say that an inmate had thrown feces at him. But, hearing Jim talk, it was clear he was happy, and that was all that mattered to her. Some of his stories were fascinating. In fact, he had been taking notes and was thinking of writing a book about his experiences once he got college out of the way. He had met nationally known mobsters, had heard murderers confess their crimes, had seen prisoners on the psycho wing who were clearly insane, and told of death-row prisoners such as Ted Bundy, the intelligent young man accused of a string of murders of college coeds. It was clear to Pat that he talked about his own life, too. Pat taught fifth grade, and one of her craft projects with the children required lots of canceled stamps. One death-row inmate sent Pat an envelope full of stamps he had saved for her class. That surprised her—not that Jim was talking about his family on the job, but that somebody sentenced to death cared enough about her kids to save stamps for them. She imagined Jim was accepted by the prisoners, as he was by everyone else he met.

Jim often had to work weekends on his new job, and on October 12, a Sunday, he drove to Starke late in the afternoon. The correctional officers mustered outside the prison for orders of the day before going on their shift, and Jim joined his shift near the parking lot at about four. His assignment for the day was on a tier in the death-row wing of the prison.

Jim stood out in the group of correctional officers—not so much because of his size or his outgoing manner, but because he was older than most of the men around him and, unlike most of the other correctional officers, he was not a native of one of the surrounding counties. Florida State Prison and the five other correctional institutions near it were some of the largest employers in north central Florida. Two or three generations of men in a family might be working at the prison at the same time. Jim, who had been raised out of the state, who had seen a lot of the world, and who lived in a suburban home on a lake near Jacksonville, was different from these men. But he was such a likable person that he didn't expect he'd be an outsider for long.

One of the first jobs Jim had to do on his shift was to escort death-row inmates to their showers. The prison is one long corridor with three floors of cells organized in wings that are perpendicular to the main corridor. Death row is on R wing. Showers are located at the ends of each row of cells. Death-row prisoners are walked to the showers individually for a ten-minute shower every other day.

For the correctional officers, the shower detail is a two-man operation. One man goes on the row and the other man stands outside the gate at the end of the row and controls the switches that open and close the electronically controlled cell doors. That Sunday night, Jim was working on the row and his partner, Roger Browne, was working the control panel.

They got up to the second floor of R wing around 6:00 P.M. Jim began going down the row. When they came to cell R-2-S-9, Jim saw Thomas Knight, a black inmate who had been on death row for five years, ready for his shower, dressed only in undershorts. Jim signaled for Roger to open the door, and the heavy metal bars trundled open.

Suddenly Thomas Knight lunged at Jim with a crude knife fashioned from a serving spoon. Jim yelled for help and tried to get out of Knight's range. Knight, according to Browne's testimony, grabbed Jim's shirt and began to stab him with the spoon.

By the time Roger Browne got his superior, Sergeant Owens, and then unlocked the grill that led on to the row, Knight was standing over Jim stabbing him. The officer and the sergeant backed Knight off, and he dropped the weapon.

Jim was unconscious and Owens could see a large puncture wound in his chest. Soon two other correctional officers were on the tier and a medical technician was with them. Knight was led away by the two correctional officers, and the medical technician began to work on Jim while he was being rolled onto a litter and then placed on a rolling stretcher and pushed to the front entrance of the prison. The prison doctor met the stretcher crew at the front gate, but there was nothing he could do. He pronounced Jim dead at 6:10 P.M.

Pat Burke was eating dinner with Carol Weidner, the music teacher at her school, and Carol's husband that Sunday night at the Weidners' house. Meg and Carolyn had not gone with her and were home when Chaplain Savage of Florida State Prison knocked on the door. He phoned Pat and asked her to come home. He didn't tell the girls why he had come.

When Pat heard that the prison chaplain was at the house, she knew immediately that Jim was dead. Her years as a navy wife had given her an understanding of what an unexpected nighttime chaplain visit meant. She was certain that her life with her husband was over. There was no agony of uncertainty, no hope for a reprieve. It was final. Carol was visibly distressed but didn't say what she thought it meant. Pat kept her thoughts to herself. She didn't cry as she and Carol drove the few miles to the Burkes'. Carol talked nervously while they drove.

Pat pulled into the garage and went through her routine of locking the car doors, pulling down and locking the garage door, and turning out the lights in the garage. She was worried about how the chaplain would give her the information, whether or not he had already told the girls, and how they would take it. She took a deep breath and walked into the house.

Chaplain Savage was quite anxious. He had not told the girls anything, and he obviously didn't want to be where he was. He told them that Jim was dead and how he died. The girls went to Pat and cried. For the rest of the night they stayed with her, each under an arm.

Pat was surprised that she didn't cry when they did. She fully expected to, but something else happened. As soon as the chaplain had given his information, Pat felt that she was standing between Jim and the Lord. Jim took one of her hands and the Lord took the other, and she knew that it would be this way for the rest of her life. She had a clear image of the three of them going on in life together.

She was probably in shock, but outwardly she was calm and able to make the necessary phone calls to Jim's brothers and sister, his friends in the Shriners, and her mother in Sarasota. Before all these calls were finished, the house began to fill with people. Jim had been such an outgoing, community-minded person that people in the neighborhood and in Orange Park who heard about the murder immediately drove to the house to see what they could do. Jim's

Shriner friends came to assure Pat that, because Jim had paid into a special fund, she would have a large amount of cash within twenty-four hours to cover the funeral costs. Neighbors brought food almost immediately. Within an hour or two of when Pat and the girls were told about the killing, the house was nearly overrun with people.

Pat, who had always liked the role of being in her husband's shadow, now found herself facing a houseful of people without him. She was overwhelmed. Sitting at the dining room table, she felt she had to have something to do. So while everyone milled around and made coffee and conversation, she began to work on an afghan she had been knitting.

Pat couldn't say why she didn't react to the news with crying or hysteria except that that was simply not what she felt or the way she expressed herself. She felt no bitterness, no sense of revenge. She had known Jim since they were kids in Rome, had dated him in high school, and then had married him in California after her first marriage had ended in divorce. While he had been in the navy, they had spent long stretches of time apart, and Pat had learned to function well without him. She had her own teaching, her own life apart from Jim. When they were together, she had been perfectly content to let him choose their activities. She had loved being with him, had loved walking into a room with him and watching the way he made people laugh. She had thought of herself as shy, a puppy dog following this big man with the twinkling eyes. But that did not mean that she had been dependent on him. When she realized that their time together was over, she felt that her tears, were they to come, would be for something that had happened and could not be reversed. When people left that night, she went to bed and went right to sleep.

The funeral was set for Wednesday. On Monday and Tuesday, the house looked like Grand Central Station at rush hour. Pat felt the momentum early Monday morning when the choir director from church arrived and began helping with phone calls and planning the service for the funeral. Jim had always loved music, and both Pat and the choir director wanted the service to be one he would have wanted to sing in, one he would have enjoyed listening to. The choir at the Presbyterian church was going to miss his deep, sonorous bass.

Pat had thought at first that she would have the funeral service at the funeral home, but when her minister, James Lowry, came to visit on Monday morning, he convinced her to have it at the church. He could see that there would be many people who would want to be at the service, many more than the funeral parlor could hold. On Monday morning, Pat didn't realize how much interest Jim's death held for many people other than close friends and family.

On Monday night, three men came to the back door and asked for Pat. One man introduced himself as Louie Wainwright, a name that didn't mean much to Pat, and the other two said that they were supervisors from the prison. Wainwright said that he was the state secretary of corrections. Pat realized, as they stood there, that this was the official delegation from the Department of Corrections. She was a bit taken aback. She did not expect any personal call from the department other than the visit by the chaplain. This was like the secretary of the navy coming to offer condolences.

The three men stood at the doorway looking apprehensive. Wainwright said that he and the members of the department were sorry for what had happened, that the governor would have been with them had he not been away on a trip to Venezuela. Pat invited them to come in, and they looked a little puzzled. But they went in and joined the group in the house at the time.

Only after Pat learned some of the details of Jim's death did she realize why the three men had come to the back door. They had probably assumed that Pat would be both hysterical about her loss and furious at the department. They knew that the department could be accused of being at fault for the death.

On the Sunday morning before Jim's murder, Thomas Knight had had a rare visit from his mother. When a guard had gone to his cell to tell him of the visit, the guard had told Knight that he had to shave; there was a prison regulation against beards. Knight had said that he couldn't because shaving caused him extreme skin irritation. The guard had said that if Knight had something called a shaving pass he could go to his visit. Knight had had such a pass, but it was outdated. The guard had refused to take Knight to see his mother, and Knight had flown into a rage and started yelling that he was going to "stick" somebody. When Jim's shift had come on later in the day, no one had bothered to mention the incident to the men who were going to escort Knight to his shower. Pat would later be told, instead, that he had refused to unbraid his hair for the visit and would feel that this was a plausible regulation, as lots of things could be hidden in braided hair. But when Wainwright came to her house, he knew what had happened the day before and he was afraid that Pat knew also.

Wainwright said that the department was planning a funeral service at the prison chapel shortly before the scheduled three o'clock service in Orange Park. He invited Pat to attend, but she said that she didn't think she could be at both services. He said that the department would like to provide an honor guard at the gravesite and that a group of correctional officers would go directly from the service at the prison to the service at the church.

That was the first time Pat suspected that the funeral would be large. Monday's news reports of the murder mentioned that there had never been a correctional officer killed at the Florida State Prison in the twenty years it had been open and that no one could remember the last time a correctional officer had been killed in the state. The fact that Jim had been killed by a man on death row made the murder all the more newsworthy. The first stories to go out over the wire talked more about Thomas Knight than about Jim.

But on Monday and Tuesday Pat and the friends and family in her house were not all that aware of the national attention the murder was receiving. They were busy going to the airport to meet relatives, arranging the funeral service and the burial. A woman who had known Jim and who did some public relations for the Clay County Sheriff's Office came by to talk to Pat. She said that she was going to write an article for a local newspaper, *Clay Today*. But other than that, the press stayed away.

The article the woman wrote was headlined "Jim Burke Was a Friend to All" and included quotes from some of his Shriner friends and the Clay County sheriff. Next to the article was an AP story datelined Tallahassee that was headlined "Guard's Death not Due to Overcrowding." The story referred to a judge having ordered, two weeks before the murder, Florida State Prison to be cleared of 372 prisoners to lessen overcrowding. That order had been delayed for forty-five days by another judge; and when the initial news of Jim's death had come out, some people in the state had linked the murder with the unfulfilled overcrowding order. In the story, a Department of Corrections spokesman was quoted as saying that, because the stabbing took place on death row, the overcrowding situation could not be construed as a cause, even an indirect one, for the murder.

On Wednesday, as Pat drove to the funeral with Meg, Carolyn, her mother, Carolyn Laird, and her mother's closest friend, Margaret Scott, she knew that she would have to be strong at the service and at the grave. She had heard that after Jim's death there had been trouble at the prison, that inmates had started to riot when correctional officers began an intensive search for concealed weapons, and she wanted to support Jim's fellow workers at the prison.

She still carried the image that had come to her Sunday night— Jim on one side of her and the Lord on the other—and it gave her strength. But another image also kept reappearing. She remembered being in California and watching Jacqueline Kennedy on television during the days after John Kennedy was killed. She had thought then how dignified the woman looked holding her head up at the funeral and the burial. She hoped that she too could look as strong to the people at the funeral. She could see that the girls would follow her lead.

In the days since the murder, they had been either under Pat's arms, at friends' houses, or in their rooms. Carolyn, especially, had always found solace in her bedroom, which was far from the living room. She was in her early teens, and whenever she and her mother or father didn't see eye-to-eye on something, she knew that she could retreat to her room and not be bothered there. Pat felt that such retreats were a necessary part of growing up, and after Jim died she realized there would be times when Carolyn and Meg would want to be alone with their grief. They had both cried when they first heard the news, but as the funeral approached, it looked as if they would be able to hold up under the pressure.

When their car pulled up to the church, it was surrounded by camera crews and reporters. There were so many people outside the church that Pat was certain no one had been let in yet. She was not aware that some fifty carloads of correctional officers had come to the funeral and that, because the church was full, there were an equal number of people outside.

Pat and her family had to wait in the car for a long time before they were escorted into the church. There were so many law enforcement people in attendance that it took a long time just to check all the guns at the door. By the time Pat was finally taken into the building, she had missed the call to worship and the processional hymn, the navy hymn "Eternal Father Strong to Save."

Reporters were everywhere in the church. Pat wasn't that aware of them except during quiet times and prayers. Then she thought all the noise from the cameras was an ugly intrusion.

She had thought that the music of the service might bring her to tears. She and Jim had never been Bible readers in their religion; they had sung their faith. They had both been members of the church choir throughout their marriage, and recently they had sung with the local community chorus. But the music didn't make her cry. She just kept thinking how much Jim would have loved his own funeral.

James Lowry gave the sermon. He said that Jim, in both his life and his death, was a person other people could learn from. He talked of how Jim was quick to see humor in the absurd, and of Jim's Shriner work for crippled children, and of how Jim was quick "to go and care for the most desperate people in our society." Toward the end of his sermon, he seemed to be speaking as much to the assembled correctional officers as to anyone else. He said, "There is one feeling that has no place here today. There can be in this house of worship no lust for vengeance. To lust for vengeance in the name of Jim Burke as we gather to worship his God would be to profane the life and faith he shared with his wife and daughters and friends, and would dull the music and laughter of his soul."

After the benediction, Gloria Hetherington played Jim's favorite song from *The Music Man*, "Goodnight, My Someone," using flute stops on the organ.

The scene at the Jacksonville Memory Garden cemetery was something of a surprise to Pat. The Corrections Department honor guard formed a long double line through which Pat and Meg and Carolyn were going to have to walk to the grave. The camera crews had beaten them to the cemetery and were waiting outside the car. Pat and her family were beginning to feel as if their every breath was being recorded by the media. Margaret Scott wondered out loud what would happen if she got out of the car and ducked behind some bushes. They all guessed that camera crews would follow her even there.

Pat and the girls stood straight and did not cry as Jim was given the Masonic rites. Louie Wainwright handed Pat the flag that had draped Jim's coffin, and the interment service was said. One of the pallbearers fainted in the heat, and the camera crews rushed to record the man being helped up by the other correctional officers. Pat carried the folded flag back through the lines of honor guards, and they drove home.

Pat felt that in many ways her experience of Jim's death had not been as difficult as the things she had gone through at the time of his heart attacks. She had always said that *he* recovered from those attacks but that she never would. The two near fatal heart attacks had come within hours of each other. After Jim had been whisked to the hospital, Pat had been unsure of just what was wrong with him. The hospital staff had given her all sorts of information about heart attacks but had never said that that was what Jim had gone through. Pat had then had days of visits to the intensive care unit. Even then she hadn't been told that twice Jim's heart had stopped completely. She had been aware that he was in great danger and she had had to struggle with her emotions, with her job, and with the responsibilities of the house and the girls. By comparison, Jim's death, from the start, had been a situation in which she had been surrounded by people who could help; she had not experienced an enormous emotional drain, and she was prepared to carry on by herself. She could see that some people expected her to exhibit more anguish or bitterness. But she was not about to tailor her feelings to their expectations.

The evening after the funeral, there were still people in the house and there was, as there had been for the past three days, plenty of food. They watched the news coverage of the funeral, and then late in the evening they went home and Pat went to bed. In her room was a sixteen-channel scanner that she and Jim had bought when he was working for the sheriff's office. It was tuned to the sheriff's frequency and was left on all day. Lying in bed, Pat heard the rescue squad being called to a familiar address, the home of Jim's aunt and uncle, who also lived in Orange Park. Pat pulled on her clothes and dashed to the hospital. She got there before the rescue squad arrived and telephoned Jim's aunt to find out for whom the rescue squad had been called. She learned that Jim's brother, Bud, who had been staying at the house, had had a heart attack. The rescue squad brought him to the hospital, but they could not save him. Pat decided to make the trip to Long Island for Bud's funeral; she made reservations to fly up on Friday.

On Thursday, the local newspapers ran stories about Jim's funeral. Pat was upset with the way the *Gainesville Sun* covered the story. When Jim was killed, the paper had printed a small story on an inside page. But the funeral made the front page. A big photo of Pat's niece, Stacy, wiping away tears was placed above the headline "Hundreds Mourn Prison Guard." The story continued on the back page, where there were just a few paragraphs of copy and nearly an entire page of pictures. Pat found the photographs offensive, and Meg and Carolyn hated them. They were both unnecessary and inaccurate. There was one of her mother wiping away tears at the church service, another of Pat and Meg looking at each other as if they had just had an argument, and one of a grinning Pat talking to Louie Wainwright. There was even a photograph of Jim lying in his open coffin. In this last picture, his best friend in the sheriff's office was viewing the body, and part of Jim's face was visible. The paper had made an effort to portray the family as sobbing and grief-stricken, even though they had not openly shown those emotions; and they had tried to wring the spectacular from the funeral by showing Jim's body in the coffin.

The coverage in *Clay Today* was nondescript, but an editorial in that edition of the paper made a point Pat had heard often in the days since Jim's murder. It said, "Let's stop the endless appeals of death sentences and start executing the people on death row." The editorial went on to make the standard arguments for the use of capital punishment and said that, without the threat of actual executions, "chaos is the ultimate result." The writer twice pointed a finger at judges who are soft on criminals.

Pat had not thought much about the death penalty before Jim's murder. She had heard Jim say that he was a proponent of capital punishment, but they hadn't talked about his reasons for taking this position, and Pat hadn't come to her own conclusions on the issue. After Jim's murder, she had no trouble making up her mind. She agreed with the *Clay Today* editorial, and she became even more pointed than the editorial in her criticism of judges. She heard that federal judges grant many more stays of execution than state judges do, and she felt that they should not have such power. She also learned that a Florida congressman was introducing federal legislation that would limit federal judges' powers in granting stays of executions.

On the plane from Florida to New York for her brother-in-law's funeral, Pat wrote two sample letters. One was addressed to the congressman who was proposing the legislation limiting federal judges in death penalty cases, and the other was a similar letter that could be sent to a variety of legislators. In the letter to the congressman, she said that Jim had been murdered by a man who had been on death row six years; she urged the legislator to "push for this [his bill] as hard as possible." She ended by saying, "I hope his [Jim's] death was not in vain. I am not bitter, but I hope his death will pave a way for better control of prisoners and quicker execution of death sentences." In the general letter to legislators, she made the same points and added, "Do we have to keep supporting these convicts at $20,000 plus a year with our tax dollars?"

Pat wrote these letters with little understanding of why she felt so compelled to act. She had never been one to write congressmen or to protest wrongs. She had spent the past year working with the legislative committee of her local teachers association, though, and in that work she had become aware of the importance of such letters. She was not all that savvy as to the mechanics of the legislative process, but she knew from experience that politicians have their ears to their mailboxes, and that one way to make a difference in the system is to write clear, pointed letters to the people who need votes to stay in office. Because of the media attention Jim's death had attracted and the concern state officials had shown, she knew that letters in which Jim's death was mentioned would have more than the normal effect on legislators. She decided to send her sample letter to friends in Florida and across the country.

Bud's funeral was to be held on Monday. On Sunday, Pat got a telephone call with even more bad news. Her father had died that morning in Sarasota. Pat had seen little of her father during her adult life. He had been institutionalized because of illness since 1945. He was eighty-seven years old when he died of natural causes.

Pat left Bud's funeral, flew to Jacksonville, picked up the girls, and went to Sarasota for a memorial service for her father on Wednesday.

The Monday after her father's memorial service, Pat went back to work. In the two weeks she had been away from her classroom, she had experienced three deaths. There had been a momentum to the events of the past two weeks that was important to her. She could see clearly the senselessness of Jim's death, and she felt it important to do whatever she could to make his life and that senseless death mean something. The sample letters she sent out shortly after she got back from Sarasota were her first attempts to give Jim's death some meaning.

A week after she went back to work, Pat got a phone call from a woman she had never met, Martha Nettles. Martha was the wife of a correctional officer who worked at Union Correctional Institution, a maximum-security prison just down the road from Florida State Prison. Martha had two things on her mind: first, she wanted to invite Pat to a big barbecue that was to be held in Union County at Sheriff Whitehead's farm. It was an annual event to which some twenty-five hundred people were invited and was a must for politicians. Martha said that she could secure an invitation for Pat if she wanted it. Second, Martha told Pat about an organization she was launching, Concerned Citizens for Correctional Officers. She said that she would like to talk to Pat about her plans for the organization and see whether Pat would be interested in participating in some of the organization's activities.

Pat accepted the barbecue invitation and said that she would be glad to talk with Martha. She realized why she had been called, but it didn't bother her. If Martha Nettles wanted to organize in order to better conditions for the correctional officers, and if Pat could help because she was the widow of a correctional officer who had been killed on duty, that was fine with her.

The barbecue was always held on the day of the Florida–Florida State football game and was a must for state and local politicians. Pat was surprised when she was asked to speak to the crowd; she had always thought of herself as a "shrinking violet." Nevertheless, she got up on the stage and said a few words to the large group, urging the people to write letters.

At the barbecue, Martha Nettles told Pat that she was planning another barbecue for the middle of November, at the same place, as a fund raiser for her new organization. She hoped that Pat would come, accept awards on behalf of her husband, and speak to the gathering. Pat had not been frightened by her first brush with public speaking, so she agreed to do what she could for Concerned Citizens for Correctional Officers.

For the second barbecue, Pat prepared a speech. She was direct and to the point about several things. First, she maintained that, although she had not openly shown her emotions, this did not mean she was not grieving. Then she quoted from Reverend Lowry's funeral sermon: "Let us dream of a world where there is no senseless

91

death and no people who kill senselessly, and then let us resolve to give flesh to our dreaming." She said that such thoughts were behind her own motives for wanting to help Concerned Citizens for Correctional Officers. She admitted that she had much to learn about conditions under which correctional officers work, but maintained that she was not so naive as to think that correctional officers themselves were not to blame for some of the problems they faced. She ended by urging her listeners to work together for improvement of their lot.

Pat realized that she was to some extent being used by the new organization; but she thought the group's work was valuable and constructive and that she could be effective in ways that no one else connected with the group could.

Pat began almost immediately to give speeches and to educate herself at the same time. One of the first things she learned was that the turnover rate among correctional officers at the prison was much higher than state officials were willing to admit, that in some years nearly 90 percent of the correctional officers in the institutions around the state left their jobs and had to be replaced. At the time Jim was killed, there had been sixteen openings for correctional officers.

There were many reasons for the high turnover: most of the state's prisons were not situated near population centers; the pay offered correctional officers was dismal; the professional image of the correctional officer was not on a par with that of other law enforcement officers; correctional officers' uniforms were usually as grubby as the one Jim had been issued and added to their poor image.

What Martha had in mind was a two-pronged attack on these deficiencies. First, she wanted to organize among correctional officers themselves by going to the jails, prisons, and juvenile homes in the state and talking to the people working there. She would urge them to work for better conditions in their institutions. At the same time, she wanted to lobby legislators at the state level in an effort to promote legislation that would bring higher pay and more fringe benefits, increased staffing of the institutions, and new uniforms.

Pat Burke

Because she was teaching full-time, Pat couldn't participate in much of the lobbying effort. But for nine months after Jim's murder, she spent practically every weekend traveling around the state speaking to clubs or organizations or helping Martha organize correctional officers at various institutions.

At several of these institutions the administration offered Martha and Pat a room in which they could talk to groups of correctional officers about their organization. At other institutions they would have to try to talk to the officers as they went on their shifts. On several occasions, Pat found that she could gain entrance to a jail or a prison even though the administration denied Martha access to the officers.

Talking to correctional officers and speaking to groups was an entirely new experience for Pat. Jim had been the organizer in the family—he had taken leadership positions in the Shriners and had founded a group of Shriners known as the Klay Kats who drove little go-carts in local parades. Jim had liked Pat to follow his lead and support him in his endeavors, and she had been very willing to do so. But when she found herself in a position of leadership, she didn't shrink from what she saw as her responsibility. She felt that being around Jim for twenty years had been a good education in how to talk with and influence people.

The image of her and Jim and the Lord going on with life together continued to reappear during her work with Concerned Citizens. When she felt that she and Martha had had some success, she would find herself talking to Jim, saying things like, "Well, Jim, we got it together again." Often she would hear Jim talking to her, giving her encouragement in the work she was doing. She could even hear his sense of humor come through: "Don't worry. Nothing to be afraid of in talking to that group. They put their pants on same way I do."

Martha had a cache of weapons confiscated from inmates which had been made from objects found in the prison. She took them with her when she spoke. She gave Pat a ring made out of a fork with a sharp protruding point that could be used to injure someone. Pat always carried the ring with her and used it to open discussion on the subject of correctional reform. She would tell how Jim had been murdered with a spoon-knife and then go on to talk more generally about the problems of correctional officers.

Shortly after Jim's death, Pat received a letter from Governor Bob Graham offering his condolences. It annoyed her. She imagined that Graham had signed the letter along with a stack of other papers and probably without even reading or knowing what he was signing. It was not the sentiment of the letter that she minded, but rather the idea of getting such an obligatory, perfunctory piece of mail. She wanted the governor and attorney general and other state officials who had written her to know who it was they were writing.

In January of 1981, she got her chance to introduce herself to both the governor and the attorney general. She was in Tallahassee for a series of meetings of the state teachers' association. Both the governor and the attorney general addressed her group. The attorney general, Jim Smith, spoke first, and after the speech Pat went to the front of the room, pushed past the press, and went right up to him. She said, "I'm Pat Burke. You've communicated with me and I'd like you to know who I am." She didn't wait for his reply; she just left the room. The governor addressed the group in his cabinet room. Pat sat in front and purposely wore a bright sweater. After he talked to the group, Pat introduced herself in the same way she had with the attorney general. He recognized the name and began, "Are you . . ." Pat said yes and that she would be back later in the legislative session to lobby for correctional reforms and that she would probably see him then. She left abruptly.

Many of Pat's friends and family thought that she was crazy to do the work she did in those months after Jim's death. Pat understood how they felt, but she really didn't give it much thought. She was so swept up in the organizing work, so soon after Jim died, that it was almost as if Jim were still out front leading the way. This had been his last work in life, and in many ways when Pat went out to speak or to organize she was carrying on for him. She realized that her effectiveness would have limits, that people would lose sight of Jim's name and his murder, but she didn't mind. She wanted to trade on his name for the reforms the organization hoped to get. And if Jim's murder somehow did some good for other officers, then it would not seem so senseless.

When Pat decided to visit Florida State Prison, some people thought she was going a step too far. She and Martha had spoken to correctional officers outside the prison; she had stood in the parking lot and heard the noises coming from the cellblocks; but she wanted to go past the double chain-link fence topped with concert wire that surrounded the prison and see the bars and the tiers. A friend of Jim's promised to enable her to go on a tour of the prison. But when he told her that the only date possible for her visit would be January 5, she hesitated—that was the date she and Jim had been married. She decided to go anyway.

Pat had already visited the nearby Union Correctional Institution, and she thought the inmates there had too much freedom and not enough correctional officer supervision. Walking through Florida State Prison, she could see that more of the prisoners were locked in their cells, and she thought it ironic that Jim had been killed in a place where there were such tight security measures.

Overall, she felt that both places fell short of her image of what a punishment institution should be. They looked too much like the free world, with their law libraries and well-decorated offices. She had begun to think about prisons from a correctional officer's perspective, and it galled her to know that prisoners were being given services she considered unnecessary while correctional officers were being paid such meager wages.

Pat didn't get to go onto death row in her tour. Her group saw the electric chair and then were taken outside the prison and around the wing that housed the death-row inmates. It was a cold day, and as they walked around the pale green building they could hear the inmates yelling to each other and to the group of visitors. Pat was neither terribly bothered by this, nor could she connect the place to Jim's death.

Pat had received a copy of the official investigation of the murder but had barely looked at it. Her only interest was in whether or not Jim had died quickly. She had glanced through the report and gathered from the times mentioned in it that he had lived longer after the stabbing than she had initially thought. But skimming the report had given her no picture of the place Jim had been killed in; and as the group went around death row, she couldn't imagine what it looked like behind those barred windows.

Meg and Carolyn didn't mind that Pat was away from home a lot working for Concerned Citizens. As teenagers, they were often out of the house too. Pat wasn't quite sure how they were dealing with their grief. After the first few days, they didn't cry. They certainly did miss their father at times, but neither experienced any abnormal emotional problems. They were used to Jim being gone a lot; in the last few years of his life he had been so busy with school and work that they had seen him only sporadically. Pat was with them on the weekdays when they were home, and on the weekends they were happy to be on their own. Pat could see that, even if she were home every weekend, they, like most of their friends, would not want to spend much time with her. Meg was at the age where she was thinking about finding an apartment of her own, and Carolyn certainly didn't want her mother going along to football games and social events with her. And the girls had no interest in joining their mother on her speaking trips. They had been forced to be on the stage when Pat accepted Jim's award at the barbecue, but they didn't want any more publicity than that.

An execution date for Thomas Knight was set for March 3, 1981. Through friends, Pat heard that one correctional officer had to do a double shift of guard duty in front of Thomas Knight's cell. For sixteen hours the guard sat there and, according to the story, Knight never said a word to the man. She thought the cost to the taxpayers of a guard in front of a death-row prisoner's cell was unnecessary. When Knight was granted a stay of execution, she felt it incredible that someone like him should be kept from the electric chair.

It became clear in the legislative session of the winter and spring of 1981 that the Concerned Citizens for Correctional Officers lobby was having some effect. Legislators listened and took up the cause with zeal. In that session, correctional officers were voted pay raises, more fringe benefits, educational opportunities, and new uniforms. As summer approached, Pat could see that the message she and Martha were trying to send to Tallahassee had been received loud and clear. She could see also that the legislators would carry the ball from this point on and that Concerned Citizens had run its course. Contributions to the organization were slowing, and Pat felt that she could no longer pay for her own trips around the state.

That summer, Pat and the girls spent a month at their family house in the Adirondack Mountains in upstate New York with Pat's mother and Margaret Scott. When they returned and Pat began teaching again, she found herself at home on the weekends watching television. She had never been one to vegetate in front of the television set, and she began to think of ways in which she could fill her time. She realized that she had spent the year after Jim's death running away from home. She no longer wanted to escape, but she didn't know exactly what to do. She was not one to join women's groups. She toyed with the idea of becoming involved in some local politics, but she couldn't see any concrete way to do so. She was up in the air.

In the middle of October, Pat was invited to the barbecue at Sheriff Whitehead's farm. She went, but she realized that it would probably be the last thing she would do for Concerned Citizens.

An acquaintance sent Pat information about a group in Florida that called itself Justice for Surviving Victims. Pat didn't get in touch with the group. She had spent a year making what she felt was a proper response to Jim's death, and she thought she had done enough.

On Halloween, Pat went out shopping in the afternoon with the widow of one of Jim's Shriner friends. Both of their husbands had been commanders of the local unit, and both wives had been quite active at the various Shriner functions. Toward the end of the afternoon the woman mentioned the Klay Kats dance, an annual affair, which was to be held that night. They both decided they would go to the dance and see old friends.

Not only did Pat see old friends, but she met a new one as well. Virgil Nettles (no relation to Martha Nettles), a sheet metal construction worker, was the guest of one of the Shriners. He and Pat hit it off from the start. Since Jim's death, Pat had dated a few times. But after twenty years of marriage, she had felt like a novice. The first time a date came to see her at the house she had had to ask Carolyn what she should do to entertain him. Carolyn had told her to stay away from watching television or playing board games. But Virgil was easy to get to know, and they began dating right after the dance.

The first time Pat cried about Jim's murder was with Virgil. She felt safe with him; she could let down her barriers with him. He was a good audience for her tears. Over the past year, she had thought that if she were to cry she would probably do it alone. Virgil understood what she meant. He told her of a time when he had fallen off a ladder at work and injured himself; his first reaction had been to look up to see if anyone was watching so that he could express his pain.

But Virgil wasn't wild about Pat's crying. He told her he didn't like it. She told him he was going to have to put up with it for a while.

Virgil was much more content to be by himself than Jim had been. He liked to dance and even belly-danced once at a Shriner dance benefit for crippled children. But he was equally at home in the woods or fishing and didn't have to be in a crowd to enjoy himself. Pat was completely happy to let him call the shots. She liked their times out in a boat on the lake, and she soon found that she and Virgil were together almost all the time. Her relationship with Virgil was different from her relationship with Jim in practically every way possible.

Meg had found her own apartment and with Pat's approval had moved out. Carolyn seemed to adjust to Virgil's presence, but one night she stayed out until 5:00 A.M. and said that she had spent the night at Jim's grave. Pat realized that Carolyn must have felt left out. Mom had a boyfriend, Meg an independent life, and Carolyn was alone. Pat could see that a couple of years would change all that.

In May 1982, Pat and Virgil were married. Pat Burke became Pat Nettles.

Pat's political activity was behind her now. She was proud of the things she had done, but she enjoyed being married again. Virgil was a man with whom she could both cry for Jim and move on in her life.

5

Iras Skinner

IRAS SKINNER can't recall what book she was reading on November 13, 1980, but chances are it was a mystery or a thriller. At lunch, after dinner, on the weekends, she plunges into somebody else's fictional nightmare and gobbles it up until the problem is solved, the crook is caught, and the mystery, which may have plagued her for days, is no longer a puzzle.

Iras, who works in the administrative offices of the Arcadia, California, Unified School District, lived with her nineteen-year-old daughter, Katy, a student at Pasadena City College. Katy had come home from her bookstore job, and she and Iras had eaten dinner together. After dinner Iras went back to her book, and Katy got a phone call and changed clothes to go out. Iras didn't pay much attention to Katy's phone call other than to hear Katy say that she didn't have either gas in her car or cash. When Iras asked her about this, Katy said she was just driving a short distance to meet a Richard from her psychology class, and he was going to drive them to a place he knew that had great pie. As she was going out the door, Iras noticed that she had changed from a skirt into jeans. She had left her blazer and a silk shirt on, though, and Iras told Katy that she looked nice. Katy said she might be late coming home. Iras gave Katy a hug, and she left.

Ten minutes later the phone rang, and Iras recognized the caller's voice. It was Paul Edwards,* a boy Katy had dated a while ago, someone Iras did not really care for. She didn't know Katy was still seeing him. She said Katy was out for the evening, and as she hung up she realized how glad she was that Katy had missed Paul's call.

Iras didn't like to read late at night because she could easily read herself awake and not be able to get to sleep. She read for a little while that night and then took a bath. Her yearly visit to the gynecologist, the man who had delivered Katy, was the next day, and as always she was a little nervous about that. But once she got into bed she went right to sleep.

Another phone call woke her up and she answered the phone in the dark. A young man's voice asked for Katy, and when Iras sleepily said she wasn't home, the voice asked, "Is this Mrs. Skinner?" Iras said yes, and the young man said his name was Bob and that he knew Katy from high school. He asked whether Katy had a key chain with a brass tag with the word *Single* on it, and Iras said she wasn't sure, and she asked why. Bob said that he worked at a liquor store on Duarte Road and that someone had found a purse and had turned it in at the liquor store because it was the only place open that late. He saw Katy's picture in the wallet and recognized her from high school. Iras thanked him for calling and asked how late they were open so Katy could pick up the purse when she got back. He said someone would be there until 12:15. Iras hung up.

When she turned on the light she realized that it was nearly midnight. Katy had said she would be home late, so she might miss the store closing. Iras guessed that Katy's purse had been stolen somewhere in her travels that night and that she was going to need it for work in the morning. She called back and asked if it would be all right if she came over and got the purse. The liquor store was only a few blocks away. Bob said sure, and she pulled on her jeans, scooped up Boomer, the silky terrier Katy had bought ten years before, and drove to the liquor store.

Bob told her that the purse had been found by a man at the gas station just down the street. He had found it in the dumpster next

*This name has been changed.

to the garage. He drank a bit too much and was worried someone would think he had stolen the purse, so he turned it in to the liquor store. Bob's boss thought that Iras ought to go over and see if there were any other things around the dumpster that belonged to Katy. He accompanied her to the gas station.

There were indeed some things outside the dumpster that looked like they belonged to Katy. The man who had found the purse at the gas station came out and showed Iras how he had climbed up on the big gray metal box to get the purse. Iras could see some other things that looked out of place down there, like an address book that she was certain must have fallen out of Katy's purse when it was thrown into the dumpster. Iras, who had always been the kind of mother to do the unusual if she thought it would help Katy, climbed into the dumpster to retrieve her daughter's things.

A police cruiser pulled up as Iras was climbing out of the dumpster. It was a young cop, and he was attracted by the sight of two men and a woman with a dog fishing around in garbage. He talked with the man from the gas station first. Then he came and asked Iras if she knew where Katy was. Iras said no, but it wasn't unusual for her to be out that late. Iras was just worried that Katy would be looking for her car keys and her purse and might not be able to get home. The policeman said that he would make out a missing persons report.

It was a chilly November night but Iras had not felt the chill while they were searching for the things in the dumpster. Now she suddenly felt cold. It was odd the way the feeling came on.

She told the policeman that Katy wasn't missing, she just might not be able to get home. The policeman asked for a description so they could be on the lookout for her. From her reading Iras knew about police procedures, and she questioned even that much police involvement at this point. "Don't you wait until twenty-four hours have elapsed before you take a report?" He said they did, but under these circumstances they might be able to help if she couldn't get home. Then he asked if anyone was home to answer the phone. Iras said no, so he quickly took the description and told her to call the station when she heard from Katy. Iras said she was just going to drive by some of Katy's friends' houses to see if her car was there. The policeman urged her to go right home to be there for the call. Iras did that.

As soon as Iras got home and collected her thoughts, she realized that the keys she had were not car keys but house keys. That made a difference. Katy was probably out trying to find her purse and her keys, not wanting to wake her mother up and get yelled at for losing her house keys. Iras called the police station to tell them about her discovery. The man at the desk that she talked to took down that information and then said, "Don't you feel relieved the keys to your house aren't out there missing?" Yes, Iras thought, and she hung up trying to feel good.

One o'clock came and went and she was into her second cup of tea. She had turned the heat up when she had come back from the liquor store, but she just couldn't get warm. The Skinners lived in a rented house on a quiet street. The kitchen was in the front of the house and looked out to a pool of light formed by the streetlight. Iras would spend fifteen minutes with a cup of tea staring out the front window and then would go into the adjoining living room and wait for the sound of a car stopping in front of the house. But none did.

She began to think that Katy had been in an accident and could not be identified because she didn't have her purse. She called the local hospitals, the ones with emergency rooms. They were curt. No, no unidentified accident victims tonight, good-bye. She couldn't have been in an accident out of the area because her purse was found here. Let's face it, Iras thought, she just doesn't want to come in and wake me up. She's going to stay out all night and come in at 6:00 A.M., when she knows I'll be awake.

By 2:00 A.M., Iras was tired and still cold. She got a blanket and wrapped herself up on the couch. But she couldn't go to sleep and she couldn't get warm. She thought of calling Katy's friends, but it was too late for that now. And she considered calling her own friends to tell them how upset she was getting. But she would have felt embarrassed having to say that Katy was missing, and she knew that once Katy got back home she'd be angry if Iras had brought others into this. She had raised Katy alone, and now she was going to have to deal with this alone as well.

The night stretched and stretched. Iras began to think that Katy had been in some trouble with the law; since she was over eighteen, the police wouldn't have to notify her that her daughter was in jail. But Katy had never even come close to being in trouble. She was in her second year of college, though, and unlike during her high school years, when Iras had known all Katy's friends and activities, there were large chunks of Katy's life that now Iras knew little about. Like this Richard she was supposedly out with tonight. Who was he? She didn't even know his last name. She suspected Katy was hanging out with some marijuana users, but she wasn't sure. Katy wouldn't even let her smoke in her room. How could she be involved with pot? But if she hasn't been in an accident, she *must* have spent the night in jail.

Daylight came late because it was November. Somehow, even though Katy wasn't home, Iras felt with daylight she was getting closer to finding out what had happened. The phone was going to ring soon, Katy's orange camper truck was going to swing into the driveway, and everything would make sense. There would be words, but they would be able to deal with whatever had caused Katy to be out of touch so long.

An hour into daylight, around 7:30, Iras called Bob Dean, Katy's closest friend. He wasn't a boyfriend in a romantic sense. He was one of "The Four Musketeers," as Iras called Katy and her three closest friends from high school. Katy didn't date often; she was overweight and, though pleasant-looking, not the prom queen type. She didn't spend a lot of time chatting with other girls about clothes and makeup. She had her music activities and, in high school, her three close friends. Bob Dean and she still saw a lot of each other, and he might just know where Katy was. Perhaps if she were waiting for Iras to leave, she might just have gone to Bob's house.

Bob didn't know a thing. Iras told him about the purse and asked if he had any clues to where she might be. Bob said he thought she was seeing Paul Edwards again. "Oh, my God," Iras said. "When did that start up?" Bob said they had been seeing each other for a

Iras Skinner

week or so and that Katy thought things might work out this time. Iras hung up with something else to worry about.

At 8:00 A.M., Iras had to call work to tell them she would be late. She reached another secretary in the office, Carol, and tried not to sound too panicky. She said that Katy had not come home and that she was probably in some kind of trouble. Carol asked Iras if she wanted her to come over, but Iras, her voice beginning to quiver, said that was unnecessary. She couldn't remember the last time she had cried, but she was coming close to it now. Carol didn't think Iras should be alone. She said, "Why don't I call Julie and have her come over? She can be spared." Julie was their boss, and this attempt at humor lightened the mood a bit. Iras said that Katy would probably be home soon and that she'd be in to work then.

The phone rang almost immediately after she hung up. It was Julie; she wanted to know if Iras would like her to come over. Iras invited her for a cup of coffee.

After Julie arrived, they sat at the dining room table, and Iras told her all that had happened the night before and her theories. Iras soon noticed that Julie's gaze was not meeting her eyes; she was saying "Oh, my" a lot, and every now and then would get up and pace. After half an hour, Iras decided to call the police again.

She was relieved to hear a friendly voice when the officer answered. It was David Hinig, the son of a man Iras worked with.

"David, this is Iras Skinner. You may not remember me. I work with your dad."

"Of course." He sounded very sober, but Iras remembered him as a serious type.

"This is embarrassing, but are you aware that my daughter didn't come home last night?"

He was very much aware.

"I guess there's no news."

"Hasn't someone been to see you?"

"No." Iras didn't understand. David put her on hold, and then came back on.

"Mrs. Skinner, there'll be a couple of men over to see you in a few minutes. To get some more information."

Iras felt better, but Julie got up and started pacing again, hardly looking at Iras.

Soon an unmarked car stopped in front of the house and two plainclothes policemen got out and came to the door. Thank God, Iras thought. This horrible night is over and they've come to make everything better. She greeted them at the door like long-lost relatives. They introduced themselves as detectives, and Iras got them some coffee before they all sat down in the living room.

One of the detectives was doing all the talking, asking questions about what Katy looked like and what she was wearing when she went out the night before. Iras felt good about the questions. The house had been so silent all night, and here they were talking up a storm. She sat on the floor at the detectives' feet and answered their questions the way a good witness in a detective novel would.

They asked about the shoes Katy was wearing; Iras couldn't remember, so she went into Katy's room to check. Iras was a little perturbed with Julie. She was being quite rude. She didn't sit in the living room. She was at the dining room window.

Iras came back out from the bedroom and said she guessed Katy was wearing hush puppies. The detective asked if it could be hiking boots instead, and Iras went back into the bedroom to check again. She didn't find Katy's waffle stompers, so she went back into the living room and said she guessed he was right, she must have been wearing hiking boots. She felt proud that she had solved that one with the detectives. She wondered why Katy had worn those boots with her silk blouse and blazer.

The policeman asked, "Did she have a mirrored heartshaped pin on the blazer?"

Iras thought for a minute. "Yes, she wore it . . ." Something clicked. "You've seen her?" She knew now that they must have seen her, must have her in custody, why else . . .

For the first time the other detective spoke.

"We think we've found her. Yes, we have her body," he blurted.

Iras was sitting on the floor and suddenly her whole body was one huge sound: a scream, a cry, a wail. Katy's dead! Katy's gone forever!

"Where?" Iras finally managed to get out.

One of the detectives said the body was found in the courtyard of a medical building at 623 Duarte Road. Iras knew the place. That was her gynecologist's building.

"How, alone?" she asked.

She heard the detective say something like "beaten to death," and everything in the room became blurry. Iras asked questions just to stop the awful images that were coming to her. She asked if it was drug-related. The detectives were curious about her question, but they didn't probe much. They asked questions about friends, who they could go talk to, and Iras gave them some names. But she wasn't really thinking about all that.

Katy was gone and she wanted to go with her. Oh my God my life is over now. The only thing that means anything to me in the world is gone. I'll go too. I'll join her. The men were getting ready to leave and she was talking to them, but all she could think was that she wanted to die.

The detectives said that they had found Katy's car on a street right around the corner from the gas station where her purse had been found. Had she taken a little drive around the block as she had told the policeman she was going to, she would have found the car. Then she might not have spent the night waiting. But she wasn't really upset with the police. They were the ones who were going to find out how this whole thing had happened, who had done it, and, most important of all, why. Why would anyone want to beat my baby, my only child, to death? The question rose with each wave of tears and crying. It seemed like the question would drive her crazy. She wanted desperately to die, but she had to live long enough to find out who killed her daughter and why. Then she could feel comfortable dying.

Shortly after the detectives left, Iras called her gynecologist to say that she wouldn't be in for her appointment. She probably could have just skipped the appointment, but something made her call the offices that she knew were at the address where Katy's body had been found. Her doctor got on the phone and said that when he came to work the police were making their investigation and he had seen the body. Katy was so badly beaten that he couldn't identify her at first. He had hoped the body wasn't one of "his kids," but it was, and he tried to offer some consolation. Iras asked him how he thought Katy had been killed, how quickly she had died. He was straightforward with her. He said that the injuries were so massive he was certain that Katy had died very quickly or was unconscious after the first blow of the attack.

Iras thanked him for the information, but she said that she really didn't believe Katy had died quickly. She imagined Katy trying to ward off her attacker. She could hear her daughter desperately calling, "Mommy!" What had Katy gone through? Over and over again Iras heard her yell, "Mom, help me!" The doctor understood.

Seeing Katy alone facing death was the difficult part for Iras. She wanted to be there to protect her daughter, but Katy was gone now, and she had been by herself in the end. Iras could not get that thought out of her mind.

During the first few days the police called Iras constantly, but they came up with no clues. They found the Richard that Katy was supposedly going to have dessert with, but he knew nothing of either the dessert date or Katy's whereabouts that night. Much to Iras's displeasure, they grilled Bob Dean for hours. Bob was an intelligent and sensitive kid, and Iras imagined that the police questioning had been a frightening experience for him. After a few days, Iras called Bob's mother to apologize for the ordeal. The police questioned lots of kids from the high school and from Katy's college, but nothing came of it.

Iras had told them about Paul Edwards and they had gone to see him, but they had gotten nowhere. In fact he had refused to talk and had retained a lawyer. That made him suspect and confirmed some of the opinions Iras had held of Paul since Katy had first brought him home. Iras didn't think that he could have killed Katy, but he might know something, or he could have set her up for someone else.

Iras was certain that the killing was done by someone familiar with the area. The dumpster behind the gas station was hidden from the street. The person who drove Katy's truck away from the medical building and then left it on the side street had probably cut through the alley behind the gas station and flung the purse into the dumpster. You'd have to know the area, know that dumpster, in order to get back there. A stranger to Arcadia, a hitchhiker who was just passing through, would not have seen the dumpster from the street.

Iras spent days trying to put all the pieces together. The police were asking a lot of questions, but they weren't answering many. She trusted them completely and saw them as her saviors, as heroes. But she felt that if she knew everything about those last few minutes of Katy's life it would make more sense somehow. A disease or an accident would make sense. She was not a religious person, but she did believe that there was a plan to life, that we each have an allotted time, and that diseases and accidents are ways in which God, or whatever is responsible, says that time is up. If Katy had died of cancer before Christmas at least that would have been her fate. But another person took Katy's life and destroyed the plan. Iras yearned to know who had upset Katy's true fate and why.

The police told her that the medical building courtyard where Katy was killed was a hangout for kids who smoked grass, but they hadn't linked Katy to any of that. They did tell Iras some things about her daughter that she would rather not have heard. Katy had not told Iras the truth about where she was going the night she was killed, and it appeared, after the police began to do some investigating, that Katy at times stretched the truth with others. The police found that Katy had been beaten by someone once, and to cover up the beating she had told Iras that she had fallen down steps at work. To others she had said that her mother had hit her. Iras called some of Katy's close friends and asked about the incident. They said Katy had not said anything like that to them, probably because she knew that they would never believe Iras capable of beating her daughter. The police soon realized that Iras was not the kind to beat her daughter, but they had to check everything out.

Iras's only living immediate relative was her brother, George, who lived in Colorado. He and his son Mike reached Arcadia the day after Katy's murder. When Iras saw Mike, she longed to have Katy with her. Mike and Katy were near the same age and had played together in the summers when Iras and Katy would spend a month in Colorado. They hadn't done that for a while, though, and they hadn't seen Mike as a grown young man. Katy would have loved to have seen her cousin as a college student. There were so many things in those first few days that Iras wanted to share with

Katy. Look how many friends are coming to the house, Katy. Listen to all the wonderful things people are saying about you.

George was very helpful in the first week after the murder. When the police no longer needed Katy's car, George drove it home; and when the coroner's office released Katy's body to the funeral home where Katy was to be cremated, George went with Iras to pick up Katy's belongings. There was not going to be a funeral and, thank heaven, they were not required to identify the body. The police had done that through dental records. Iras wouldn't have viewed the body no matter what. She had seen her first husband's body after she had watched him slowly die of tubercular meningitis. She vowed never to view a body again. She wouldn't do it at her first husband's funeral, she wouldn't do it at her father's funeral when Katy was four, or her mother's funeral several years before. She thought she might want to go and look at Katy's hand once more, see the round, dimpled fingers, but she knew that wouldn't be possible. She didn't want to be present when Katy's ashes were scattered up in the mountains, so she knew that picking up Katy's personal effects at the coroner's office was going to be her last contact with Katy's body. She was glad George was with her.

They went to a small room in one of the corridors of the county office building. There was a man standing behind a window covered with wire mesh. They told him why they were there and he went to get an envelope. He emptied the jewelry in the envelope onto the window ledge and then checked off each item in front of them and had Iras sign a paper. They were out of the building in minutes.

After they got home and George and Mike went out for a while, Iras took the envelope from her purse and looked over the jewelry. The first thing she took out was a pearl drop on a gold chain that Katy had been given when she was five or six by Iras's Aunt Ethel. Iras held the drop in her hand and thought that Ethel would have liked to know that Katy was fond of that piece of jewelry. As she held the piece of jewelry the reality, the finality, of Katy's murder came and she went to the bathroom to throw up. But she could not put the envelope away without looking at everything else, even the blood-stained, mirrored, heart-shaped pin. She had to know everything, no matter how morbid. With the pin she could gauge how far down on Katy the blood had come. She picked up a ring that had blood on it and wondered if Katy had put her hands up to protect herself when she saw that she was about to be attacked.

Iras and Katy had never gone to church, and Iras knew that Katy would not have wanted a funeral. But when Edwin Linberg, the minister of the Christian Church in Temple City and the father of one of Katy's close friends in high school, called to ask if it would be all right if they held a memorial service for Katy the first week of December, Iras was pleased. One of Katy's achievements in high school had been to sing in the elite group drawn from the school's concert choir, the Brighter Side Singers. Dr. Linberg said that he and his daughter, who was also a member of the group, would put together a service, and that many of the people who had worked on music and drama programs with Katy at the high school had already come forward and asked about doing such a service.

A few days before the memorial service, Dr. Linberg dropped by the house and went over the program with Iras. Fifty past and present members of the Brighter Side Singers were going to be in the choir loft, and Katy's choir director would be playing the organ. John Higbee, who had been in the Brighter Side Singers when Katy was, and who was now doing professional work as a tenor, was going to sing a solo of the Lord's Prayer. Iras had always choked up when she heard John Higbee sing solo, and she had kidded with Katy that she would like John Higbee to sing at her wedding. Katy had been certain that John Higbee wouldn't want to sing at her wedding, and here he was volunteering to sing at her memorial service.

Iras knew she wasn't going to be able to see all of these people without breaking up, so she went into the service after everyone was seated and left before the congregation went out. But there was no way she could avoid the emotion around her. On her way in, she saw a clutch of young men huddled together at the back of the church crying. As she sat down, Bob Dean reached out his hand to her. His eyes were swollen from crying, and Iras's heart went out to him. He was as close as she had come to having a son. In the last few days she had wished she had been given other children, but seeing Bob Dean's suffering, she wasn't sure. She realized that if she had had other children, they would have suffered terribly over Katy's death.

Dr. Linberg's comments surprised Iras. He began by saying that Katy had not been a member of his church, but that in her senior year in high school she had come to his office when she was working on a term paper and had talked with him for an hour or so about Christianity. She had wondered if a person who did not attend church could be considered a Christian, and she gave him her views on people who did go to church but did not act like Christians outside of church. Dr. Linberg said that as far as he was concerned, knowing the care and concern Katy showed for others, she was a Christian even if she was not a church-goer.

Iras had known nothing about Katy's visit to the minister. When she heard that, she felt Katy was, in some ways, back—not the Katy who had been murdered, but the Katy who had always wanted to stop at Indian reservations on their way back from Colorado, the Katy who had joined Greenpeace, a political group advocating ecological policy reform, the Katy who had wanted to picket with the handicapped students on campus when they were seeking access to buildings.

When the Brighter Side Singers began to sing, Iras was sure Katy was there. She turned to look back to the choir loft. It all looked so familiar. How many times had she seen those same faces lined up in just that way singing those songs! She even got angry while they were singing because she was sure Katy was up there and another girl, a tall girl, was standing in front of Katy's spot and blocking Iras's view of her.

Feeling that Katy was there at the memorial service made Iras glad that Katy could see her friends, see the tears they were crying for her. Tom, her partner in the Brighter Side Singers, someone she had been especially close to in high school but who had been out of touch in the year they had been in college, was crying along with the rest. Katy had always been somewhat self-deprecating, like her mother, and yet here were all these people she admired admiring her. Iras knew that this was the time and the place to say good-bye to her daughter.

After her brother went back to Colorado, Iras was alone in the house. Her cousin Var and his wife, Ann, had been very helpful in the first few weeks and had told Iras to call anytime and to come to their house whenever she wanted. But Iras is not an outgoing person, and inviting herself out or asking others to come over is not her style. For the nineteen years before Katy's murder, her life had consisted mainly of working and taking care of her daughter. After Katy had left high school, Iras had felt less needed, but she had not branched out socially. She was not a club joiner; neither did she have any hobbies. And she was not a drinker. Her housework didn't take up much time, so the majority of her hours outside of work were spent with Joseph Waumbaugh, Robert Ludlum, and the like. When Katy was out at night, Iras acted as a switchboard operator, taking messages for her. When Katy was home she would more than likely hole up in her room and talk on the phone or play the guitar and sing. There was always either live or recorded music in the house. Now there was only Boomer waiting for Iras when she returned, and the only sounds in the house were the clock chimes every quarter hour.

Iras went back to work to fill up the hours during the day. Her frequent tears made it hard to go to the office, but the embarrassment of crying in front of others was easier to live with than all those daylight hours at home alone. She had seen a doctor who recommended that she try to structure her time as best she could, that she plan her weekends in advance. But she couldn't plan every minute, and there would inevitably be those days when 5:00 P.M. would come and the hours between then and 8:00 the next morning would yawn like a horrible void. Panic would set in if she came to a Friday without anything planned for the weekend. She feared going days without hearing another human voice.

Her nightmares were vivid. In them Iras would see the scene at the medical building courtyard played out before her eyes. She would hear Katy scream and she would know who it was who killed her. She would wake either screaming or with a migraine headache that threw her entire body into a rigid arch. But upon waking, the identity of the person she had seen beating her daughter would slip from her mind.

In the first month after Katy's murder there were any number of things that would bring Iras to tears. The day after Katy's death, Iras heard a song, "What Are You Doing the Rest of Your Life?" on the radio and she couldn't get it out of her head. She would find herself humming the tune, and then it would trigger thoughts of Katy. She had hundreds of thank-you notes to write, but she could never get through more than two or three in a night. She would cry and then find herself overcome by inertia, sitting at the dining room table staring for hours at a time. Katy's death certificate arrived and gave the date of her death as November 13, when Iras was certain that Katy had been killed before midnight. Time of death was not listed; it simply said she was "found." Iras knew that was a small point, but "found" sounded so forlorn that the tears came as soon as she read the word.

Iras spent much of her time those first few weeks either in bed or in a stupor. The only thing that would help her stop crying was thinking about how Katy would react to her tears. Iras felt that if the Hindus were right, if death is simply a move to another plane of consciousness, perhaps Katy was aware of her mother's crying. And she could just hear her daughter chiding her. "Go ahead, Mom, grab the spotlight. Who are you feeling sorry for? Me, because I'm not going to have a life anymore, or yourself?" That would be the way Katy would deal with her mother's tears, and imagining it helped Iras pull herself together.

In many ways, the self Iras was feeling sorry for was one that was radically different from the self Katy had known. Iras had been widowed at age twenty-five. People had told her then that she was young, that she had her whole life in front of her. And she believed them. When Katy was born, Iras, who had always avoided committing herself to a career, saw motherhood as her vocation, and for nineteen years she devoted herself to that vocation. Iras was married to Katy's father, her second husband, only briefly, and was divorced from her third husband before Katy entered kindergarten. But Iras was content with her role as a single parent even at a time when that role was not socially acceptable. In many ways Iras lived through her daughter, and as Katy approached an independent life, Iras was looking forward to a wedding and grandchildren to make her old age full and complete.

All that was gone now. There would be no grandchildren. Iras was nearly fifty and considered herself over the hill. She could see no wide open life in front of her. Katy would always be nineteen, and Iras was going to get old and wrinkled by herself. When she thought of Katy, it would always be as one who had hardly tasted the world. The high points of her life had been a summer trip to Europe that she took after high school and a starring role as Mother Abbess in a high school production of *The Sound of Music*. Iras would reach her sixties, her seventies, maybe even her eighties, and the gap between her and her teenage daughter would grow wider each year.

Iras used to be afraid of dying, but now she was only afraid of growing old alone, of suffering without others, of being helpless. Since the moment she knew Katy was gone, the notion of suicide had entered her consciousness, but it was never anything concrete. She didn't know how to do it, and she didn't want to make things difficult for her family. She didn't want to be here in life, but she didn't know how not to be here. Some days her solution was just to stay in bed as long as she could.

Katy's car, actually a compact pickup truck with a camper top over the back, sat in the driveway for weeks. When George had first driven it home, Iras had immediately cleaned off the finger-printing dust and emptied it of notes, parking lot stubs, and books. Then she didn't know what to do with it. She didn't drive a standard shift, so she couldn't use it herself. A neighbor told Iras that seeing the orange truck in the driveway made her feel sick. Iras didn't say anything, but she wondered if her neighbor realized just how sick it made her feel.

The local paper had run a picture of the truck when the police were looking for anyone who had seen the car the night Katy was killed. Now Iras worried that the car in the driveway was an advertisement to people who drove by that Arcadia's recent murder victim used to live there. She didn't want people gawking at her or at the house. She didn't want to be looked at as the mother of a murder victim.

The car in the driveway was sometimes a sudden reminder of Katy. In the morning, Iras would get up and have something else on her mind, but when she went to the kitchen window and saw the orange vehicle, it would all come back to her. Or when she drove home from work and turned onto South Third Street, getting her first glimpse of the car, for an instant she would think, "Well, Katy's home," before she would snap back to reality.

Iras had always had trouble asking people for help, and so the car just sat there for a while. One day a woman she worked with approached Iras with an offer of help. She said that her husband passed by the truck every day on his way to work and wondered whether Iras wanted to get rid of it. He had told his wife that he wanted to do something for Iras and thought that, if she wished him to, he would take care of selling the car for her. Iras was touched by this offer, and after a little thought said that she would appreciate his help. It wouldn't start, so he had it towed to the garage and then sold it for Iras.

Calling other people to plan outings, dinners, anything social, was difficult for Iras. She knew that people were sincere when they said "call anytime," but it wasn't easy to call someone for no reason other than simple loneliness. Sometimes an empty Saturday afternoon would come around and Iras's panic would overcome her fears and she would call someone.

Often, though, she would make plans with someone and then she would get sick. She wondered if she were as fearful of the contact as they were. Her friends' embarrassment was obvious to her; she could see it when they exchanged recipes in front of her, and she could see it when she spoke of Katy. Iras found that it was much easier to have dinner alone at a restaurant with a book for company. She liked the sounds of voices around her, and small talk—asking the waitress something about the menu—was much preferable to embarrassing scenes or an empty house.

Small physical ailments that Iras had had some trouble with for years now became serious. Migraine headaches came with frequency, and a small ulcer grew to a painful size. She took medication for these ailments, but she didn't want to take anything like Valium. She was afraid she might become addicted to tranquilizers. Once though, for a month, she did take a pill her doctor called a mood elevator. She had gone to see him because Katy had been dead for four months and she could not stop crying. Her throat was raw from trying to choke off cries, and she was sick of walking around with swollen, puffy eyes. She thought nobody would want to be around her if she couldn't put a stop to the constant tears. The first few days, the mood elevators did quite the reverse; but then the sleepiness wore off, and she found that her crying came less frequently.

At about this time Iras's office sponsored a one-night seminar on the use of small canisters of tear gas for self-defense. The local police had offered the class to any interested group, and there was a sign-up sheet in Iras's office. She really didn't have a great interest in the class, but she signed up because, first, she felt that people would think it very strange if she didn't attend after what had happened to her daughter, and second, the class was to be given by the chief of police, and she knew that he would know who she was. She wanted to sit right up front for him to see. She was starting to feel very frustrated by the irresolution of Katy's case. She didn't feel the police were doing a bad job or were incompetent, in fact she felt just the opposite; but she was beginning to sense that they were at the end of their day-to-day work on the case, and she didn't want them to forget her.

Iras had become, as she called it, a "cop groupie." The two detectives who worked on Katy's murder were considerate men, and a call from them, even if it was just to ask some more questions or report that there was nothing to report, could keep her going for days. These men were the heroes who were going to tell her why someone had killed Katy, if anyone could.

Fearing that there would be too many memories if she stayed in Arcadia for Christmas, Iras went up to San Francisco to stay with an aunt who was a near invalid. In her ten days there she only went outside for a few hours; most of the time she slept or cried. The day before New Year's Day she came home, but did nothing to celebrate the first of the year. On January 2 she was lying in bed not wanting to get up, thinking she might spend the whole day there, when the phone rang. "Happy New Year, Mrs. Skinner." It was the voice of one of the detectives. If she had told the detective just how happy her New Year's was now that he had called, he probably wouldn't have understood.

From the first, Iras didn't feel comfortable initiating calls to the police. She didn't want to pester them. She would have loved to have called every morning to ask how things were going, to see what was new. But she didn't. She realized that they couldn't manufacture evidence. She was angry that they couldn't get Paul Edwards to talk. She was certain that he knew something about Katy's murder. He had called so soon after she had left the house. And then when the police had tried to question him he had hired a lawyer and had refused to provide any information. The longer the case remained unsolved the more Iras grew to dislike Paul Edwards. But she really couldn't blame the police for his silence. They were doing all they could, she felt.

As spring came in 1981, the calls from the police became less frequent. They mentioned the possibility of offering a reward, but they didn't feel it would be all that helpful. Iras thought about hiring a private detective, but she decided that bringing a private detective on the case might jeopardize the work the police were doing; and besides, she really didn't know where to tell the private detective to begin.

In April, she asked the police if she could see the autopsy report. The police had given her little information about the murder, perhaps because they wanted to spare her feelings and perhaps because they wanted to save those details to check against the story of anyone they might arrest for the murder. But she had gone months imagining what had happened to Katy and she wanted some facts. She told one of the detectives that she understood she had the right to see the autopsy report. The detective said that she should check her rights further; he thought that in an open homicide investigation things might be different. Did she want them to close the investigation? No, she replied without hesitation, that was the last thing she wanted. She stopped thinking about it for a while.

In July 1981, the calls from the police stopped altogether. Iras passed a difficult summer. In her talks with the police she had been able to say things, ask questions, that she couldn't mention to even the closest of her friends. She could wonder out loud whether Katy had faced her assailant, whether she had put her hands up to block the attack, how hard she had been hit, what her last minutes had been like. She knew that such thoughts would horrify her friends, and she couldn't do that to them. When the police calls stopped, she really had no one to talk to in any depth about the murder.

At the end of the summer she got a phone call from a friend, Hope. She called to ask if Iras had seen an article in the *Los Angeles Times* about a self-help support group called Parents of Murdered Children that had just been formed. Iras said she hadn't, but promised to read the article. Iras had always seen support groups as social gatherings and had never had much use for things like single parents' meetings. In the article, though, members of the group talked about the kinds of things she had only been able to talk to the police about. She read the article many times over, but she wasn't motivated enough to call the phone number given for the group. Hope kept calling and asking if Iras had contacted the group. She even volunteered to make the call herself. Finally, Iras called and drove into downtown Los Angeles for a meeting.

In the very first stages of her grief Iras would not have been able to go to such a meeting. Now that she was able, she worried that people would just be sitting around crying with each other. She didn't want to wallow in self-pity. That was part of the reason she had resisted calling Parents of Murdered Children. Her first night at the group, though, was a revelation. She thought that *nobody* but nobody knew what she was going through, but she soon found out she was wrong. Not only did the people there know about the feelings of grief and loss, but they knew about other aspects of Iras's experience as well—the police, the gore, the awkwardness with which most people approach you. There was even another single mother there who said that the only people she wanted to talk to were the police. Iras realized almost immediately that these people were going to be very important to her.

In one of her first Parents of Murdered Children meetings, a woman told how she and her husband had wanted to see their child's autopsy report and how they had asked their lawyer to get it for them. They had gotten the report, but they really hadn't needed to have the lawyer do the leg work for them. Autopsies are readily available to parents in such cases. Iras no longer feared that the police would close the case if she got Katy's autopsy report. She called the number listed in the phone book, got a recorded message that told her the steps to take to get the report, and followed them. Within a week she had a transcript of the tape the coroner had made during the autopsy.

The words of the report were difficult to decipher and, once deciphered, were horrible to read. But Iras learned a lot about Katy's death. There were no bruises on the back of Katy's head, nothing to indicate that she had been struck from behind or that she had fallen heavily after she had been hit in the face with an object like a rock. Iras thought that perhaps someone had stood behind her while she was hit from the front. The report went into gruesome detail about the obliteration of Katy's face. The medical examiner could not even tell the color of her eyes. Her teeth were almost completely gone. She had inhaled blood. There were few bruises on her body other than those around her face. There were, however, bruises on the backs of her hands, which told Iras that she had indeed tried to protect herself.

Iras knew that Katy bruised easily, so she assumed there had not been much of a struggle. And because Katy was a heavy girl, she would certainly have bruised herself had she fallen. After reading the report, Iras formed a picture of the killing that included someone standing behind Katy when she was struck.

Why anyone would so brutally destroy Katy's face was not answered by the autopsy report. Iras, of course, had not expected it to, but she thought that perhaps the more she knew the closer she could come to an answer. Reading the report brought back images of Katy's death, nightmares that would once again wake her in the middle of the night. But she felt that she had done the right thing in getting the report. She was coming to see that she might never have answers to her questions and she wanted to do all she could to know more.

Several months before she got the report, Iras had a surprise visit from Paul Edwards's mother. She was a schoolteacher, and she had always had difficulty with her son. Her visit had been prompted by a letter she had found in Paul's room, which Iras had written months before. In the letter Iras had pleaded with Paul to tell the police all he knew about the murder.

Their conversation was a tense one. Mrs. Edwards said that she wished Paul would talk to the police, but that she could not make him do so. She did not remember much about the night Katy was killed other than that Paul had been at the park and had come home early. She knew that Paul had called Katy that night and that Katy had called him once. That last bit of information did not sink in until Mrs. Edwards had left. Iras wished she had followed up on it.

Parents of Murdered Children gave Iris an outlet that she needed, but it was not a cure-all. There were difficult times that Iras simply had to experience on her own. She went back to the bookstore where Katy had worked and back to the medical building where Katy was killed. She did not go into the courtyard, but just going to the building was enough to convince her that she had conquered her fears.

In February 1982, on Katy's twenty-first birthday, Iras planned to take the afternoon off work and visit a friend. The year before, Iras had been in such shock that she had not been all that bothered by the birthday date. But this was different. Iras had always looked forward to Katy's twenty-first birthday as the beginning of her adulthood, her take-off point. As the day approached, Iras found herself becoming more and more upset. She thought that taking the afternoon off would help. When she went into work there were all sorts of things she wanted to say to people—about how this would have been Katy's twenty-first birthday, about how much she missed her daughter, and about how she was still plagued by both the horror of the murder and the unanswered questions surrounding it. But she said none of these things. She felt sure that other people wouldn't want to hear them. By noon, however, these unsaid thoughts and feelings bubbled up in the form of a searing migraine headache that, by the time she struggled home, nauseated her, made her cancel her visit to her friend, and put her in bed for twelve hours with excruciating pain. After talking about her experience at the next Parents of Murdered Children meeting, she knew that she would never hold such thoughts and feelings in again no matter how strongly she felt other people might not want to listen.

In the late spring of 1982, the Parents of Murdered Children group decided to sponsor a luncheon, open to the public, at which they would have speakers talking about various aspects of the criminal justice system. Iras had been feeling for a few months that the group really needed to *do* something in addition to talking about their experiences. She encouraged other members of the group, who were somewhat reluctant about the idea, to become involved.

As the luncheon shaped up, it began to look like one that would draw the press in numbers. Doris Tate, whose daughter Sharon was killed by the Manson family in the highly publicized murders of 1969 known as the Tate-LoBianca murders, was going to make her first public statement. She was doing so because she had been trying for several years to block any efforts by members of the Manson family to be paroled. She was going to speak only about that aspect of the case and not about the murders themselves. George Nicholson, a candidate for state attorney general and a strong advocate of victims' rights, was also going to speak.

Shortly before the luncheon, Connie Adelman, a psychiatric nurse who helped organize and facilitate the group, asked Iras if she would speak at the luncheon. Iras declined; she couldn't imagine talking in front of such a group. Connie persisted, reminding Iras that it was she who had pushed others to do something. Connie felt that people coming to the luncheon would need to know something about the grief process parents go through when they lose their children through murder and that Iras could, through her story, help. After a few days, Iras agreed to say something if Connie would help her by asking questions. They would do an interview in front of the luncheon.

The week before the luncheon, Iras was a nervous wreck. She was afraid that she might break down in front of all those people. It was all right to do that with members of the group; they understood. But she didn't know how outsiders would react. She got Hope and her cousin Ann to come for support.

Iras spoke first. Connie asked her to say something about Katy, and Iras described her as a normal child who had musical ability. Then Connie asked how she learned about Katy's murder. Iras told the story of her long, horrible night and getting the news from the police. Iras's voice cracked now and then, and when she told of the brutality of the murder and then asked out loud, "Why would anyone want to do that to my baby?" she stopped for a while to wipe away the tears.

The people at the luncheon cried with Iras. She remained strong, answered the remainder of Connie's questions, and spoke of how she had made it through her long ordeal. She said that her first reaction was to want to die, that she never thought she would be able to live without Katy, but she was here and she was living.

When Iras finished, there was little more that needed to be said about the ways in which parents are devastated by the murder of a child. Out of turn, George Nicholson took the microphone and tried to capitalize on the emotion of the moment with some remarks of his own. But Iras's words and feelings were still in everyone's ears. She had come a long way from the time she hadn't been able to tell her co-workers that it was Katy's twenty-first birthday.

There was an article about the luncheon in the *Los Angeles Times* with a picture of Iras and Doris Tate. Iras was quoted extensively in the first part of the piece. Soon after that article appeared, Iras got her first call from the police in over a year. They asked her to come to the office to look over some new information on the case. Iras was ecstatic. The detectives she had worked with on the case were no longer there, but as she drove to the police station, all her old "cop groupie" feelings returned. They showed her a number of mug shots and asked questions about them. Iras didn't know any of the faces, and soon she saw that the "new information" they had for her did not have much to do with Katy's case. She tried for two days to make the information fit. She went back over Katy's journals, personal papers, checkbooks, and address book, but there was no way she could connect any of the faces to her daughter. The officers saw the disappointment on Iras's face, and they explained how they had obtained the "new information." All the people she had looked at in the mug shot books were in custody and were claiming that they had something to do with Katy's murder. This happens all the time, they said, when details of an unsolved murder are in the paper. People in custody often try to up the ante in their plea-bargaining by saying that they will provide the police with information on an unsolved crime. The police were fairly certain that none of the people who read about the luncheon and then claimed to have knowledge of the murder really did, but they wanted to make sure. Iras was crushed.

In the summer of 1982, she got some sketchy information through a friend who used to work with the Arcadia police department that the police were quite certain they knew who killed Katy, that they had known all along, but that they had no evidence. Without evidence, all they could do was wait for a slip-up by their suspect. They would say nothing to Iras of who they were investigating, but she had her own suspicions. Those suspicions became a bitter hatred of the person first on her list.

In many ways, Iras felt herself healing. And there were times when she could even accept the possibility that she might never know who killed Katy. But what she couldn't accept was not knowing whether or not her awful hatred was misplaced.

6

The Besses

DOROTHY BESS woke up in the middle of the night. Her bedroom was dark, the television that had lulled her to sleep was silent, and her husband, Lee, was asleep beside her. The neighborhood, a middle-class one in the Brentwood section of Los Angeles, was quiet. She didn't know the time, but Dorothy knew from experience that it would be hours before morning and that she would not be able to go back to sleep. The nightmare that had brought her out of her sleep was a familiar one, one that had returned at least once a week for the past year and a half.

In the nightmare, Dorothy is sitting on a hard, oak bench looking at some old, abandoned desks. The hard bench and the cold-feeling room add to her subconscious dread. A gruff man comes up to her, does not look her in the eye, and without an introduction of any sort, tells her that her son has been murdered.

The nightmare is a memory. On December 1, 1980, Lee and Dorothy Bess drove from their boat, a modest cabin cruiser outfitted for sleeping that is moored at Marina del Ray, to the Venice Division of the Los Angeles Police Department. Given the chain of events of the preceding twelve hours, Lee and Dorothy were relieved somewhat. They were only going to the police station to fill out a missing-persons report. Their twenty-four-year-old son, Sheldon, their only child, had not shown up. In the morning they had heard a news report on the radio that said a young man fitting

Sheldon's description had been murdered by someone with a shotgun the night before. They immediately called the police, gave their names and, much to their relief, were told only that they should come down and fill out a missing-persons form.

Lee and Dorothy identified themselves at the front desk, and the police officer told them to follow him. He ushered them into a room that looked like a repository for old furniture. Along one wall were several old oak benches, and in the back of the room were desks. The police officer told them they could sit on the benches. Dorothy, a bit confused now, asked the officer why they should do that, they were just there to fill out some forms. The officer said that a detective would be in shortly and would explain everything. He left the room.

Lee and Dorothy sat on one of the benches to wait. The small relief they had felt coming to the police department vanished and was replaced by the fear and anxiety they had experienced all night long. In a little while a plainclothes policeman came into the room. He did not identify himself and, before either Lee or Dorothy could stand or say a word, said, "Your son was murdered last night."

Dorothy's arms and legs went numb. The words hit her in the face like a brick. She couldn't move; the bench was like stone and offered no comfort. She was out there alone with those words and this detective and the unbelievable thought that her Sheldon was no longer alive. As soon as she could, she began to pound the hard bench and to scream and cry that it wasn't true. Through her screaming, Dorothy asked where Sheldon was. The detective's voice had the same mechanical, almost breezy tone of before: "He's in the morgue; you can go identify him if you want." He said little else to them, and they left the police station.

The horror of being lured to the police station and being bludgeoned with the news of Sheldon's murder was only the beginning. In the next year and a half Lee and Dorothy would suffer enormously because of the loss of their only son. But added to and greatly exacerbating their suffering would be their experiences with the police department, especially with the detective, who later identified himself as Detective Ravens.

*　　*　　*

Sheldon Bess called his parents at least three times on the night he was killed. He called the boat from the Bess home to say he would be later than he expected, they should eat without him, and he would have a sandwich later. Their boat, a thirty-six-foot tri-cabin cruiser, was outfitted with a phone hook-up. The first time he called, about 9:30, he said that he was going to bring an early Christmas present for his mother down to the boat. Dorothy said she couldn't stand surprises and that he had to tell her what he was bringing. He gave in and said he was bringing her a pair of boot roller skates like his own and that the next day he would take her roller-skating on the walks around the harbor in Marina del Ray. Dorothy agreed to give it a try.

Then Sheldon said that he was on his way to the boat, that he was going to stop by the house of a former construction employer who owed him money. Dorothy said she wished he wouldn't, she feared he'd be in danger; she said that she would give him the money. Sheldon said that he couldn't always keep taking from his parents. He said that if he didn't call back in fifteen minutes they were to call the police. Sheldon had been having trouble collecting money owed him, and there had been threats from his former employer. Dorothy didn't like the whole business. Sheldon sounded scared.

Sheldon was not the type of young man who got into scrapes and upset his parents. He was their only child, born long after Dorothy had given up hope of every carrying a child to term. She and Lee adored him, gave him all the material things he wanted, as well as their time. He returned their affection and found no reason after high school and a few years of working to move out of the home he shared with his parents. He had been open with them about his activities outside the house. They knew some of his close friends. Lee and Dorothy felt they had raised Sheldon well, though they would admit that he was spoiled.

When Sheldon didn't call or arrive after fifteen minutes, Dorothy called the Venice police. She was in the middle of that conversation when Sheldon had the operator interrupt the call. He said that he was at the Hughes Market at Sawtell and National Boulevard and that he would be down in a few minutes. He said that he had gone to the employer and had the door slammed in his face. He asked them if they would cash a check he had received that day. Dorothy said they would and asked him if he needed more money. Sheldon said he had money for the weekend and that he was looking forward to having turkey sandwiches with them. "I love you guys and I'll see you in a few minutes," he said and hung up.

That was the last they heard from Sheldon. When it became apparent that he was very late, Lee and Dorothy thought that he had stopped off at some friend's house and may have decided to spend the night. He would have called, but since they were no longer worried about him confronting the construction employer they went to bed.

Dorothy couldn't sleep. She went from their forward stateroom to the master stateroom, Sheldon's room, in the aft part of the boat. She was up and down all night. She called some of Sheldon's friends, but got no answers.

By morning there was no one else to call, and Dorothy was exhausted and extremely worried about Sheldon. The ten-thirty radio news Lee tuned in caused more concern. The lead story was about four people who had been injured by shotgun blasts during a two-hour period near Inglenook Boulevard and Charnock Road. A fifth person had been shot to death with a shotgun about twenty blocks away. The dead man was described as a blond, slender, twenty-four-year-old male from the Brentwood area, a description that would fit most of the young male population at any one of the beaches in the area. Lee and Dorothy called the police nonetheless.

After being told of Sheldon's murder, Dorothy could hardly walk out of the police station. She went home, cried, sobbed and was in a state of shock. Lee called an old family friend, Dr. Miller, who came to the house immediately and prescribed medication for Dorothy.

Dorothy wanted an active part in the preparations for the funeral and the search for Sheldon's murderer. But whenever she thought about the photos of Sheldon she wanted to have printed on the memory folders or about what clues she might be able to give the police, her whole body began to tremble and she would cry.

Lee felt utterly helpless. Sheldon was gone and it was too late to do anything for him. Lee had loved the father role, one which included a lot of late-night runs to pick up Sheldon when his car broke down or he needed a ride. Lee had felt this was a labor of love and had often gone out of his way or been woken up in the middle of the night to perform these tasks. But now he was lost. Lee had to think of the ways he could help, something he could do.

When the Besses came home from the police station, Lee started making phone calls and glanced at the *Los Angeles Times* that had been delivered while they were on the boat. He was shocked when he saw an account of Sheldon's murder that expanded on the one they had heard over the radio. The *Times* had printed Sheldon's name, spelling it Bass in the first part of the report and Bess at the end. One of Sheldon's friends called to say the Rams football game had been interrupted with the announcement of the murder and all the details. A reporter from the *Los Angeles Herald Examiner* called and wanted more information. He had been at the scene shortly after the murder. The police had obviously released the name to the press before they had notified the next of kin.

The *Times* story said that the police believed that one man had been responsible for the five shootings of the night before. Lee knew from the phone calls Sheldon had made during the night that it was unlikely that this theory applied to Sheldon's case. He and Dorothy were certain that Sheldon had been shot by someone who had had it out for him or by someone who had been hired to do the killing. While he was trying to help Dorothy, handle the funeral arrangements, and contact friends and relatives, Lee began to put together a scenario of Sheldon's last hours so that he could be ready when they had their interview with the police.

Whenever she could in the first few days after Sheldon's murder, Dorothy would put in a call to Detective Ravens. She never had much luck getting through to him. She would leave messages for him to call but he never did. He was never in his office. At first this reassured Dorothy; he must be out tracking Sheldon's murderer. But by Tuesday she had heard nothing from anyone at the police station, and the distrust that her first contact with the police had engendered grew.

The morgue wouldn't release Sheldon's body until Tuesday because an autopsy had to be performed. Dorothy, who teaches radiologic technology at Los Angeles City Community College, has been active in the Radiologic Technology Society for many years and has many friends and associates working in Los Angeles hospitals, was able to find out later that the autopsy had been held up because Detective Ravens demanded to be present when the autopsy was performed. Just why that was Dorothy didn't know.

The first call the Besses had from the police was about Sheldon's car. They said that it was parked in a red zone and that if they didn't get it out of there it would be ticketed and impounded. Lee reminded the desk sergeant that the keys were still at the police station. The sergeant said they could come and get the keys. As Lee began to ask about Sheldon's other property, it occurred to him that it would be very difficult to pick up the car while Dorothy was in the shape she was in. She certainly couldn't drive. He mentioned this to the officer. The desk sergeant said nothing, made no effort to help out with Lee's dilemma. Lee called a friend, who said he would come right down and drive Lee to the station. The friend lived about a half hour away in Torrance. Before Lee's friend made it to the house, the Besses got a second call from the police saying that someone would be driving Sheldon's car over shortly.

Sheldon's funeral was on Saturday, December 6. Dorothy with Lee's help had managed to write a poem for the memory card to be handed out at the church. She selected a photograph with Sheldon sitting on a beach chair, back to the camera, facing the ocean, which had been taken when the three of them were on a vacation in the Virgin Islands only months before. For the cover of the memory card she selected another picture from the cruise, a full-face one of him smiling his warm, charming smile. His shoulder-length blond hair and white mustache with the suit jacket, white shirt, and tie he was wearing might have looked incongruous to some, but for Dorothy that picture said a lot about Sheldon. Perhaps he was unconventional, but at least he would put on a suit and tie to go out to dinner with his parents. Dorothy cried often as she got those photographs together for the memory card.

At the funeral, Dorothy was escorted to the family room by several close friends. She couldn't talk to anyone. She cried and tried to listen to the words of the eulogies three of Sheldon's friends gave. She and Lee drove out to the cemetery with friends. Lee and Dr. Miller helped Dorothy get to the gravesite services. At the end of the services Dorothy lost consciousness. Dr. Miller put her in a wheelchair and friends took her home. She never saw Sheldon's interment.

On December 16, sixteen days after Sheldon's murder, Detective Ravens visited Lee and Dorothy. They had expected him much earlier, but they were glad that he was finally going to get the information they had for him. Lee had spent long, tear-filled hours putting together a five-page summary of Sheldon's activities on the night he was killed. Lee had Dorothy correct his English, and then he put the finished work on the home computer so that it would be printed in a legible form for Detective Ravens. Lee also worked up a list of Sheldon's close friends and arranged for two of them to be at the house when Detective Ravens came. Lee has worked for twenty-five years as a project manager with Hughes Aircraft, and writing a scenario is second nature to him. But the task was a wrenching one. He had to sit for hours and imagine what roads in his son's life had led to the trap that killed him. He tried to dispense with the everyday appreciation he had of Sheldon, that of a somewhat spoiled, perhaps naive, slightly adventurous youth who could charm the pants off you and who made up for any of his faults with the caring attitude he showed those people who were close to him, as well as those who were down and out. Lee tried to see Sheldon as the object of a killer's wrath. He had to wrestle with the ugly question of why someone would want to do such damage to Sheldon. And he had to open up his own guilt about why, in those last few minutes, he had not been with Sheldon, helping him out, substituting for him.

Both Lee and Dorothy had been appalled at the treatment they had gotten at the police station, but they were ready to say that the shock of the news and not Ravens himself had been at the core of their difficulties. They were not willing to accept what had happened, though. Now that the funeral was over, they just wanted to have their questions answered. They were certain that the police, with all the leads Lee and Dorothy had worked up for them, would have some information soon.

Detective Ravens stayed at the house only a short while. He said that he still felt that all the shooting incidents of that night were connected and that he had some leads he was working on. He sat in the living room, never looked around the house, or even asked to see Sheldon's room. Ravens never said a thing to Sheldon's two friends. When Lee gave him the five-page report he had worked up, Ravens didn't give it more than a glance before he set it down on the coffee table. He did not take it with him when he left.

Lee was furious. He didn't care whether or not the work he had done was what Ravens needed. He could have understood it if the man had taken the pieces of paper and thrown them in the garbage as soon as he had gotten out of the house. But to not even have the courtesy to take them with him, to acknowledge in some way the work that had been done, was a slap in the face.

When she could see that Ravens had no interest in their theories of the murder, in their information, Dorothy asked him about Sheldon's belongings, especially an expensive gold chain she had bought Sheldon while in the Virgin Islands. He said he would look into it. Shortly after he left he called to say that he had found the chain and could he come back so they could identify it? The chain was a dime-store one that the police were trying to pass off as the expensive one Sheldon had worn when he was murdered. They were incensed and told Ravens so. He left, saying that he would see if he could find the other chain. The Besses are still waiting for his call saying he found the chain.

Regardless of Ravens's behavior, Lee and Dorothy had no choice but to try to deal with him. In the weeks after the funeral Dorothy called him for information on a regular basis. He was never in, would never return phone calls, and never initiated any himself. Once when she called she thought she heard Ravens in the background say, "Oh, that's her again. Tell her I'm out."

After several weeks of trying to work with the police and getting nowhere, Lee called a friend of his who had a cousin on the Venice division homicide squad. Lee wanted to find out what recourse he and Dorothy had. The report back was not encouraging. The source said that each detective handles his own cases and that it would be near impossible to get a detective taken off a case. He said that Detective Ravens is a hard man to talk to and that Lee and Dorothy ought to hire a private detective if they weren't satisfied with Ravens. During the last week of December they did just that.

The private detective got nowhere. He said that he had to go through the police department, and he went directly to Ravens. He took the information Lee and Dorothy gave him, and a healthy fee, and gave nothing in return.

A week and a half after Sheldon's murder, a bill came to the house, addressed to Sheldon, from the hospital where he had been taken the night he was shot. It showed that Sheldon had been in the emergency room for half an hour before he died, that he had been given nine pints of blood and four X-rays. The bill totaled $2,572.

Dorothy called associates to ask what they could find out about the bill. She soon realized that practically every item on the bill was inflated. She talked to some other friends, who assured her that only one X-ray of Sheldon had been taken after he had died and none before. Lee and Dorothy decided not to pay the bill.

From the beginning the Besses had been troubled by the fact that Sheldon had been taken to Brotman Hospital, which was five miles away from the scene of the shooting, and not Marina Mercy Hospital, which was only a mile and a half away. They had asked Detective Ravens about it, but he had told them nothing. When they realized that they were being asked to pay a padded bill, they wondered whether the decision to take Sheldon to Brotman had had something to do with money.

Christmas was a bad time for the Besses. They did not trust the police, and they feared that Sheldon's murderer would never be found. Lee had been able to go back to work sporadically, but Dorothy still had not returned to the classroom. She could not stop crying, she could not eat, and sleep came only for short periods of

Lee Bess   *Dorothy Bess*

time. She kept thinking about the trip she and Lee and Sheldon had planned to take over the Christmas vacation. They were going north to look over a college in Santa Cruz that Sheldon wanted to apply to. Now there would be no trip, no college. She and Lee bought a Christmas tree, but they had nothing to put underneath it except for a present they had bought Sheldon before his death. They went to their boat the night of the marina Christmas party, but they didn't mingle with the others on the dock. When the temperature dropped later in the evening, Lee invited a few people they knew into the boat to keep warm, but that proved a bad idea. Dorothy could not stop herself from crying, and the people who had come on the boat didn't know what to say. They handed her tissues and left.

Dorothy had been raised a Catholic and partially a Presbyterian, but had not been in a church for years. She did believe in a supreme being, though, one who didn't come to people through all the trappings of the Church. And she had certainly believed in such a benevolent spirit when Sheldon was born. She had spent the first seven months of her pregnancy in bed and was afraid at seven months, when her doctor made her go into the hospital, that she was going to miscarry once again. She prayed for two months solid. She wanted a child desperately. Not only did she want a child, she wanted a healthy, blond boy. God didn't let her down then.

From the beginning, Sheldon was all she had hoped for. The sun rose and set on her child. She had never known such a wonderful feeling of love and symbiosis. Her only worry was that she would devour her son with her love.

Dorothy went back to work while Sheldon was still an infant. She didn't want to become the kind of mother who stayed home all day doing things for her only son, smothering him with abnormal amounts of affection. When Sheldon went off to school, she also feared being the sort of mother who had nothing to talk about with her son. Her work, she thought, would make her interesting to him.

Even with all these precautions, Dorothy could not keep from worshiping Sheldon. She organized her class schedule so that she could be home with Sheldon after school. She could deny him almost nothing material. She came to see most things outside her relationship with Sheldon as trivial. Sheldon had a keen sense of humor and warm personality and used it to charm his mother anytime she resisted his requests.

With Sheldon dead, Dorothy saw no reason to believe in anything resembling a supreme being. Her family had done nothing wrong that she was aware of; they had always tried to be helpful to friends, students, elders in the neighborhood, and now they had been dealt this dirty, underhanded blow. How could a supreme being give her such profound joy and now such intolerable pain?

Dorothy had never espoused violence before, but that changed with her loss of faith. She wanted to know who had killed her son, and she fantasized about what she would do to his murderer. She wouldn't hesitate to take vengeance on him. In fact, she would have loved to pull the trigger. Revenge requires an object, however, and neither the police nor the private detective had come up with a suspect.

After Christmas, Dorothy went back to work. The people there were understanding and there were several she could talk to about the murder, but she also came to see that she would have to put up a front in order to make it through the day. Lee had the type of job that allowed him to go off by himself and work. He could choose the kinds of projects he wanted to work on, and in the first few months back on the job he chose ones that put him off in a corner. Dorothy didn't have such a choice. She was required to be out in front of students for hours at a time.

That first semester back was hell for Dorothy. She had a room to go to when she needed to cry and she used it often. But she really felt she needed to cry all the time. She found herself in the middle of a lecture drifting off, thinking of Sheldon, and then crying. More than once she would collapse in class and have to be taken out of the school in a wheelchair. She didn't want to eat and she couldn't sleep. She was tired constantly, tired from lack of sleep, tired from trying to maintain the front that kept her from crying. She felt over and over again that people expected her to return to normal, but she didn't feel normal and she couldn't pretend she did for very long. The effort left her exhausted. One day she nearly fell asleep at the wheel and drove off the San Diego freeway on the way home from work. She had not slept more than a few hours a night for weeks. She decided to take a sleeping pill that night, but it just knocked her out for the next day.

After Christmas, the Besses had a brief meeting with Detective Ravens. They had called the office of the Los Angeles county coroner and much to their surprise had been given an hour and a half appointment with the coroner, Thomas Noguchi. Noguchi's reputation in Los Angeles was that of "coroner to the stars," but Lee and Dorothy found him both sympathetic and helpful. He called the Venice Division police and arranged for the Besses to get some of Sheldon's belongings returned. It was when they went to pick up Sheldon's wallet that Lee and Dorothy had their third meeting with Detective Ravens. He said almost nothing to them. Noguchi had said that the coroner's office was not responsible for notifying next of kin (as Ravens had said it was). When the Besses brought this to

Ravens's attention, he said that patrol cars, not detectives, are responsible for informing next of kin.

Lee and Dorothy were not naive or unworldly when it came to dealing with officialdom. In 1973, their house had nearly burned to the ground, and they had spent seven years in court trying to get what they felt was a proper settlement from the insurance company. In the end they came out with far less money than the insurance company had offered in the first place. There were parts of that experience they could accept even though they felt they had been done an injustice. But after several months of dealing with the police after Sheldon's murder, they knew that they could never accept what was happening to them. They felt that the police are civil servants and are obligated to tell the truth and to keep the public's trust. In their case, they could see the police doing neither. Lee realized that it takes only one bad detective to taint the rest, but he wasn't dealing with percentages. When people would ask he would say that he had a lot of "animosity" toward the police. For a man as self-controlled as Lee, animosity is a strong word.

Lee had never shared Dorothy's religious feelings. For him, Sheldon's murder did not entail the loss of faith that it did for Dorothy. But Lee had always believed in certain values, such as honesty, trustworthiness, and respect for other people's feelings and property. He had always abided by these values and felt that the strength of the United States was due to belief in them. His disillusion with the police, his "animosity," was followed by a loss of faith in some of the things he held most sacred.

While Sheldon was alive, Lee saw a lot less of him than Dorothy did, especially in Sheldon's last few years. Sheldon worked for five years after high school at the UCLA Medical Center and would usually get home around 4:30 in the afternoon. He and Dorothy would talk, catch up on each other's activities, and then he would go out for the evening. By the time Lee got home from work Sheldon was gone. Lee's time with his son usually came late at night. Sometimes Lee would still be awake and sometimes Sheldon would wake him up. Sheldon would think nothing of waking Lee up out of a sound sleep to ask him to get him up early for work. Often Sheldon would come home late, wake Lee up, and kiss Dorothy goodnight. Lee and Dorothy lived for Sheldon, and any form of contact with him was all right by them.

Shortly after Sheldon's death, Lee started to wake up in the middle of the night. He would find Sheldon standing in the room, just as if he were there to ask Lee to wake him in the morning. It would take a few seconds for Lee to realize that Sheldon was not really there, and it would take hours for him to get back to sleep. Two years after Sheldon's murder such apparitions still appeared to Lee on a regular basis.

For Dorothy, one of the most difficult aspects of Sheldon's death was Sheldon's age. Sheldon had spent several years after high school living a carefree life. Lee and Dorothy wouldn't allow him to have dates home overnight or to smoke pot in his room, but they didn't mind him having such freedoms outside the house. Sheldon, with his thin, muscular frame and long blond hair, had more girlfriends than he knew what to do with. For several years he lived a full social life that included little time for his parents. They had bought the boat specifically for him (they had hunted two years for one that would suit his needs), and while he was in high school he had spent all his free time down at the marina or out on the water with Lee and Dorothy and his friends. But as he neared twenty-three, he had little interest in going out on the boat.

Just before his death he seemed to be coming around again. He was applying to colleges, he was spending more time on the boat, and he was talking about living at home at least until he was thirty, perhaps even bringing a bride back to live there. The house, after all, was one that was meant for a large family.

Dorothy was haunted by what might have been. She remembered the sparkle in Sheldon's eye when he teased her about how she was going to look as a grandparent. Sheldon's friends were going to get older and have families, but for Dorothy Sheldon would always remain twenty-four.

Sheldon had been very particular about his room. He wouldn't let his parents go through his things, and he would instruct new cleaning women not to go into his room unless he was there. When Sheldon died, Dorothy could not bear to do anything to the room. After Christmas she took the Christmas present from under the tree and put it in his closet. But she left the room as Sheldon had left it, the bed unmade, the rock posters on the wall, the last record Sheldon listened to on the turntable. Every time Dorothy would think about doing something to the room she would be overcome with grief and renewed pain, and she would put it off.

The same was true of Sheldon's memorial tablet. Forest Lawn Cemetery requires certain payments for decorative headstones. Lee and Dorothy wanted outlines of birds and boats on Sheldon's headstone, so they asked what the price for their design would be. The cemetery requested a fee just to give an estimate. Dorothy, who was handling the arrangements, could not follow up on such details without being torn up by memories. She had trouble trying to contact the Forest Lawn counselor, who didn't return phone calls. Two years after he was buried Dorothy still had not been able to arrange for a headstone.

Late in the spring of 1981, Lee and Dorothy talked to Detective Ravens again. They had gotten some of Sheldon's belongings back but were still missing his set of keys to their house and boat and the clothes he was wearing the night of the murder. Ravens said he did not know where the keys were. The Besses had to get new locks made for both the house and the boat. Dorothy wanted very badly to have the clothes back. Ravens asked her why in what she perceived as an accusatory, suspicious tone of voice. Angry, Dorothy said, "Why? I want to sleep with them, that's why!"

At this meeting, Detective Ravens said that his investigation had changed course. He was now convinced that the person who killed Sheldon was also involved in what were known as the "Bob's Big Boy murders," killings that had occurred, after Sheldon's death, in a Big Boy restaurant. The people believed to have committed those murders were in custody, and Ravens said he was trying to get the girlfriend of one of them to link one of the men to Sheldon's murder. Lee and Dorothy later found out that he never attempted to contact the district attorney about the plan.

Lee and Dorothy saw this as nothing more than an effort to close the case, to obtain a false confession so that the paper work on Sheldon's case could be wrapped up. They asked about one of the people on the list they had shown Ravens who, they understood, had a long record and was now in jail again. Ravens looked up the name, but said that he could do nothing without direct evidence. He said that the only way they were going to get a conviction now was for the killer to confess or for a friend of the killer's to point a finger. To any other questions Lee and Dorothy asked Ravens replied that there was confidential information involved. That was the last Lee and Dorothy heard from Ravens.

Detective Ravens told the Besses that they could recoup funeral expenses by applying to the state Victims Compensation Board of Control. Lee and Dorothy looked over the form he gave them to fill out and decided not to file for the money even though they might have been eligible for reimbursement of medical expenses. Lee had already decided he would not pay the padded hospital bill, and he and Dorothy felt that if they signed the form and received money for the funeral expenses they would be legally liable for all of Sheldon's debts, the only one they knew of being the hospital bill.

Through her hospital sources and through the coroner's office, Dorothy had obtained the hospital reports both of Sheldon's emergency-room treatment and of his autopsy. Her familiarity with the language used in those reports and her hospital experience with similarly injured patients allowed her to understand every detail, to get a vivid picture of what Sheldon had suffered.

After studying the reports, Dorothy had mixed feelings about the methods and procedures the hospital had used. Why hadn't he been taken to the closest instead of the farthest hospital? Sheldon had been shot in the upper right leg and had nearly bled to death by the time he had reached the hospital. She learned from the autopsy that the force of the shotgun blast had broken the bones in his upper leg and pelvis. She realized then that Sheldon's killer had stood very close to him when he shot.

Images of Sheldon being shot, Sheldon bleeding profusely on the steps of a bungalow near where he was shot, Sheldon being opened up in the emergency room—these images recurred with greater frequency as the months went on. In class she would remember how Sheldon would at times call the college and take her out of a lecture, how he knew that she was always there for him. Then she would see him, imagine his body on the street or in the hospital, and she would be wracked by the thought that she had not been there for Sheldon. At these times she wished over and over again that she could have taken Sheldon's place, that she could have done something.

A year after Sheldon's murder Lee and Dorothy were no closer to understanding why someone had killed Sheldon than they were the day they were told the news. Then Dorothy saw a television program featuring a psychic who specializes in unsolved murder cases, and she decided to give it a try. Any chance of knowing what had happened to Sheldon had to be better than the state of limbo they were in.

The psychic came to the house with a man who identified himself as a private detective. She said that her services were free but that there would be a fee if they decided they wanted to use the private detective. Lee and Dorothy didn't hesitate to hire the detective.

Without looking through the house or seeing any of the pictures in the den, the psychic went straight to Sheldon's room and sat there for a long time. She came back downstairs with a sketch of what she thought Sheldon looked like and another sketch of the man she thought was responsible for Sheldon's murder. The sketch of Sheldon was remarkably accurate. Lee and Dorothy couldn't place the sketch of the murderer until months later when they realized that it matched someone in a photograph Sheldon had taken, someone Lee and Dorothy could not identify.

The private detective returned and spent eight hours going over Sheldon's room, talking to the Besses, and taking the lists and information they had worked up for the police. He approached Detective Ravens but not directly as the other detective had. He told Ravens that he had a grant to work with the psychic, to check her accuracy. Ravens was insulting to the psychic and did not want to cooperate with the private detective. The detective began to work on the case.

He found that the address carried on all the police records as the location of the shooting was inaccurate. The shooting, in fact, had occurred across the street from where the police said it happened. Hearing this Lee and Dorothy assumed that the police had never even investigated the scene of the crime.

After making inquiries, the detective learned other things of interest to Lee and Dorothy. He found that the brother of the employer who had owed Sheldon money had left town for Alabama the day after the shooting and that another person who had been owed money by the same employer had been paid off shortly after Sheldon's murder. The detective told Lee and Dorothy his theory of the murder: someone had been hired to kill Sheldon and had followed him to the place where the shooting took place. Later he told them that he had a suspect in the case, but that the suspect had already been convicted of second-degree murder and was serving a sentence for that offense. The private detective told Lee and Dorothy that he was getting his information from someone on the list Lee had worked up, someone who had decided to talk.

The information Lee and Dorothy got from the private detective was helpful. They had to pay over four thousand dollars for the two detectives they had hired, but they thought the money was worth it.

As time passed, life didn't get any easier for the Besses. Dorothy no longer cared about anything. She didn't cook, barely ate, and was not able to take care of the house the way she used to. She stopped all activities that once had been important to her, and had no desire to go anywhere. Increasingly, she refused to act the stoic. She broke down in front of friends, over the phone, even with her mother. Though people in the neighborhood and at the marina knew of Sheldon's murder, they did not want to deal with Dorothy's crying and depression. Dorothy had trouble sleeping and was exhausted all the time. The doctor said it was emotional fatigue and it would go away. But it didn't. She would watch the television next to their bed, have a few sips of Amaretto, and try to drift off. When sleep came, she hoped it would be without nightmares.

In the beginning of their ordeal, Lee and Dorothy could not help talking with friends about what they were going through. They would try not to deluge people with their grief and with the details of their problems with the police, but the subject always came up and was frequently cause for Dorothy's crying. Friends started pulling away. Lee and Dorothy had entertained a lot on the boat before Sheldon's murder. They knew their friends enjoyed being down on the water, going out for a ride. Now when they invited friends to the boat and bought food, beer, and soft drinks, they were never sure people would show up.

Dorothy was relieved when people didn't come by because it meant that she would not have to struggle to maintain her composure. She could talk to some of the people in Parents of Murdered Children and to one of her students, but otherwise she just wanted to blank out, to avoid the hurt.

Friends no longer called. They were tired, Lee and Dorothy thought, of hearing the same old depressing story. When they went to boating club meetings and social events they didn't jump into the activities and mix with other people as they had in the past. They had stopped going to their professional meetings because they were tired and depressed and didn't feel like holding up their front around people who didn't understand.

Dorothy wanted to find out who murdered Sheldon and why. Two years after Sheldon's murder, Dorothy could still feel the hardness of the bench she sat on when she was told the news, the numbness in her arms and legs. Until she could get over such feelings, until she could understand what had happened to Sheldon and why, Dorothy could never commit suicide. She no longer cared about living, but she was consumed by a desire to live long enough to take a gun to Sheldon's murderer.

While Dorothy grew more and more despondent, Lee began to realize that their marriage was not the way it used to be. Before Sheldon's death they had been a happy couple. A picture of the two of them laughing with Sheldon at his twenty-fourth birthday party hung in the hallway and was a constant reminder of the change that had come over them in a year and a half. There would be no wedding and no grandchildren to carry on the family name. Now there were just the two of them. Why go on living?

At work Lee felt comfortable with people, enjoyed himself, and sometimes felt like he was beginning to live again. He kept busy solving his job-related problems and tried to forget what had happened to Sheldon and what it was doing to Dorothy. By the time he had left work and arrived home his mood had changed radically. Now he had to face the home problems. He had to do some of the shopping and cooking on the nights they ate at home and some of the cleaning around the house. Dorothy would try to get her crying and sobbing over with before Lee came home. There were times when he would feel the depression himself, when his day would be full of thoughts of Sheldon. He would have to be prepared to put up with such days, but Dorothy seemed always to be down.

Late in 1981, Lee and Dorothy started going to meetings of Parents of Murdered Children. There they saw others who were having just as difficult a time in the aftermath of their child's murder as they were. Lee and Dorothy talked to the group about their situation, especially their problems with the police. At one meeting Lee surprised Dorothy by talking about how he didn't feel depressed at work and how depressed he felt seeing Dorothy so low.

Dorothy was hurt by Lee's statements, but she came to realize what the tragedy had done to her relationship with to Lee. When they got home that night, Dorothy told Lee that he should divorce her. She realized that due to Sheldon's murder she had not been the wife she had once been. But she expected Lee to understand. If not, he could divorce her and move on. He wanted to pick up the pieces and get back into the world. Dorothy felt perhaps he didn't love Sheldon the way she did. How could he want to go on? She knew she would never be herself again. Lee felt differently.

Lee, however, did not want a divorce. He felt that there were cycles to the grief and adjustment they were going through, that he himself was not immune to deep depression, and he hoped Dorothy would one day want to enjoy life again. Lee thought that once the pressures of the school year lifted, Dorothy would revive. When summer came in 1982, though, Dorothy still hadn't pulled out of her despondency. Trying to appear normal exhausted her. She would get up at 11:00, nap from 2:00 or 3:00 until dinner, and use television to put her to sleep later on. The most Dorothy could do was take care of the laundry.

The more depressed Dorothy got, the angrier Lee got—not at Dorothy, but at what he saw as the lingering effects of their mistreatment by the police. He wanted to tell the world what had happened, but he is not the sort of person to openly show such feelings.

Dorothy began to see her material possessions, her gadgets, the boat, even the house as toys, things that could distract her for a while. But the distractions never worked for long. Even sleep didn't keep her away from the pain. Always it was there, always it was the same. The cold, hard bench, the gruff man, the words, the news that her son had been murdered, the numbness in her arms and legs. And then she was awake again.

7

The Lewises

W HEN SCOTT LEWIS visited his parents' new home in San Jose, California, in June of 1980, they had just barely moved in, and he spent the ten days of his visit helping his mother Jean put the house in order. They unpacked boxes, hung a chandelier, and strung a wash line in the backyard of the large, middle-class home.

One day, after they had finished their work, Scott, who was twenty-one at the time, turned on a portable radio and used the open area next to the kitchen for a dance floor. Jean watched her budding Fred Astaire twirl around the tile near the sliding glass doors and had to laugh. He was in his element, and for the first time in several years, she was certain that her oldest son was truly happy.

Scott had a lot to be happy about that June day. After two and a half difficult years at the Air Force Academy, he had resigned in January, and in the coming fall, he was going to enter the University of Colorado in Colorado Springs and major in psychology. The Academy had been much too confining for Scott's restless energy, and Jean and her husband, John, had seen Scott's normally cheery spirits sink during the years he was there. John, a recently retired career military officer who was beginning his first civilian job in San Jose, had supported Scott's decision to leave the Academy.

Outside of the Academy, Scott found a whole new life for himself. He worked several jobs during the semester he took off, had his own apartment, and was hoping to be accepted as a dance instructor at the local Arthur Murray Dance School. Ballroom dancing had always been Scott's love, and the prospect of doing it professionally thrilled him. On top of all this, Scott had met an instructor at Arthur Murray, just before he had come home, a woman a bit older than he, named Janet, about whom his family would hear a good deal in subsequent phone calls from Colorado.

As she watched her wiry, five-foot nine-inch son dancing to the music coming from the portable radio, Jean could sense that her own life was also at a high point. After twenty years of moving from army base to army base, mainly in the South, she and John had finished off their time in the service with a flourish, spending four years at a NATO installation in Belgium and then at a prestigious language school at the Presidio in Monterey, California. John had gone back to school, had gotten a master's degree in organizational development, and had landed a job with an electronics firm in San Jose. Scott's life seemed to be smoothing out after a rocky few years; their daughter, Sandra, two years younger than Scott, was about to begin junior college in Monterey; and thirteen-year-old Steven, their youngest, finally seemed to be in good health after several serious childhood diseases. Jean, who had met John while she was at Russell Sage College and he was at Dartmouth, could now begin to think about a career for herself.

Jean and John took Scott to the airport for his trip back to Colorado. As he boarded the plane, he turned around to wave and yelled, "See you at Christmas." The year before, they had all gone down to Mexico for Christmas. It was there that Jean had seen how affected by the Academy Scott was when Sandra went para-sailing over the ocean and the normally adventurous Scott, who had had a bad experience in an Academy parachute program the summer before, watched his younger sister from the beach. This Christmas so much would be different, she thought.

Scott called home several times during the summer and was full of good news. He had been accepted at the Arthur Murray studio and was beginning his job as a part-time instructor. He and Janet seemed to be hitting it off, and he talked about how they would leave their work at the studio and go sit out under the stars at a rock formation known as the "Garden of the Gods" and wait for the sun to rise. Then Scott reported that he was enrolling in school, buying books, and getting ready to study again.

One Monday evening in September the phone rang; the call was from Colorado, but not from Scott. It was from his employer at the dance studio. Mr. Schweiger and his wife were a middle-aged couple who had just bought the studio, and Scott had often spoken of them with affection. Mr. Schweiger was upset. He began by saying that he hoped he had done the right thing. He had reported Scott and Janet missing. They were very dependable employees, and they had not called or shown up for work in five days. After the first day, the Schweigers had called Scott and Janet to no avail and then gone to Scott's apartment, gotten keys from the landlord, and found the apartment intact with fresh food in the refrigerator. Scott and Janet had disappeared.

The Schweigers didn't know much more than that. The last night Scott and Janet had worked at the studio, Scott had gotten a phone call to meet someone after work. As far as the Schweigers knew Scott and Janet were going to the meeting and then were going dancing at a nearby disco. Janet had had her car and Scott his motorcycle.

Jean was upset; she was certain that Scott and Janet had gone dirtbike riding after the disco, had taken a fall, and were somewhere out in the rugged foothills in need of help. John called the Colorado police, but they didn't seem very concerned. They told him that they were looking into the disappearance but that a young male and a young female who are missing, along with a motorcycle, usually turn up in Florida or California on a lark. Twenty-four hours after the Schweigers reported Scott and Janet missing, the police had found Janet's car, abandoned, two miles from the disco. Her purse, with her glasses, contact lenses, and i.d.s, was on the front seat, one door was unlocked, and one door locked.

John and Jean knew that Scott was not the type to abandon a car and head out for Florida without calling his employer, parents, or friends. They were certain that the two had had an accident. John paced the floor the entire night. He is a very organized person, and while he paced the floor he began to jot down questions for the police. He called the police and asked whether he could come out to Colorado Springs to talk with them. They urged him not to, but finally said that there was no way they could stop him. John was on a plane the next day.

On Monday night, after the Lewises got the call from the Schweigers, they got a call from Sandra, who was in school in Monterey. John answered the phone, and when he found out who it was he barked, "Why are you calling?" Sandra couldn't say for sure. The weekend before she had had a strong feeling that she should call home, but work had kept her from doing so. On Monday the feeling was even stronger, and Monday night she found the time to call. Her father handed the phone to Jean, who came to the phone crying and told her that Scott had been missing since the previous Tuesday. Sandra's mind raced back to what she had been doing that Tuesday. She had gone dancing with a friend, and while they had been out on the floor, she had suddenly had a strange, hollow, empty feeling. She had seen herself drained and lifeless. Her religious beliefs at the time could probably best have been termed atheistic, and in a sarcastic sort of way she had dealt with the empty feeling by laughingly thinking to herself that God could fill her up. Shortly after she had thought that, a friend, who was a born-again Christian, had come up to her on the dance floor, grabbed her by the arm, and said, "Excuse me Sandra, but were you just thinking about God?" Sandra had nearly flipped out.

Her mother was certain that Scott had perished in an accident. Sandra felt that with his Academy training he might be able to survive several days out in the wilderness, and so she hoped a search party would find him. But she couldn't help thinking that she was the oldest child now, that the man she trusted most in the world, more even than her father, was gone.

John spent three days in Colorado Springs and was able to go over his list of questions with the police. He met with them twice. The first time they grilled him for over an hour to learn everything they could about Scott, who he was, what he was like, and who he knew. Both times he met with police they briefed him on their investigation and the searches they had made on foot, horseback, and by helicopter. A detective took John to the place where they had found Janet's car. The first evening he called Jean with disappointing news.

The police, he said, were thorough and had covered all the bases before he had arrived. The search team was hopeful of finding the motorcycle because the brush in the area was not thick and the gas tank of Scott's motorcycle was a bright orange color; they would be able to spot it from the air. But after several days of searching they had turned up nothing. The police, however, were quite certain that Scott and Janet had not had an accident, once they learned what responsible kids they were.

John also said that the police suspected something about Scott that he and Jean could never have imagined, that he was a minor dealer in marijuana. Scott dealing drugs? An Eagle Scout, accepted at both the Air Force Academy and West Point, a straight, all-American kid if there ever was one? The police tried to reassure John that in the drug world Scott's buying and selling was minimal and that his disappearance most likely had nothing to do with his dealing. But both John and Jean were dumbfounded by the idea. Jean remembered having felt, in March, when Scott turned twenty-one, so relieved that they had made it to his majority without any of the drug problems that so many of the teenagers of his generation seemed to have. And now they had to learn that he was hustling small amounts of marijuana.

During his three days in Colorado Springs John spent most of his time searching all of the areas he thought Scott and Janet might have gone to, including ones the police had already searched. Hiking over hills and through wilderness territory, John would call out Scott's name, wishing desperately that he would get a response and at the same time fearing what he might find. The days were hot and John had to stop for water every now and then. But when he did he would be flooded with guilt; how could I be taking this refreshment, he thought, when those kids may have been out here for days with no food or water.

The police helped John find Scott's landlord and, after promising to keep the rent up to date, got the key to Scott's apartment. In the evenings John searched the apartment for clues, even though the police had already done so, washed dirty dishes, and put away clothes. He didn't know what to do with the fresh food in the refrigerator. He couldn't let it rot, but if he threw it away he would symbolically be admitting Scott was gone forever. It took a long time to decide to throw some of it away and give the rest to Scott's neighbor.

The first week of Scott's disappearance was a hell for Jean. She couldn't eat, sleep, or do anything. She couldn't stand to hear music. Steven reacted to the disappearance by going to his room and blaring the radio. Jean sat on the couch downstairs wanting to scream, "Shut that off!" through her crying. A small, normally thin woman, she lost fourteen pounds in the first three weeks after the disappearance.

In the third week there was new information. Some kids out rabbit hunting in a remote area near Colorado Springs fell into a shallow hole covered with brush and found Scott's motorcycle "very cunningly concealed," as the police later said, under the brush. There were no fingerprints on the motorcycle, and there were no signs of violence.

Janet's father had been in Colorado closing up her apartment when the motorcycle was found. He went with the police to the scene, and he called the Lewises to tell them what he had found there. It appeared that someone had driven the motorcycle around and around to gouge out a hole large enough for the motorcycle and then had made a clever effort to cover the hole. It was only by accident that the cycle had been found. Hearing this, Jean was certain that Scott and Janet had been killed, that some methodical mind was behind their disappearance. She got off the phone and half screamed, half cried, "Let them be found!"

But they were not found, and over the next two months, Jean and John experienced a helplessness and a despair that seemed to have no end. They cried together in the beginning, they both felt anger;

but since no bodies were found, they had to hold out hope that their son was still alive. They didn't know what else to do. The detective in charge of the investigation, Detective Spencer, kept in touch with them and said that they could call collect anytime. But they couldn't keep bothering him. The president of John's company suggested that they consult a psychic. When they asked Detective Spencer about that, he said the police would follow up on any leads the psychic turned up that looked good, but he warned them that psychics can play on emotions.

They went to one psychic who said she could see the two of them in either California or Florida on a motorcycle with Janet's hair blowing in the wind. They consulted a second psychic who said that they would know something in November. Jean hung onto that hope as if it were truth.

When November came and there was no news, John and Jean went out to Colorado Springs to close up Scott's apartment. The small scale and baggies with marijuana residue they found there convinced them that Scott had indeed been dealing marijuana.

His new books for his course work were in the apartment too. They went to the university to withdraw him and watched as his papers were stamped "deceased." As hard as it was to see that, and as much as she cried over that cold word lettered on those papers, Jean came away from the university saying to herself that it was true, that she would never see Scott alive again.

John's day was organized around his work, but Jean did not have the advantages of such structure. She watched him get ready for his job each day and wondered how he could get through his schedule. She was spending hours at home crying, feeling at a complete loss. At times she thought that John simply was not going through the same amount of pain. One morning she could no longer take it and confronted him with the fact of her own deep anguish. He calmly looked at her and said, "Why don't you try scream-therapy?" Jean was furious. John had taken some course work in counseling and therapy in his master's degree program, and he meant the suggestion as both a real possibility and a challenge to her to try to deal with her anguish straightforwardly. He had been concerned about Jean's anger and the despair she often sank into. Nevertheless, his remark that morning cut deeply.

After he went to work that day, Jean felt she was going to burst with anger and frustration. She wanted to scream, but she was afraid the neighbors would think something awful was going on in the house. She went upstairs to the walk-in closet in their bedroom, closed the door, and screamed her guts out.

It worked. The tension of the months since Scott's disappearance had eased somewhat, and she was much better able to accept John's business-as-usual approach. She had learned, too, how to deal with such a build-up of tension and would use her new knowledge in the future when she thought she was going to fold from the pressure. In among the suits and dresses and shoes she could just explode.

The family dog, a Shepherd mix named Samantha, was her only companion during the day. Sandra asked once if she could take Samantha to Monterey with her, but Jean would hear none of it. Samantha was a godsend. He and Jean walked miles every day, and that helped. When she cried, Samantha sensed her sadness and lay at her feet. Jean wasn't about to let Sandra have her.

Jean worried a lot about Steven. She worried that he was keeping too much inside. He would not talk about his brother's disappearance, and he didn't want to be around when the family was talking about it.

Steven was trying to adjust to a new school and new friends. He was bright for his age and was placed in advance classes in which the kids were older, old enough to drive. Once, after Scott's disappearance, when John was away, Steven asked if he could go to the movies with a friend who was going to drive them to a theater across town. Jean was confronted with a new situation, and in the state she was in over Scott she gave Steven a flat no for an answer. He was livid. He went out back and for an hour threw stones at the back fence with all his might.

Sandra talked to many of her friends about Scott's disappearance. She learned quickly which ones could handle her crying and her sense of loss. Three days after she learned that Scott was missing, she decided to wear a black ribbon wristband until he was found. She felt that it would always remind her of Scott, and that with it she could go out and have a good time and not feel that she had forgotten her lost brother. She wore it on her left wrist because her left arm was closer to her heart.

The first time she saw her parents after she learned of Scott's disappearance she found herself in a new role. She held both her mother and her father as they cried and she cried with them. Only recently had she and her father been physically affectionate. He had learned to express his feelings through hugs while doing his master's work. Sandra had been surprised the first time he hugged her. That had never been his style. Now, with Scott gone, she found herself cradling him almost as if she were the parent and he the child.

Sandra could not see Scott as dead. She had dreams in which he was skiing with his girlfriend. Sandra had always known him as a lively older brother, a go-getter who could bring quiet people out of their shells. She had visited him once in the Air Force Academy, and he had looked so old and sad there. But he was through with all that, and the last time she had seen him he had been the good old Scott she had loved for as long as she could remember. He wasn't dead. He was still the Scott who had chased her around the backyard in their house in Texas and who, after catching her, instead of throwing her to the ground as she had expected, had given her a big kiss on the cheek.

Sandra stayed in school, but studying and working part-time were hard. Some of her teachers understood when she told them about Scott's disappearance. Others demanded that she do her work as she normally would. Sandra felt that she was going to need help and began to see a counselor.

Jean wasn't looking forward to Christmas at all. After the disappointment of November, she began to think that they would never know what happened to Scott. She dreaded the meals without him, Christmas day itself. John's mother came out to California from the East for the holidays. Jean didn't know what her presence would do to their Christmas, but it turned out to be helpful. With another person in the house, the family was not as acutely aware of Scott's absence.

In October, Jean had found that she was at the end of her rope. As in the beginning, she could not sleep properly, and she lost her appetite altogether. She thought that she needed tranquilizers and went to see a local doctor, a man who was recommended to her by a friend.

She told the doctor her problem and what she was there for. She did not expect him to work miracles, she simply wanted something to calm her nerves. He heard her out and then delivered a sermon of sorts. He began by saying, "I don't know what your religion is, but I'm a Christian," and he went on to imply that if she, too, were a Christian, she would see Scott's disappearance and possible death as the work of the Lord and have no need for tranquilizers.

Jean was overcome by guilt and incensed by the implication at the same time. She had always considered herself a practicing Christian, but "the work of the Lord"? The doctor eventually gave her twenty Valium tablets; but after she got home she was so mad that she only took one and then adopted an "I'll show him" attitude and took no more.

The doctor's sermon stuck, however. After several days of anguish and guilt, she got in her car and drove to Monterey to see an Episcopal priest, Father Ken Barta, whom she had been close to when they were stationed at the Presidio. As soon as he heard her out, he put his arms around her and said, "Jean, things of this nature are not part of God's plan." That helped, but Jean's visit to the doctor scarred her for a long time.

Though their experience with psychics had not been fruitful, Jean could not shake the feeling that a true visionary might be able to see things the police were missing. In January, she and John got the name of a psychic who knew nothing of their son's disappearance. They called her and gave her the barest of details. All Jean said was that she was the mother of a missing son. The woman replied that her son was about five-feet nine-inches with brown hair and that there was a girl with him. Jean was amazed and scared at the same time. She felt that she didn't really want to hear what this woman had to say about Scott. "I think they've been shot," the psychic continued, adding that they were covered with snow and they would not be found until spring. Jean could only pray that this psychic was as inaccurate as the others had been.

One April day John came home from work at two o'clock. Jean saw him coming into the house and thought he looked horrible; he had no color. He never came home early, so she assumed he was sick. He came into the house and blurted out, "They found their bodies!" and burst into tears. Jean was stunned and relieved at the same time. She had given up on them ever being found and now, without warning, all the shock of the disappearance returned. While they cried together, John told Jean what Detective Spencer had told him.

The bodies were found by accident when hunters near Raton, New Mexico, about 170 miles from Colorado Springs, stopped along the side of a road to urinate. They found the badly decomposed bodies in a culvert. It took only a day for the police to identify them as Scott and Janet.

The image of Scott's body lying all winter in a culvert was a horrible one. Scott had always been proud of his trim physique. To think that he died and then his body simply rotted in the elements was ghastly and ironic.

There were so many questions that the discovery raised. Detective Spencer had said that it appeared the two had been shot to death. But he had not said how long they had been dead, or how long they had been held before they were killed. Jean wanted very much to know, but she was afraid to ask.

With the discovery of the bodies, there came a flurry of activity that didn't allow John and Jean time to brood. They decided that they wanted to have Scott's body cremated and his ashes scattered at the Garden of the Gods. Because they were new to San Jose, they thought that a memorial service there would not be appropriate. The huge, futuristic chapel at the Air Force Academy was their first choice, but there was a snag. The Academy did not allow such services for anyone not on active duty at the school. After some hesitation, however, they allowed the rules to be ignored, and Jean began to plan for the service. She thought that Scott would have been pleased that a regulation had been bent for his memorial service.

Jean was left to do the planning of the service herself. After the bodies were found, John and Sandra and Steven were just not available to help. But Jean wasn't bothered by their absence. After several months of feeling absolutely helpless in the face of her son's disappearance, planning for the memorial service gave her something to do.

While she was planning for the service in Colorado, Jean got a call from one of John's ex-colleagues at the Presidio in Monterey. News of the bodies having been found had been run in the Monterey newspaper. The man called to say that he and others who knew the Lewises were going to have a memorial service for Scott in Monterey because, "we want to share your grief." He said that he realized they would be busy with the other memorial service, but that they were going to have the service even if Jean and John could not make it. Jean was touched and was happy that Monterey was close enough that they would be able to attend.

Before they went to the memorial service in Monterey, Jean sat down with Steven and tried to prepare him for what might happen. She worried that he had not shown emotion, and she wasn't sure how he would react to the service. She told him it would be all right to cry.

The service in Monterey was a very emotional one for the whole family. The men there, military men who are not accustomed to such displays of emotion, hugged and cried with John. Before the service, the narthex of the church was filled with men who had broken down on seeing the Lewises. Steven stood with three of his friends from Monterey and watched this. He didn't cry himself, but Jean could see that the openness of the men was an education for Steven and his friends.

Sandra was shocked by the emotional atmosphere. She had grown up thinking of her father's friends as stiff and uptight. But here were men hugging her and crying openly. She could tell when a hug was perfunctory and when it came from real emotion. Most were of the latter type.

The memorial service at the Air Force Academy was attended by eight of the Lewises' relatives from back east. The cadet chapel was a beautiful setting for the service, and the Academy chaplain had, with Jean's help, prepared a fitting memorial. A cadet friend of Scott's read an essay Scott had written, the chaplain delivered an appropriate meditation, and they chose hymns that Scott would have liked, especially, "I Danced in the Morning When the World Was Begun."

After the service the family went to the Garden of the Gods to scatter Scott's ashes. It was an overcast day, and against the gray sky, the red sandstone rock formations seemed even brighter than they normally were. The family stood in a circle with a rose and the box of ashes in the center. They held hands, and each member of the family in turn took a handful of ashes, said his or her name, and then said, "sister of Scott" or "father of Scott" and then "whose Spirit lives within me" as they scattered the handful of ashes. It was a beautiful and peaceful moment for the family. When they had finished and were leaving, the gray clouds divided and a glorious sunset spread over Pike's Peak.

Before going back to San Jose, John went to the dealer Scott had bought his motorcycle from only months before he disappeared. The bike which was at the police pound was in good shape and John had the $900 bill of sale. The dealer seemed to know about the bike and offered John $200 to buy it back. John was amazed; the book value of the motorcycle was much more than that. John asked him if he knew the circumstances under which he was selling the bike, and the dealer said yes. "And you're still only offering this amount for it?" John asked. The dealer said he was in the business to make money. John stamped out of the motorcycle shop. Months later the Lewises donated it to Goodwill.

Jean carried some of Scott's ashes back to California with her so that they could be scattered over a favorite spot of his in Pacific Grove, near where they had lived before they moved to San Jose. She had the ashes in a box in her tote bag as she went through airport security. After she went through the metal detector, she noticed that her tote bag had been placed on a table and a woman security guard was asking whose bag it was. Jean said it was hers. Brusquely the woman asked her to open it up. Jean did, and the woman pointed to the box. "What is it?" she asked. "My son's remains," Jean replied. "I know that," the woman said. "Where are the papers?" Jean was nearly in tears. She threw down the necessary papers, and after the woman examined them, she then demanded three kinds of I.D. Jean went to a corner and cried.

Within three weeks after the discovery of the bodies the police had arrested the suspected murderers. Three men in their twenties were charged, and each time the police made an arrest they notified the Lewises. Detective Spencer also asked permission to give their phone number to the press.

The police had suspected the three men all along, but they had not had anything to link them to the disappearance. When the bodies were found, a woman who was an accomplice panicked and turned herself in. Once the police had her confession, they were able to make the other arrests. In searching the apartment of one of the three, they found Scott's motorcycle helmet. When they called the Lewises, the police were able to tell them the motive for the killings and the details of the murders—at least as many of the details as the Lewises wanted to know about. Detective Spencer answered all of Jean's questions. John didn't have any desire to be briefed on the details of Scott's death.

The motive for the killing appeared to be a threat that Scott had made to the leader of the four, Roger Cullen, a twenty-three-year-old drug dealer from whom Scott had bought marijuana. Scott felt that he had been cheated by Cullen and threatened to go to the police if he wasn't given his money back. That threat was made six weeks before the disappearance. In those six weeks, Cullen plotted the abduction and the murders and hired someone to do the killings, someone who eventually turned state's evidence. Janet, it appeared, was killed only because she happened to be with Scott when he was lured into Cullen's trap.

The night they were killed, Scott and Janet were to meet Cullen at the apartment of a woman accomplice. She called the dance studio, set up the meeting, and when the two were abducted, supplied the macrame rope they were tied up with. The police had suspected her involvement from the beginning and had even tried to get her to take a lie detector test. She had been arrested previously for drug charges, though, and refused to aid in the investigation. She was granted immunity for her testimony when she turned herself in.

The police weren't certain just how Scott and Janet had been abducted. They knew that after they were tied up they were put in the trunk of a car and driven to New Mexico. Once there, the man who had been hired to do the killing backed out at the last minute, and Roger Cullen stepped in. He shot Janet once in the back of the head, and then the third man, Randy Wilson, shot Scott at least twice. They drove directly back to Colorado after the killings because one of the men had to be at work at 7:00 A.M.

Jean felt rage and horror at the calculated premeditation of the murders. That one human being could plan and carry out something so ghastly and then lead a normal life while the bodies rotted in a culvert in New Mexico and while the families of the victims were in agony for seven months was incomprehensible to her. The world she had grown up in, the world she had brought her children into, did not prepare her for such viciousness.

At the same time, Jean felt anger toward Scott. How could he have been trafficking in drugs? And why had he threatened those people? Hadn't he had the sense to know that you don't challenge people like that? She and Sandra had talked about the drug dealing that Scott had been doing. Jean realized that he had always liked ways to earn money and that the dealing he had been doing was not big time. But she couldn't help being angry at him for his stupidity.

And she felt so sorry for Janet. She had done nothing, had made no mistake other than being with Scott at the wrong time. Knowing what she did about the motive, Jean didn't see how she was going to be able to talk to Janet's parents again.

Sandra too was angry with Scott. She initially felt this anger when she heard the news of the discovery of the bodies. At first she thought that her anger was directed at his murderers; but then, after a long crying session, she realized that the anger she felt was toward Scott. He had abandoned her. He was her closest friend in many ways, and he had just left her. It was an unbearable feeling, almost sacrilegious. She couldn't tell people about it, so she hid it deep inside. Months later, in a poetry class, she read a poem in which Anne Sexton curses her father for having died early. After seeing the therapeutic value of such expression, Sandra realized that she was going to have to let her own feelings out in one way or another.

Sandra's feelings toward her brother were not only angry ones, of course. She had dreams after the bodies were found in which she was watching Scott from a distance, across a cafeteria for instance, and it was enough for her just to see him. She had no urge to go talk to him. In another dream, he was riding a bicycle next to a car the family was riding in. Suddenly he fell over and the car continued on. Others went rushing to help him, but Sandra told herself that there was nothing she could do. Instead she went to a monastery-type place to find someone to talk to.

The black wristband she had worn all the time Scott was missing fell off by itself three days after Scott was found. She had wondered when she would take it off. It had become a part of her. She was working in a day-care center at the time, and while painting with some of the kids she suddenly felt naked. She looked down to see the wristband hanging from her shirt cuff. She realized that it was time for it to come off.

For John, the discovery of the bodies and the memorial services were an end point of sorts. He no longer wanted to talk about the murders with his family. It was over and he wanted to get on with his life.

Jean felt differently. She was plagued by the unreality of all that had happened. The guilt that she had been made to feel when she

John, Jean, and Steven Lewis

had seen the "Christian" doctor had stayed with her throughout the ordeal. For months she had struggled with questions of faith. Janet's mother had said that as far as she was concerned it had been Janet's time to go, that God had planned it that way. Jean could not accept such a faith; yet she had nothing with which to replace her former trust in God and the world that had been crushed by Scott's murder.

The church she and John began to attend in San Jose after Scott disappeared was pastored by a young man named Jerry Drino. After Jean had the disastrous visit to the doctor and then had gotten some reassurance from her former minister in Monterey, she asked Jerry if he would talk to her about her doubts and questions. He had come to the house after Scott and Janet had been found and Jean was impressed that he listened rather than preached. He implied that it was he who had to learn from them, that he had never been through such a situation.

Jerry felt Jean had to resolve her religious questions in order to ease her pain. She did not feel deceived by God, and she held no anger toward Him. But she did feel extremely uneasy about certain parts of her faith. Jerry didn't try to tell her he was with the angels in heaven. She would have shown him the door if he had. He began to give her books that he said he hoped would bring her to her own understanding of God's plan, of creation, of good and evil. Jerry didn't have any pat answers. Jerry's help with Jean's religious dilemma and his more concrete aid in helping to get Scott's body back from New Mexico, helping to plan the ashes-scattering service at the Garden of the Gods, and introducing Jean to people in San Jose who might be sympathetic to her—all of this made him invaluable during the ordeal.

After their return from Colorado, Jean learned that, in some people's eyes, having a son murdered was like having a highly contagious disease. When people avoided talking to her, she realized it was because they were afraid. They could see that Jean was as normal as they were, and if Jean's all-American son could be killed so violently, what was to stop it from happening to their children? For Jean this problem was compounded by the fact that she was new to San Jose and her close friends were all in Monterey. She had to overcome not only her identity as the mother of a murdered son but also her status as an outsider in the community. At the time the bodies were found, a large, well-done obituary appeared in the local paper. In meeting people after that obituary ran, Jean could not avoid the subject of Scott's murder.

Before the bodies were found, Jean would often, when asked, say that she had two children. Sitting with three virtual strangers at a bridge table at the Newcomers Club and having to explain that your oldest son had been missing for seven months was too difficult for her. But there were times when she was forced to mention Scott's disappearance and then, after the bodies were found, she would often have to say that her son had been killed. Most often, people changed the subject after hearing this. Once, though, at the Newcomers table, a woman leaned across the table, gave Jean a big hug, and said how sorry she was to hear that. But that kind of reaction was rare indeed.

Jean did find several people to whom she could talk. In the main these were people who had suffered a loss of some sort. Margaret Trapp, the mother of Steven's best friend in school, Evan, had lost her only daughter in a drowning accident; she spent long hours with Jean listening and crying and sharing her grief. A friend in Monterey introduced Jean to two of her friends in the San Jose area, Fred and May Gere. Fred, an Episcopal priest in nearby Milpitas, had a daughter who had been killed in a car crash. May's first husband had been killed during the Korean conflict and her son in Vietnam.

In talking with these people, Jean found that she was reassured that her own feelings weren't abnormal under the circumstances. She could talk of pain so intense that she thought she was going out of her mind, and she could see from the nods, the tears, and the responses of Margaret and the Geres that their experiences had been similar. There were aspects of Jean's ordeal—the premeditation of Scott's murder especially—that they had not known personally, but they all understood the pain of loss. And the Geres, like Jerry, were reassuring when Jean broached the subject of doubts about her religious convictions. They clearly understood how her experience could cause her to reexamine her lifelong understanding of Christianity.

Jean's relationship with her sisters underwent a change in the first year after Scott disappeared. The youngest of three daughters, Jean had always been closer to one of her older sisters than the other. But during the year, Jean saw that configuration reverse. By the end of the year, she found it much easier to talk to the sister she had not been as close to before Scott's disappearance.

Her parents had called frequently while Scott had been missing, but there really hadn't been much to say. When Scott's body was found, they were not able to come to the memorial service because Jean's mother was in failing health. In June, her mother died, and Jean went east for the funeral.

Returning from the funeral, she saw almost immediately how people she knew casually could handle her mother's death but not Scott's. There were those who had never said anything about Scott's death but who went out of their way to express their condolences about Jean's mother's death. To one such woman Jean replied that it had been a rough two months because she had lost her son in April. Even with that opening, the woman, who knew of Scott's murder, did not say anything about Scott. She said, "I heard about that. I'm sorry about your mother."

When the Lewises were in Colorado for the memorial service, Margaret saw a "Donahue" television show that featured Charlotte and Bob Hullinger, the founders of an organization called Parents of Murdered Children. She jotted down some information and gave it to Jean when she returned. Jean wrote for a transcript of the show and then wrote the Hullingers directly. When the Hullingers visited San Francisco in June, John and Jean went to meet them.

John didn't want to go to the meeting, but he knew that Jean preferred not to make the drive herself at night so he went along. Jean was surprised at how effective the Hullingers' simple method was: each of the parents told the story of their child's murder, their feelings about it, and anything else they wanted to add. Jean sensed that others in the room felt the same release she did in verbalizing their feelings. John talked a little at the meeting, and driving home, he and Jean talked more than they had in months.

A group formed in Oakland, and John and Jean went to two of their meetings; but because the commute was long, they didn't continue attending. During the summer, Jean and John became charter members of a chapter of Parents of Murdered Children in the San Jose area. The group met once a month starting in September 1981. The meetings were intense and wrenching, but they were often cathartic. In those meetings, Jean saw a wide range of responses by people to the murders in their families. Many of those responses and feelings were ones that she had had at one time or another. In some cases, she marveled at the strength of people who had experienced situations that she considered even more horrible than her own. In other cases she saw people being consumed by bitterness; she wondered if the group was strong enough to contend with such unmitigated, raw hatred.

The group got a lot of local publicity and began to grow in size.

Sandra Lewis

Jean was most surprised when an Associated Press reporter came to a meeting and John opened up in front of her. He cried when he told of coming home from work one evening, seeing a boy on a motorcycle who, from the back, looked like Scott. Before that meeting, he had not told Jean about seeing the boy.

Jean realized that many couples had difficulty talking to each other about the murder of their children, and that a marriage is put under an enormous strain by the ordeal. At crisis points in their marriage—when Steven had been so gravely ill, when John had gone to Vietnam—she and John had been able to pool their strength to get through. Jean had thought that with Scott's disappearance and murder she could lean on John as she had in the past. But he hadn't been able to give; he was going through so much himself that he had no strength left for her. In the Parents of Murdered Children meetings Jean realized how common that sort of reaction was and how lucky she and John were to still be together. In her small group alone she heard several stories of marriages breaking up after the murder of a child.

*   *   *

Sandra took time off college during the fall semester of 1981. She had taken incompletes on some of her courses the year before, she saw her life becoming scrambled by the fallout from the murder, and she knew that she had to take time to reorganize herself. Scott's disappearance and death had given her more problems than the apparent grief and anger. She lost all confidence in herself to the point where she began to stutter. And when she wasn't stuttering she was running a whole sentence of words into one big word. Normally an outgoing person, she no longer went out of her way to meet new people, and she found it very hard to trust men. She was certain that if anyone ever tried to attack her she would kill that person first. She also found that she could no longer watch television. Nothing she saw there had anything to do with life as she now knew it.

Sandra's atheism also changed. At the memorial service in Monterey, she had met a friend of her father's whom she liked very much. He was one of the sincere huggers, and the Lewises had gone to his house after the service. He told Sandra about something called the Religious Science Church. She went back several times to visit him and his family and to learn about his religion. In the Religious Science Church there is an emphasis on the god within the person and the personal power that can be derived from recognizing that god. While she was out of school for the semester, Sandra adopted some of the tenets of this church and tried to prepare herself for her last semester in junior college.

When she visited her parents, Sandra missed Scott terribly. He had been the kind of brother who would comment on her new clothes, or her haircut, and generally show her that he cared for her. She knew that Steven cared for her as well, but he was not demonstrative, as Scott had been. Her big brother gone forever, Sandra felt on her own in the world.

In the fall of 1981, Jean decided that she would do some volunteer work to fill up her days. She began working at the Milpitas High School, volunteering in a remedial reading program. Soon after she started there, a girl who attended Milpitas Junior High School was raped and murdered by a student at the high school, who then took a number of his friends up into the hills to view the body before the police discovered it. Such a gruesome murder made national headlines, and there were scores of editorials questioning the character of the students who had viewed the body and yet had not reported it to the police for days. Jean was thoroughly dismayed by the reaction of the students. She got the impression that the murder was not bothering them deeply and that they were more upset by the tarnished image of the school than they were by the murder of one of their classmates.

Worse than the students' reaction to the murder, however, was the reaction of the girl's family minister. He was quoted, in an article in the *San Jose Mercury* that was a collection of rumor and gossip extremely degrading to the victim, as blaming both the young girl and her parents for personal conduct that had led to her murder. Jean was livid. She wrote a letter to the paper that appeared a week later along with another letter denouncing the *Mercury*'s style of journalism. In her letter, Jean harshly criticized the minister and tried to make readers aware of the ways in which society denies the victim and the victim's family rights or consideration in the aftermath of a murder. Jean had heard much from other parents about the ways in which their rights had been abrogated, about problems with the courts, with the press, and with parole procedures. Her sense of their frustration, coupled with her own, went into the letter.

After the arrests, Detective Spencer said that he would keep John and Jean informed about the trial. He didn't phone them for months, though, because he didn't feel they should be notified of each pretrial hearing, each delay. Late in March 1982, he called to say that the trial was about to begin.

He said that there was a lot of local interest because the prosecution was asking for the death penalty for Roger Cullen, the first of the three to be tried. He also told them that Roger Cullen was admitting to having shot Janet and was professing to having become a born-again Christian; his attorney was going to extraordinary lengths to keep him from getting the death penalty. He had even gone so far as to call Janet's parents to ask them to plead for mercy on behalf of her murderer. Janet's father, according to Detective Spencer, had gone to pieces when Cullen called.

Jean asked the detective what was going to be said about Scott and Janet in the courtroom; he said that very little about the two could be entered in the record. Detective Spencer said that they were trying to work it out so that John could take the stand to identify Scott's motorcycle helmet; in so doing they would at least be able to show the jury what the Lewises were like. He asked that they send a picture of Scott that they could enter as evidence.

The judge in the case ruled against the prosecution having John take the stand. John was relieved; he didn't want to be in the courtroom and he didn't want to know any of the details that would come out in the trial.

As the trial began, reporters from Colorado started to call. They had called first when the bodies were found. John had answered the first calls and had been incensed by what he thought the reporters were looking for in their questions. They seemed to want some crude, raw, sensational quotes for their stories. He had simply refused to talk to them. When reporters began to call at the start of the trial, they mainly wanted to know how the Lewises felt about the death penalty. John once again would say nothing to them. Jean talked to the reporters, though, and said that, as far as she was concerned, the issue of the death penalty was up to the jury. She had been educated in a time when criminologists were emphasizing rehabilitation instead of retribution, and she took a middle-of-the-road position on the death penalty. She couldn't really see how taking Roger Cullen's life was going to solve anything, though. She was glad that Scott's murderers had been caught and held without bail, however, and she hoped that the outcome of the trial would be that they would not walk the streets for a long time.

She didn't want to say much to the reporters who called. The district attorney had not been in touch with them at all, but she didn't want to say anything to a reporter that might jeopardize the case against Cullen. To one reporter she said that she felt very distant from the proceedings and that she wasn't about to go to

Colorado and sit in the courtroom for weeks. She suggested Jean call the librarian at her paper and have her send clippings of reports of the trial. She did, and every few days during Cullen's five-week trial she would receive a batch of newspaper stories in the mail.

The reports of the trial were horrifying and infuriating. The testimony of the man who had turned state's evidence gave the court and Jean a chilling look at the way the crime had been planned and carried out. He detailed the ways in which they had plotted to cover up the murders once they had been accomplished. He said that they had taken butchering equipment with them when they had driven to New Mexico with the intent of dismembering the bodies to foil identification. But it had gotten late and they had had to be back in Colorado in time for work, so they had decided against it.

The premeditation of the crime, the six weeks of calculation, and then the methodical way in which four human beings had ended the lives of two others was so far beyond Jean's comprehension that it was almost impossible to make sense of the news articles.

As the trial went on, Jean went in to see Jerry Drino to talk to him about the depression she was sinking into. She told him that everything she had ever believed in or valued seemed to be shaken to the roots. She said that she had spent the better part of her life raising her children, keeping her family in tow, and then all of a sudden everything was topsy turvy. All that she had done in her life seemed worthless. Someone could just come along and eliminate her son with a few seconds of gunfire. It was as if Scott had been worth nothing. Goodness and propriety had always been as sacred to Jean as her belief in God, and yet now those values seemed so meaningless in the face of the cold murder of her son. Jerry could only listen. He said that he had no idea just how deeply an experience such as Jean's would cut into his faith and his understanding of life itself.

Jerry encouraged Jean to examine her dreams. Jean had never thought much about her dreams and remembered few of them. Jerry said that she shouldn't worry, that they would come and she would be able to remember them. One night during the trial a particularly vivid dream did come. In it she and Sandra were walking down a papier-maché street lined with glossy papier-maché houses. The street and houses were all painted in dark, somber colors. It was a dead-end street, and there was a house at the end of the street that one entered through a dutch door. The top half of the door was open and Jean and Sandra could look into the house. But instead of seeing a house inside, they could see a street scene that looked just like Belgium, where they had lived before coming to California. The streets were narrow and quiet, and the gray and dark red houses were very compact. Old women dressed in black were quietly doing something with their hands.

Jerry offered an interpretation of the dream that was something of a surprise to Jean. He said that he thought the papier-maché world Jean and Sandra had walked through represented their relative state of innocence before Scott's disappearance, and that the world they had glimpsed through the dutch door and the old women all dressed in black represented a world of pain, Belgium having suffered so much bloodshed during the World War. That world, Jerry surmised, was the one where Jean now saw her own pain could be understood.

Jean had heard parents in Parents of Murdered Children meetings talk about their guilt. She had not felt guilt in the same way that they discussed it, she did not feel that she had in some indirect way been a part of the murder. But in looking at her dream and Jerry's interpretation, she saw that in some ways she was carrying guilt. She felt that her family had been isolated from the reality of the world, that they had been naive about life and that this naivete had not prepared Scott for a world that included the likes of Roger Cullen. Their world had been one of Boy Scouts, church picnics, army base life, and family vacations. As far as violence was concerned, they had been untouched. Even in Belgium they had not really understood the pain of the people living around them. They had been isolated there too. Her guilt about this isolation and naivete had its limits, however. Scott, had, after all, been killed by another human being.

Along with the horror of the news articles there came some very disturbing information about the approach Cullen's defense was taking. His attorneys were not contending that he was innocent; however, they were trying to paint a picture of him as a changed man: he had committed murder a year and a half before, but now he was someone different. Character witnesses who had known Roger as a youth were put on the stand, as well as a minister who had converted Roger while in jail. Oddly enough, among the character witnesses were two convicted rapists and a convicted burglar. Cullen's defense seemed to be that the jury should judge him by what he is today and not by what he was at the time of the murders. There was some mention of his drug dealing, his cocaine habit, and his part in a larger, regional drug ring. But the parade of witnesses was intended to give the jury a very narrow view of the man.

Scott and Janet were also presented at the trial through a very limited set of facts. Whenever they were mentioned by the defense it was almost always in very subtly negative terms. Reading the newspapers, Jean came to see, would make one think that Roger Cullen had killed another drug pusher and his girlfriend. The Schweigers testified because they were the last to see Scott and Janet alive, but they were not allowed to say anything about the character of their two dance instructors.

Jean was furious with the defense posture and the absence of any positive mention of Scott and Janet. She vented some of her frustration on John, who was not reading the articles and had not been as affected by the trial as Jean. She also let some of her frustration loose on her father when he called to tell her about a distant uncle of Jean's, an older man she had never been close to, who had passed away. After letting Jean talk for a while, her father interrupted her and said, "I think you've said enough for now. I'm going to hang up. Goodnight, Jean."

A phone call from her sister came right after the one from her father. Her sister reminded Jean that their father looked on the bright side of things. Even though she understood that, Jean was still deeply hurt by her father's reaction. She had been the youngest daughter and had been like a puppy dog to him when she was growing up. She had not spoken to him of her feelings about the murder, but in her frustration over the trial, she felt the need to talk to him. His abruptness stung for months afterward.

Jean and Sandra were able to talk about their mutual frustration over the way the trial was going. Sandra, too, was deeply depressed by the trial, by Roger Cullen's assertion of being born-again, and by the impossibility of mentioning Scott's good qualities in the courtroom. She was juggling her final semester in school, two jobs, and her depression. One of her instructors, a man who taught a course in magazine journalism, was unable or unwilling to understand what Sandra was going through and made some callous remarks about course papers in which she had tried to express her feelings about Scott and the trial. Another instructor, however, was quite helpful. He taught a course in literature of the Vietnam war; he had been there himself and had written a book about his experiences. He encouraged Sandra to take her time and to write about her feelings. In writing papers about antiwar protest, Sandra was able to put many of those feelings on paper, and her instructor felt that what she had written was superb.

Jean's way of expressing herself was similar to Sandra's. She found that when she had no other outlet, she turned to the typewriter. At the end of the trial, after the jury had convicted Roger Cullen of first-degree murder but had turned down the death penalty, Jean spoke with Detective Spencer and asked what had been done for the victims in the trial. He was quite upset. He had followed the trial closely and had wanted the jury to give Cullen the death penalty, but he could only say that the system was such that information about the two victims was not permissible evidence. He had spoken to the jurors after they delivered their verdict and had told as many of them as he could about some of the more positive things about Scott and Janet. He reported to Jean that several members of the jury had cried when they had heard what he had had to say. Jean asked whether he thought it would be all right if she wrote the local newspapers and the judge who was to pass sentence on Cullen. Detective Spencer thought it was a good idea, but he told her to check with the district attorney's office before she did anything.

A prosecutor from the district attorney's office said that writing letters would be fine, but Jean didn't get a good feeling from talking with him. He had said that he thought the "outraged parents" should be heard from. Jean did not like being classified as an "outraged parent." It was almost a dismissal of what she wanted to do in her letters. She was not going to write only from anger. She had a reasoned argument to present.

Her letters to the editors and her letter to the judge were similar:

> For one year I have been obsessed with the horrendous vision of the bound, gagged, brutally murdered, decomposed bodies of two Colorado Springs young adults "lying intermingled in a remote culvert of New Mexico." Now this vision is superimposed by the picture of two defense attorneys of Roger Cullen (Apr. 17th, Colorado Springs *Sun*) smiling insidiously over the jury's decision to spare his life.
>
> One of those murdered young adults was my first born son, Scott Jonathan Lewis. Since the first phone call notifying me of his disappearance, I have struggled to be able to experience a moment of spontaneous joy or one of inner peace.
>
> For the survivors, the loved ones of a murdered victim, there is no time off for good behavior. There is no parole from the anguish over their staggering loss of a life precious to them. A child is irreplaceable and, in losing him or her, you've lost a part of yourself as well as a part of your future. The world of siblings is likewise devastated. It is a constant, strenuous effort to regain some kind of normalcy, to maintain some kind of balance and not to succumb to bitterness and anger. Your values of home and family are shaken to the roots.
>
> For the murdered victim there is no second chance; never again the opportunity for life, love, laughter. For Janet and Scott, both caring, gentle, family-oriented young people, there will never be marriage or parenthood. Theirs were not natural deaths and, for them, death came early.

> I grieve for Janet Marie Bunkers, 26.
> I grieve for our own Scott Jonathan, 21.

> And I shudder over our criminal justice system, a system which did not permit the victims' parents or friends to testify in their behalf. Would our pain have been so obvious and thus have prejudiced the jury? But the same system, by permissible defense techniques, convinced the jury to back away from condemnation of the most vicious crimes, premeditated kidnapping and first-degree murder. The intention of the murderer never to have the bodies found is inhuman

cruelty beyond my comprehension.

At least "criminal justice" is not a misnomer. It is precisely that; justice for the criminal and a travesty of justice for the victim. When all the compassion and all of the so-called rights are reserved for the defendant, we, in our society, are all victims.

The defense brought up the subject of God. I agree, Roger Cullen is a child of God. I believe we are all God's children. I also believe that our Creator has shared our shock, our anger, and our tears because Roger senselessly stripped away from Janet and Scott God's most precious gift, that of life. I think God would want justice for the victims.

Sentencing is to take place May 21st, and I urge Judge Richard Hall to exercise justice in their behalf. If legally possible, I urge him to advocate two consecutive life terms for convicted murderer Roger Cullen.

Jean E. Lewis

Jean did not want her letter to be seen as a call for revenge. Sandra and Steven had expressed feelings of revenge, had read a book called *Death Wish* and agreed with the vigilantism of the protagonist. But for Jean revenge was not the answer. She just wanted to make certain that Roger Cullen would spend many years behind bars. His partner in the crime, Randy Wilson, had already tried twice to kill himself in jail, and the second time he had come close enough so that now he was in a coma and probably would be forever. Jean felt that the woman who had set Scott and Janet up and had supplied the rope should have been held responsible for her actions, but she was never charged. The man who had turned state's evidence had plea-bargained his way to a light sentence, but his life, now that he had snitched on a large drug operation, was in danger no matter where he did his time. Jean couldn't quite express how she felt, but she knew that if Roger Cullen's sentences were to run concurrently and he only got twenty years for what he had done she would not feel satisfied.

In writing her letter, Jean had hoped for some response from the public, but she had not been prepared for one of those responses. Roger Cullen had requested, and been denied, counseling by a psychologist in preparation for his jail term. The unlicensed psychologist Roger had wanted to see responded to Jean's letter with one of her own. In it she said that Jean was bitter because she had not accepted the fact that God loans his children to us. Roger Cullen notwithstanding, she went on to say, it had been Janet's and Scott's time to be called home to God. Jean laughed at this at first, then she got angry, and finally she was able to see that she had opened herself up for such claptrap by writing the letter.

Cullen's sentencing was delayed several times, so Jean was surprised when a reporter finally called to say that Roger Cullen had been given two consecutive life sentences, which meant he would have to spend a minimum of forty years in prison. "You must be very happy," the reporter said. Happy? Hadn't the reporter seen her letter? She tried to restrain herself, but she had few calm words to express how she felt, so she hung up. The second reporter who called for her reaction asked the same question. Jean fell apart. She spit out all the anguish she and her family had been through since Scott had disappeared. When she finished there was silence on the other end of the line.

Jean had been struggling to find words to express the way she felt, and just before the sentencing she had come across a review of a book about a murder in upstate New York. The author of the book had concluded that somewhere along the line in the criminal justice system society has to say to the criminals, we abhor what you have done and we're not going to tolerate it. That was what Jean had been asking for in her letter and that was what she really had wanted to say to the reporter. Though the criminal justice system had failed Scott horribly during the trial, she felt that Roger Cullen's sentence was an appropriate expression of abhorrence by society.

After sentencing Jean began to think about her own future. She was still plagued by questions of faith, and she agreed with Jerry that those questions could not be shrugged off. She knew that no matter what she did in the future however there would always be that reservoir of sorrow lying just beneath the surface of her life.

177

8

The Giffords

"**W**AS SEAN SLEEPING over at somebody's house last night? His bed's still made up."

Lavada Gifford woke to these words on Tuesday, May 20, 1980. Her husband, who was up early to go to work, had noticed their fourteen-year-old's bed and had come into the bedroom to ask about him. Lavada and her husband, whom everyone called Buddha, had gone to bed early the night before. Sean had been out visiting a friend and was expected in shortly after his parents went to bed. The Giffords live in Southgate, a section of Los Angeles, and it had been a hot night. Lavada and Buddha had slept in the back room with the fan on and had not waited up for Sean. Sean was the kind of kid you could trust to come home when he said he would.

Lavada was up in a flash and was near panic. Sean had gone to visit a new girlfriend who lived in Downey, the next town over. He had his bus pass, and he was going to take either the 9:00 or 9:30 bus home. The girl's name was Charlene something. What was the last name? Fisher, Frazier? She couldn't think. Her head was crowded with other, horrible thoughts as she threw on some clothes. Then she remembered that just the night before she had asked Sean about a phone number where he could be reached and he had left his address book with her. Strange that he had done that. Normally he took it everywhere with him.

Lavada found the number for Charlene Frazier. Even though it was only 6:00 A.M. she called the Fraziers' house. Charlene said that Sean had left at about 9:00 the night before and that a friend of his, Billy, had gone to the bus stop with him. Chris, Charlene's younger sister, got on the phone to confirm this. Lavada called Billy and he said that he had walked Sean to the bus stop. Sean had intended to catch the 9:30 bus. Billy had gone home before the bus came, though. Lavada envisioned Sean sitting on a bus stop bench, and a frantic feeling gripped her stomach.

There was a chance, a small chance, that he had stayed out all night with a friend or gone to somebody's house or forgotten to tell them about some overnight plans. Lavada called his school at 8:30 praying that Sean was in his classroom. Her prayer wasn't answered. There was no one else to call but the police, but she didn't want to do that because once the police were in the picture it meant that Sean was in real danger, that something serious had happened to him. She didn't want to admit that.

When she called the police they were polite and matter-of-fact. They said that boys Sean's age leave home now and then and that he would probably show up soon. The police couldn't investigate the case until forty-eight hours after the disappearance because so many kids Sean's age turned out to be runaways. They told her that if Sean didn't turn up by Thursday she should give them a call.

In the meantime the police said that she could give them a photo of Sean and information about him, names of friends and the like. Lavada called her daughter at work and asked her if she would take a photo and information to the police station. Lavada didn't drive, and Buddha had already left for his job at the Western Auto Store.

Lavada could see why the police might wait forty-eight hours to investigate disappearances, but she was certain Sean was not a runaway. He was the youngest of her six children and in many ways the happiest. He had been born two years before Lavada and her first husband were divorced, three years before Lavada and Buddha had married. Buddha had been a wonderful husband and father and had taken on Sean as his own right from the beginning. Sean's older brothers and sisters had experienced a lot of turmoil growing up, but Sean had missed most of that. He certainly had no complaints about his parents other than the normal ones of a fourteen-year-old. He hadn't run away. Something had happened to him.

As her fears for Sean mounted, Lavada's anxiety about her own well-being increased. In the past, Lavada had found all sorts of ways to deal with emotional problems. She had overeaten, taken a variety of medications, and used amphetamines. Several times things had gotten so bad that she had checked herself into mental hospitals. Her family had always worried that Lavada would encounter a problem too big for her to handle and would go over the edge.

Lavada called the answering service where she worked as an operator to say that she wouldn't be coming in. She talked to one of her co-workers, who was convinced that Sean had just taken off for a little while. During the next two days Lavada didn't leave her phone. The only thing she could do for Sean was to be available constantly. At times she was hysterical and at other times she was numb. The phone was a blessing when it brought the voices of her family and friends and a curse when it brought no news of Sean.

On Thursday morning she called the police to say that Sean had not returned. They told her that detectives would begin work on the case right away. Shortly after she spoke to the police, she got a call from one of Sean's school friends, a girl named Angie. She said that Chris Frazier was going around the school showing kids a handwritten poem entitled "I am Dead," which she claimed Sean had written the night he disappeared. Angie told her what was in the poem and Lavada went crazy. Sean was predicting his own death. This had to be a hoax. She called the school principal, who was already in conference with the detectives who had come to inquire about Sean. One of the detectives got on the phone and said that they had heard of the poem and had intercepted it. The detective was certain that Sean had not written the note and that Chris Frazier was just trying to grab attention. The detective said that they would bring the poem to Lavada when they came to interview her.

Lavada could see immediately that the poem, written with a red pen in a hand that was not Sean's, was a fake, and she read only the first two lines. It was garbage, but it played on emotions in a cunning way. Lavada, who is naturally given to theatrics, and who was trying desperately then to keep control of the real-life drama she was caught up in, had to fight not to become hysterical in front of the detectives.

She was impressed with the concern of the two policemen. They asked questions about Sean, about his family life and about any problems he might have had at the time he disappeared. They said that, no matter how much you thought you knew about your child, sometimes there were things you could never know. Perhaps Sean had taken off to escape something he couldn't talk to his family about.

The police had no leads to go on in their investigation. A friend of Sean's had been driving by the bus stop with his parents the night Sean disappeared and had seen him sitting there alone waiting for the bus. But that was it. The police called daily to ask if Lavada had heard anything, but they could find no trace.

Everyone in the family dealt with the lack of information in their own way. Buddha worked harder than he ever had. He is the sort of person who keeps himself busy almost all the time. But during June and July Buddha overworked. He would come home from his job and would do hours of yard work or house repairs until it was time to go to bed. Lavada's children would come to the house and sit and stare and not know what to say or do. Lavada's mother and sister would call or visit every day, as much to keep an eye on Lavada as anything else. Lavada experienced wild swings of emotion. There were times when she would cry and scream, and there were other times when she would find herself washing a dish four or five times in a row. One morning she came out of the bedroom and screamed at the top of her lungs, "I want my son!"

There was little the family could do. The local newspapers ran Sean's photo, and a reporter from Channel 5 came out to inquire about him. He said that they had had good luck with stories about missing children. Channels 5, 2, and 7 ran stories about Sean's disappearance, but nothing turned up. Chris Frazier circulated a rumor that Sean was holed up in the apartment of a drug dealer in Downey. Lavada called her and pleaded with her not to lie about Sean. Chris said she wasn't lying, and so on Memorial Day weekend the police,

Buddha, and Derek staked out the apartment. But nothing came of it, and under pressure Chris admitted that she had lied.

Late in June, the Los Angeles police arrested a truck driver from Downey, William Bonin, and charged him with a series of murders that had occurred over the past two years and that had come to be known as the "Freeway Killings." Bonin, it was alleged, had picked up hitchhikers, usually young teenage boys, on the freeways around Los Angeles, sexually molested them, murdered them by strangulation and stabbing, and left their bodies beside the freeway in plastic trash bags. The Freeway Killings had been much in the news during 1979 and 1980, and the arrest was front-page news in Los Angeles and throughout the country.

Lavada had been well aware of the Freeway Killings. She is an avid television watcher and followed the reports as the victims were found. Shortly before Sean disappeared, she had watched the news with him one night, and they had had a long talk about the killings. Sean had realized the dangers of getting into a stranger's car and promised never to hitchhike. It was after that conversation that Buddha and Lavada decided to get Sean a bus pass. He liked to go to the beach and he was starting to notice the opposite sex. They felt he needed his freedom and that with a bus pass he could go when and where he wanted.

The family never connected Sean's disappearance with the Freeway Killings. Lavada was certain that Sean would have done as he had promised and would not have hitchhiked. But when she saw the news of Bonin's arrest she wondered whether he might have a circle of friends who were involved in crimes similar to the ones he was charged with. She thought it a remote possibility that Bonin might know something about Sean. After all, he was from Downey, and that's where Sean was last seen.

Bonin was arrested on a Friday, and Lavada didn't talk to the detectives working on Sean's case until Monday. During that conversation she asked about Bonin. The detective told her that a friend of Bonin's, a man named Vernon Butts, had also been arrested in connection with the Freeway Killings and was talking. The media had not been told of the second arrest, so she knew nothing about

Butts. The detective didn't say anything more about the information they were getting from Butts, and Lavada put the Freeway Killings out of her mind.

Buddha, the children, and Lavada's mother all worried that Lavada was going to have a breakdown, but they didn't know what they could do to help her. Lavada realized that she was on the edge, but she was determined to hold herself together for the sake of her family. She knew that her past breakdowns had been escapes, and she did not want to escape this time—she wanted to stay and fight. As time passed, though, she had violent headaches and had to get medication. She found that she had no appetite and lost twenty-five pounds.

At the end of July, the police called to warn her that they were making a statement to the media about Sean's disappearance. They said that after a certain length of time in the case of a missing child they are required to give their opinion on the case to the public. Even with the warning, the newscast that night was shocking. The police had reported to the press that they were assuming Sean had been the victim of some sort of foul play, that he was not a runaway. Lavada knew the police conclusion was true.

On August 1, one of the detectives called Lavada at work and asked her if she would meet him at her house. The detective called Buddha too, but he was out on a delivery run, so he wasn't home when Lavada arrived. Lavada's heart went out to the detective; he was clearly upset and did not want to be the one to have to bring the news. Lavada tried desperately to prepare herself for the words she was about to hear, words she had suspected she would have to hear sooner or later.

It was worse than she had imagined. Sean was dead, and the police were certain that William Bonin had murdered him. Vernon Butts had been with Bonin the night of May 19. They had driven past Sean sitting at the bus stop, and Bonin had suggested to Butts that they "get" Sean. Butts, who had helped Bonin before, declined this time, but Bonin had later told him that he had killed Sean and dumped his body in a secluded area. The police had searched where Butts thought the body might be, but had no luck.

Lavada couldn't stop crying and screaming. The detective tried to help, but couldn't. He waited until Buddha arrived.

Buddha knew as soon as he arrived that Sean was dead, and he did what he could to help Lavada. When he heard the details and learned that Sean had probably been molested and killed in Bonin's van, he too experienced more of a shock than he was prepared for. He had been around enough as a bar bouncer, a biker, and an ex-convict to know what an ugly, degrading, and vicious thing Sean had been through. His grief was compounded by the contact he had once had with people like Bonin. He called the kids, Lavada's mother, and Lavada's first husband, Sean's real father, who was a close friend. After he finished the last call, he began to cry and to pound his fist against the wall next to the phone. His big Buddhalike body shook so that Lavada was afraid he would collapse. She leaned against him, and they held each other up.

The family knew now that Sean had suffered a horrible death and they also knew that they would most likely never recover his remains. Sean had just been torn from them and was gone completely. The information they had was both scant and repulsive. They didn't even have a body to bury. Nothing offered them consolation.

Religion had never been central to the Giffords, but it had at times been present in the house. Lavada had grown up in a Baptist home and considered herself a Christian. She worried about her own lax attitude toward Christianity, though, and feared that by not raising her children in the church she was keeping them from salvation. Buddha usually described himself as an agnostic. He didn't deny God's existence, but he didn't think of himself as a Christian.

At the time Sean disappeared his brothers and sisters held a variety of opinions about religion. Derek and Brook didn't have much use for it. Ricci, who had been an atheist all her life, was beginning to listen to friends who were telling her what a help Christianity had been in their lives. Roni had been converted and baptized with Sean several years before, but in the spring of 1980 she had lost interest and had nearly stopped attending church.

Without really letting his family know the extent of his involvement or commitment, Sean had been attending a local, community church and had been active in the youth program there. Lavada had known that he went to services, meetings during the week and vacation Bible school, but she had assumed that the church was just a good place for Sean to meet girls. He had given her a drawing of Christ he had done and she liked the artwork, but she hadn't understood it as an expression of religious conviction.

A month or so after Sean disappeared, Lavada had gotten a call from one of the girls in Sean's church who said that some of the members of the youth group wanted to come to the house and pray with the family. Lavada was at her wit's end at that point and didn't see how a prayer circle could hurt. She was familiar with that sort of thing anyway, having grown up in a Baptist family.

They were a nice group of teenagers and they were sincerely concerned about Sean. Lavada and Buddha couldn't really connect with a lot of what they said in their prayers, but at that point simply having people in the house expressing concern was a comfort. Lavada began to see that perhaps Sean had been going to those meetings for reasons other than purely social ones.

Shortly after the news got around that Sean was dead, Lavada got a call and then a visit from Sean's pastor and his wife. They asked Lavada if the family would have any objection to a memorial service for Sean at the church. With no body, Lavada didn't know what to do about a funeral, so she said a memorial service would be fine.

It was held two weeks after they learned of Sean's death. The pastor had been frank in saying that he hoped to be able to minister to people through the memorial service, and Lavada was not certain what that would mean. She did expect the atmosphere to be somber, perhaps even morbid. It was far from that, however.

The place was packed with children and adults, and there was hardly anything in the program that could be labeled morbid. The Giffords were swept up by the singing and the eulogies. The service could only be described as uplifting; that was the word that came to Lavada as she stood greeting people in front of the church for forty-five minutes after the service. She was not dissolved in tears as she had expected to be. She wasn't sure just what had gone on, but she felt better than she had in months. Somehow Sean was alive among these people.

Derek was quite shaken. He had been feeling for weeks that it was he who should have been killed, not Sean. He, not Sean, had gotten into trouble several times. When he heard the singing and the words of praise for his brother, Derek felt even more deeply that it was he who should have died. The pastor invited any people who were interested in joining the church to meet after the service. Derek went to the meeting.

One of the people Lavada greeted after the service was a woman named Barbara Biehn. She was the mother of Steven Woods, who, along with Sean, had been one of the last victims in the Freeway Killings. Several days before, Lavada had seen Barbara on a newscast talking about William Bonin and about a program in California that provided hospital and outpatient treatment, rather than jail terms, for mentally disordered sex offenders, whom she called MDSOs. Bonin, she had said, had been an MDSO and one of a number of such sex offenders who had been released from the program. On the newscast Barbara had said that the laws regarding MDSOs should be changed and that she and others were forming an organization to push for such legislative action. Lavada liked the idea of the group and called Barbara.

The organization was soon off the ground and went by the acronym VICTIMS, Voter's Initiatives Concerning Tougher Imprisonment of Molesters and Sex Offenders. Bonin had by that time been linked to some thirty-three murders, and most of the parents of the children he allegedly killed eventually came to VICTIMS meetings. Lavada was an active charter member. She attended meetings and spent many hours in the fall of 1980 writing letters to legislators. The group was a political action committee, but for Lavada it served as a support group as well.

Lavada was terribly depressed after the memorial service. She left her job for three months because she couldn't be the helpful, professional operator she had been before Sean's death. She was so short-tempered that when she heard small complaints from customers she wanted to scream into the phone, "You think you've got problems? My little boy's been killed!" She went to see a psychologist, but that didn't work out. He said that she would feel guilty about Sean's death (which she never did), and he predicted a date when the raw, angry feelings would leave her. When they didn't leave according to his schedule, his attitude toward Lavada changed, and she stopped seeing him.

During the fall, Lavada kept in touch with the Southgate detectives assigned to the case, but they didn't have much to report. The only way they were going to find Sean's body was for Bonin to tell them where he had left it, and they didn't have any hope of that happening. In desperation, they asked Lavada if she would, in her own handwriting, send Bonin a letter. She agreed to, and the detectives composed the letter. She wrote Bonin that she wanted Sean's body so that she could give him a Christian burial.

Lavada was back at work on December 20 when one of the detectives called to say that the San Bernadino police had found some remains that they thought might be Sean's. Lavada couldn't speak. Remains? My God! Is this how we're going to find out what happened to Sean? The detective said they needed hospital records, X-rays, and dental records to make the identification.

That afternoon was like an abbreviated movie of Sean's life. The police and Lavada went to the hospital where he had had his appendix out and to another hospital where he had had a broken arm set. Suddenly Sean was there for Lavada. He was once again the kid who liked to swim and surf, the kid who had tried Pop Warner football but hadn't been very good at it. And yet here she was riding around with two detectives picking up medical records so that they could identify his remains.

The Giffords tried to have a Christmas. They decorated the house but, as the day approached, no one in the family felt like being festive. At 7:00 P.M. on Christmas Eve the phone rang and Lavada answered. It was a San Bernadino policeman. He said, rather bluntly, that they had identified the mandeval jaw they had found as Sean's. Lavada blew up. "Why did you call me on Christmas Eve!" she screamed into the phone.

Christmas Day was horrible. Images of Sean's body decomposing, being picked at by animals in some remote canyon in San Bernadino wouldn't leave them. Lavada had always thought that the days of her breakdowns would be the worst time of her life, but this was far worse.

Two weeks later, the police found a skull, identified it as Sean's, and called to tell Lavada. Again she screamed at them. "My God! Are you going to find a different piece every week?"

Sean had said once or twice that he would like to be buried at sea. Lavada and Buddha decided that they would cremate his remains and scatter them in the ocean. It took them almost four months, however, to get the remains from the San Bernadino police.

As it turned out, the police called on Good Friday in April 1981 to say that they would release the remains. Sean was buried on Easter morning. It was a cold, dreary day and only the family came. Buddha's boss took the ashes out on his boat and pulled near the beach so the family standing there could see. Derek wore a tuxedo, but the others were dressed informally. They took pictures of the boat out on the water and of the family standing hugging each other on the beach. They tape-recorded a collective prayer that they said as Sean's ashes were dropped into the water. They all told Sean how much they loved him.

As they walked back to the parking lot, Lavada noticed that the noises of the surf and the traffic of the adjacent highway stopped and a quietness settled on the beach for a minute. She mentioned this, and the family looked back to the water. The clouds had parted slightly and a shaft of sunlight seemed to hit the water just about where Sean's ashes had been scattered. They were all stunned. They didn't exactly see this as a sign, but they were all taken by the sudden calmness and the beauty of the light on the water. They cried, held each other, and then left.

The months preceding Sean's burial had brought a growing, unfocused anger into the house and an unspoken fear of Bonin's trial, which was about to begin. Buddha expressed this anger more than the rest of the family. At work he would yell at employees and customers alike and his boss, who understood the anger, would try to cover up for him. At home he was short-tempered. As he was normally an easygoing sort of person, the change was radical and only increased the tension.

Lavada was fighting her own battle with the specter of a breakdown, and her body was showing signs of the fight. She was willing to take any kind of pill doctors would give her, but she was determined not to escape by checking into a hospital. She hadn't done that in nearly ten years. She had surprised her family by sticking with her job through most of the worst part of the ordeal, and now she was trying to hang on and get through the trial. She and Barbara Biehn had decided that they would attend as much of the trial as they could stand; there were so many questions that they wanted answered. Lavada just wasn't sure that her mind and her body could take the strain.

Of all the emotions the Giffords experienced in those days, none was stronger than the pure and utter hatred they felt for William Bonin. No matter what they were doing, that hate was never far from the surface, and it took very little to activate it. They saw the hatred as something natural and organic to their ordeal. In VICTIMS meetings they heard others express the same sort of hatred, so they knew that their rage was not abnormal.

One evening late in the spring, Lavada was watching the evening news and was surprised to learn that a local reporter, Dave Lopez, had interviewed William Bonin at length. Lavada listened as Lopez described the details of the interview. He said that Bonin had led police to Sean's body after he had gotten a letter from Sean's mother. What? Usually when there was to be anything like this on television or in the papers the detectives or the D.A.'s office would call to warn her. Lopez said that Lavada had written that she forgave Bonin for killing her baby, but that she wanted to give him a Christian burial.

Forgave him! Lavada soon had Lopez on the phone. She yelled at him and asked him where he got his story. He said that he had just gone by what Bonin had said and had not read the letter himself.

Part of Lavada's anger had nothing to do with Lopez. The news that Bonin had taken police to the site of the remains was something she had not heard from the detectives. She had assumed that a prison snitch, not Bonin himself, had informed the police.

Lopez seemed nonplussed and asked to interview Lavada. Lavada had no desire to sit down with him. She had already done a number of interviews with the press. A woman reporter from the *Los Angeles Times* with whom Lavada had gotten along well during one such interview called, and when Lavada told her about Lopez, the reporter said that he was relentless and would "camp out at your gate" to get a story.

That's exactly what he did the next morning. Before he came Lavada went to a girlfriend's house. Derek talked briefly to Lopez, which angered Lavada. She never did grant him the interview and she stayed angry with Lopez for quite a while.

During the fall of 1980, at Ricci's urging, Randi and Lavada had started watching Sunday morning television sermons broadcast from the Crenshaw Community Church with the Reverend Fred Price preaching. Ricci had been watching his televised sermons for a while and had found them helpful. Lavada and Randi soon made Fred Price's sermon a staple of their week.

He talked a lot about what being born-again meant. He used words and phrases that Lavada had heard before, but he used them in ways that gave them more meaning than she had ever remembered them having. Although they didn't discuss it much, the sermons seemed to be having an effect on the three women. Ricci had accepted the idea of giving everything—pain, sorrow, tears, anger, hate—to Jesus. Lavada and Randi couldn't imagine doing that, but Reverend Price had such a clear way of putting things that it almost made sense.

But Lavada and Buddha were not ready to give up their hatred of Bonin and were certainly not ready to forgive him. They had no desire to give up the pain either. In all the meaninglessness and horror of the past year, the pain was at least something concrete to hang onto. Give that up to Jesus, or anyone, and what would be left?

Still, on Sunday mornings Lavada found herself in front of the television with her daughters.

Out of the blue one day, shortly before the trial was to start, Sean's death certificate came in the mail from the San Bernadino coroner's office. It listed cause of death as stabbing and strangulation. The only way the coroner's office could have known that was through a confession from Bonin, as there weren't enough remains for a medical examiner's assessment. Seeing those words on paper, feeling them in the pit of her stomach, gave Lavada an indication of what she was going to have to go through at the trial. She wanted to know what had happened, she wondered how Bonin had lured Sean into his van, she wanted to have all sorts of details cleared up. But whenever a detail would be uncovered, the knowledge of the detail brought more pain than her prior ignorance had. She began to see that the trial, which the district attorney's office was telling the families would be a long one, was going to be a string of such horrible revelations.

Buddha decided that he would not go to the trial. He was certain that it would make him much too emotional and that he might cause a mistrial by standing up and shouting. Lavada and Barbara Biehn, who had become good friends through their work with VICTIMS, were determined to go to as much of the trial as they could even though it was being held in downtown Los Angeles and neither of them drove.

The preliminary hearings began in May 1981. Lavada had to testify and get on the witness stand. Bonin would not look at her, though he had looked at other parents who had taken the stand. Being in the same room with Bonin, only a few feet from the man who had taken her son's life, she could understand why some of the other parents did not want to come to the trial.

The trial was supposed to begin in May, but there were four continuances on procedural matters, and it didn't actually begin until September. The district attorney's office had a good idea of when the trial was going to start, so Lavada and the other parents didn't have to go to the false starts over the summer. But the continuances only served to increase the pressure. On July 5, Lavada woke up with severe stomach cramps and bleeding. She went to the hospital and was eventually hospitalized for three weeks for an ailment the doctors called Chron's disease. They said that it was a permanent condition of the intestines that could flare up in the presence of strain or pressure.

Before the trial began, Vernon Butts hung himself in his cell. Lavada learned from the detectives that, when Bonin had led them to the place he had left Sean's body, he had done so under the condition that it could not be used as evidence against him in court. Without a body and without Butt's testimony, there was only one way that Bonin could be convicted of Sean's murder. Bonin would have to confess.

When Lavada first went into the courtroom, she was almost certain that Bonin would not be found guilty of her son's death. That and the fact that there would be no testimony about Sean or pictures of his body was going to make her experience of the courtroom different from those of the other parents who came. But she was a vital part of the group. It was she the press felt comfortable going to for their stories. Some of the other parents had trouble expressing themselves with the lights blazing, tape recorders running, and cameras clicking. But the press found Lavada, even under these circumstances, an articulate and open woman, a good interview.

Lavada felt that she had something she needed to say to the press. She was certain that the court would not officially blame Bonin for Sean's death, and yet she and everyone else knew the circumstances of the murder. The press would listen to her and do stories about Sean's case. If the courts would not publicly condemn William Bonin, then she would.

But going to court took a heavy toll. Randi often went with her. Their trip on the bus was exhausting. Added to that were the emotions raised by the details of the trial.

The families were given help by people from the victim witness program and were always within earshot of a detective. They had a room of their own on another floor, which they could go to any time the pressure was too much. Lavada rarely used the room, but the pressure did get to her. There were times when she wanted to stand up in the middle of some testimony, point at Bonin, and tell everyone in the courtroom that he had led the police to Sean's body. But she and Buddha and Barbara had talked about such things, and she knew that to do so might jeopardize the other convictions. They all wanted the trial to run smoothly so there would be no possibility for reversal on appeal.

The trial began in September and ended in December. As she sat through the first few weeks, Lavada kept thinking how bizarre the whole affair was. The testimony all had to do with the murders, of course, and any mention of the victims outside their victimization was not allowed. Parents heard mention of their children in the most gruesome of situations and never had an opportunity to tell the court about the full lives their children had once led. And each body, except for Sean's, was well documented by color photographs. As soon as Lavada saw some of those photographs, especially the one of the boy with the ice pick in his head, she was thankful that Sean's body had not been photographed. She never saw her son dead. She had no image of her son's mutilated body to carry out of the court-room with her. But her heart went out to the parents who did have to suffer that.

Barbara and Lavada weren't able to stand being in the courtroom for several days after the testimony of two of Bonin's accomplices. One of these men had the sense neither to lie nor to use anything but common street language to describe certain acts. His ghastly, detailed accounts of hearing necks snap and the like was enough to turn even the strongest stomach and sent Lavada back to the hospital with a flare-up of Chron's disease.

Many times during the trial, Lavada's mother and friends would call to tell her not to look at a certain article or news broadcast. She always obeyed.

While the trial was on, the family was shown a tasteless joke in *Hustler* magazine. It was a mock advertisement for a game called the "Freeway Killer." The copy beside a picture of the game read:

How about a road-race set that brings you the *real* danger of a California highway? Not nine-car pileups and trucks jackknifing, but the murder and mayhem wrought by the mysterious Freeway Killer. This kit has all the accessories you need to commit the crimes: young male victims, a Highway Patrol chase vehicle, the deadly Freeway Killer pickup van, heavy-duty trash bags, and a combination body-counter/lap-timer. See who can commit the most hideous murders before the cops catch up. This is the kind of fun you can have only on the West Coast!

A little inset picture of the box the game supposedly came in read: "Get ready for the ride of your life." Lavada had seen it before and had dismissed it; but with the trial growing more grisly each day, she could not remain as calm the second time she saw it. She showed it to the other families, and they all took it with them when they went to see a lawyer about another matter. He drew up plans for a suit against *Hustler* and wanted to begin right away, but the D.A. told them to hold off until the trial was over.

The other matter the parents went to see the lawyer about was their concern that several journalists and perhaps the defense attorney were thinking about writing books on the Bonin case. The families were furious that these people were going to make money off their children's murders. The lawyer said that there was little they could do to stop the publication of any books about the case.

The testimony about Sean was not as gory as that about some of the other children. The only picture of him shown in the courtroom was his school picture. Three of his friends, the last three people to see him alive, told what they knew, but there was no official mention of how or where Sean's body was found.

For Lavada, however, even this mild testimony was horrifying. She felt that anything that put the children in the limelight, anything that connected them to the acts Bonin was accused of having committed, was a denigration of the children's lives. Her close contact with the press gave her the sense that, beyond the cameras, the public was squirming with each revelation of new horrors, but that they were doing so without the full knowledge of who the boys were and what their lives had been like before Bonin had killed them.

Two journalists, Tim Alger of the *Orange County Register* and Dave Lopez, had each done extensive interviews with Bonin and were subpoenaed to testify. Both said that they would not do so, citing journalistic privilege. As the trial came to a close, however, it became apparent that strong testimony, such as that which Lopez could give, was needed to seal the case and bring in convictions. Lavada had softened some in her attitude toward Lopez. He and she talked now, and early in the trial she had grabbed him playfully by the scruff of the neck once and asked him what he would do if his testimony were needed. The families of the victims were upset by Alger's and Lopez's refusal to testify, but Lavada had a feeling that Lopez would testify if he had to. She certainly hoped he would. If he took the stand, he could tell about Bonin taking them to Sean's remains. Even if that couldn't be used against him, at least the jury would know that Bonin was Sean's murderer.

When the trial had to be postponed because Bonin was beaten up by other inmates in the county jail, Dave Lopez saw this as a sign that he was being given a last chance to testify, and he did so. His change of heart was headline news and was applauded by almost everyone in the press except for Tim Alger. Lavada and the other family members were, of course, ecstatic.

When the jury was in deliberation, Lavada was not completely certain that they knew of Bonin's involvement in Sean's murder. The evidence was sparse and Lopez's testimony had only touched on it. But the other cases were so much more specific. She made sure that she got the truth, as she knew it, out to the press. She didn't care that she was trying Bonin in the papers; she felt that she had to make up for the deficiencies of the justice system.

But once while they were deliberating, the jury returned to the courtroom to ask a question of the judge. During the trial a chart had been used to chronicle the various dates of each of the cases— when the boys had disappeared, when their bodies had been found. In Sean's case, the date of the discovery of the remains should not have been on the chart because that date was not allowable evidence. It had appeared on the chart by accident. The jury returned to ask the district attorney to verify that date, but he could not. Lavada realized then that the jury knew Bonin had killed Sean, but she also realized that they would have to acquit him of the murder.

The press coverage of the trial had been very heavy. There were cameras and reporters in the courtroom, and more cameras and reporters in the hall outside, and as the trial drew to a close and the jury stayed in deliberations for two and a half days, the media seemed to be everywhere. Lavada and some of the other families dealt with press requests as best they could, but they were all starting to feel the pressure of a long trial.

There were ten murders being tried, and each murder had various other charges connected to it, such as kidnapping or sexual molestation. As the jury foreman read down the lists of these charges for each murder, there was a string of guilty verdicts until they got to Sean's name; then there was a "not guilty." This happened a couple of times before it became too much for Lavada. They were about to read his name and "not guilty" again when she realized that she could take no more. She got up and walked toward the door with her head down, crying. The press waiting in the hall outside, watching the proceedings on a monitor, didn't miss her exit. Ricci and Brook were out there too and could see the camera men getting ready. This was the shot the press were looking for; the tearful mother unable to sit through the verdict, coming out of the courtroom. There was a lot of jostling near the door in anticipation of Lavada's exit. Ricci knew her mother was going to need help getting through the swarm of reporters, so she moved close to the door.

When a detective opened the back door of the courtroom to let Lavada out, there was a blinding bank of lights, and microphones were thrust into her face. Questions came from all over. She felt like she was going to be swallowed up by the lights and the noise. This time Lavada didn't want to look at anyone, be photographed, answer any questions. She just wanted to be alone. The detective tried to push people back, as did Ricci, but it was slow going. The reporters knew Lavada and knew that their readers and listeners and

Lavada Gifford

viewers wanted those tears. They couldn't miss this part of the story. Lavada inched toward the elevator, but the lights didn't get turned off and the questions didn't stop. Ricci yelled at several reporters, but it did little good. The whole crazy scene continued even while Lavada, Randi, Brook and the detective were waiting for the elevator. Lavada felt for the first time as if she were being used by the press. She had been so conscientious with them, and here they were pushing and shoving the one time she really needed to be alone. Her opinion of the press though generally favorable would always be tainted by the memory of that crush of reporters.

Lavada, Randi and Ricci watched Reverend Price on television for a year before they finally went to Crenshaw Community Church in August 1981. The church was so crowded that many people who went to the services never made it in the door. But through a friend who was an usher at the church the Giffords were able to make it in. Lavada knew when she went to the service that she wanted to make a commitment, that she was ready to return to the religion she had left when she was twelve. Being inside Crenshaw and hearing Reverend Price in person was a very moving experience for all three of the women, and at the end of the service they went to the altar and were born again in the Lord.

Being born again was a wonderful experience for Lavada. So many of the things that had happened to the family in the preceding year had been so horrible, so depressing, so profoundly negative. But coming to the Lord was not like that at all. It was the most positive set of feelings she and her daughters had ever felt. For the year after Sean's murder she had often felt as if she were trying to find her way through some dark swamp. Being born again was a combination of dry land and bright light. She began to know a comfort and peace that a year before she would have thought impossible. In accepting Jesus and in beginning to give her life over to him she became certain of a heaven in the afterlife, a heaven Sean was already a part of and one that she and Randi and Ricci were now destined for. At times the thought of that would flood Lavada with a calmness unlike any she had ever known.

After becoming born again Lavada's life began to change greatly but the change did not come all at once. The trial was such a devastating experience and brought back so much of the pain of the murder for the family that much of their growth as Christians during that time came slowly.

A turning point for Lavada came near the end of the trial. So much of the testimony she had heard over the course of the trial had made her confront death and loss in ways that were very uncomfortable. Sean was so far away, lost to her forever. It helped tremendously to know that Sean had died a Christian, but she wasn't at all sure what that meant, how that affected his death and how that could help bridge the huge, uncrossable chasm she felt between herself and her son. Then one morning Reverend Price talked about death. He said that death isn't a slow process for the Christian who has been saved. And it is not a difficult problem. He moved to the side of the podium and took one step down the altar steps. He said that death was just like that, from this world to the next world, and that for the Christian it was like stepping off your back porch into the arms of Jesus. You never lose consciousness.

Lavada was transfixed. Sean was not dead and gone, separate forever. He had simply taken one step and moved on. A detective had once told the families in a meeting that, if it was any consolation to them, strangulation was the least painful way to die. Lavada had been particularly upset by that remark. But suddenly that sort of thinking, imagining what horrors Sean had gone through, was hardly important. Sean had taken a step into a new world, one they were all destined for. He had gone on ahead of them, saved.

Sean was alive. She no longer could think of him as dead, murdered. She no longer said "when Sean died" but "when Sean went to heaven." It was a wonderful revelation for her, one that changed her thinking tremendously. She began to see that so much of the pain that she and her family had been through was pain that they had held onto, had refused to let go of. Anger, too, she saw as a fire, a destructive fire, that she and the rest of the family had fed in the days before she became born again. Once she got to the point where she could give things like pain and anger to the Lord she realized that, had she not done so, they might well have destroyed her. She felt saved in so many ways.

The change that came over Lavada after she made her commitment to the Lord was a radical one but not one that closed her off from the secular world altogether. She would begin her day with Christian television and she would listen to Christian radio, but she still followed the Los Angeles Dodgers as avidly as ever. Outwardly she had changed little, but inwardly she felt like a completely new person. And in the months after the trial, the first few months of 1982, she could see that something amazing was happening to the whole family. Buddha and Derek and Brook were starting to see just how important Jesus had become for Lavada, Randi, Ricci, and Roni.

Buddha listened to the sermons on television and went to Crenshaw with Lavada, but at first he saw the services as entertainment. Lavada understood that it would take time for him to see what she was seeing. One day she looked over at Buddha during a service and saw tears streaming down his cheeks. It was wonderful to see him crying in the Lord. She realized then that he was starting to get the message. On the day after Easter Buddha made his commitment to the Lord. Lavada was with him at home and she read a prayer. It was a glorious time for Lavada. She knew that Sean was their own little angel, who had gone on before them, and she knew that she and the girls were saved, washed in the Lord, and would one day join Sean. Now Buddha as well would be part of their family in heaven. Lavada was certain that it would only be a matter of time before Derek and Brook would join them as well.

There were many things about their faith that the Giffords could live by every day, but nothing was more important to them than the understanding that "all things work for those who love the Lord." Lavada could never have predicted on Easter Day in 1981, when Sean was buried at sea, that a year later her family would have come to the Lord and would have changed so radically. If she ever had predicted change it certainly wouldn't have been the positive sort that the family now experienced. But that is exactly what happened and Lavada knew that it was the love of

Buddha Gifford

the Lord that made the changes possible.

Probably the most difficult part of their change was the family's attitude toward William Bonin. When Sean's death certificate had come in the mail Lavada had been so enraged by the information that Sean had been stabbed and strangled that she would have done the same to Bonin if she had been able to. When, in January 1982, Bonin was sentenced to death, Lavada stood up in the courtroom and shouted, "Praise God, thank God, all right!" She believed in the death penalty, believed the Bible supported it and certainly believed that Bonin was one who should suffer it. At the same time, though, Lavada realized that one day her growth as a Christian would show her the way to forgive Bonin. Listening to Christian radio she felt guilty when she heard talk of forgiving your enemies. Even after she was born again and saw almost everything in a different light she found it hard to imagine praying for William Bonin. But other Christians assured her that such a thing would eventually happen and it would happen because God would cause it to happen. And eventually it did.

Lavada's health improved greatly in the first few months of 1982. The Chron's disease that the doctors had said would be a permanent condition disappeared. She was able to stop taking the medication that she had needed to combat migraine headaches, and she started to think about going back to work. She had never been one for exercise, but in the late spring and early summer she began to take long walks in a nearby park in the evenings.

The Giffords realized that many people who were not Christians, had not been born again, could not understand the change that had come over their family. They could see that other people were often skeptical when they talked of their faith. But that didn't bother them. They had once been a family that did not love the Lord and they remembered both their own skepticism and the negative feelings of those days. They knew also just how positive life had become for them in the Lord and they hoped and prayed other people would experience the changes they had gone through.

In the two years after the night of Sean's disappearance there had been two upheavals in the Gifford family. The first was caused by the horror of Sean's murder and the second was caused by the family coming to the Lord. The Giffords could see that the two were connected. Sean's death, as horrible and unnecessary as it was, became in the end a victory for the Lord. He had died a Christian, he had gone on ahead of the family, and now the family had turned to the Lord and would follow him.

Early in the summer of 1982 the Giffords decided to repaint their house and, after some discussion, chose a color that in many ways summed up the changes that had come to them. They painted the house a bright yellow.

9

Camille Bell

THE FIRST POLICEMAN who came to Camille Bell's apartment after Yusuf disappeared said that he had seen the nine-year-old walking to the corner grocery store two hours before. He remembered seeing Yusuf—after Camille described him as wearing only shorts, no shoes and no shirt—because it was a hot October afternoon and the policeman, sweltering in his patrol car, had envied the carefree, cool-looking kid. It was Sunday, October 21, probably the last summery day of 1979 in Atlanta, Georgia.

Yusuf, his older brother, Jonathan, ten, and two neighborhood kids had been watching Tarzan on television at a neighbor's apartment when Miss Pearl, a seventy-year-old woman who often had youngsters do errands for her, asked Yusuf to go to the store to get her some snuff. Actually, she asked whether any of the kids stretched out on the floor would go to the store, but Yusuf was the only one who would go for the offered price of seventeen cents. Jonathan turned his nose up at any errand that would not net him at least a quarter. Yusuf had a policy of taking the low-paying jobs and getting kickbacks later in the form of one of Miss Pearl's homemade cakes. Yusuf left the television watchers, went to his apartment, asked Camille's permission, and then headed up Fulton Street for the short walk to the corner store.

The apartment house the Bells lived in was a private one in the Mechanicsville section of Atlanta on the south side, near the new

Fulton County Stadium. The area is a mix of empty lots, wood-frame houses, apartment buildings, and old city housing projects, and most of the area's residents are black and poor. The convention-eers who flock to Atlanta's flashy new downtown hotels usually miss Mechanicsville. Since this section of the city is not troubled by much of the street crime that plagues Atlanta, Camille Bell, who grew up in a middle-class black home in Philadelphia and who was divorced in 1978, found the neighborhood a good one in which to raise her two boys and her daughters Maria, a year and a half younger than Yusuf, and Cici, three at the time.

Unlike Jonathan, who might wander into a ball game on his way home from the store, Yusuf was predictable. If he went someplace like the store he was back quickly, and if he wanted to play ball he would come home and ask permission. At 3:30, when Yusuf had been gone a half hour, Camille started to get worried, and she and a friend went looking for him. They quickly learned that he had been at the store and had bought the snuff; but there was no trace of him. Kids in the apartment house fanned out to search for Yusuf but turned up nothing. Camille, who knew the Mechanicsville community well, called Marie Fletcher, a woman she knew at the closest housing project, and had her organize a search. When after nearly two hours that produced no results, she called the police.

The police, who remembered having seen Yusuf, did their own search, also to no avail. They took information from Camille but told her that nothing would be done with their report until Monday morning, and that, because Yusuf was nine, there would be no investigation until twenty-four hours after that, Tuesday morning. At the time, the Missing Persons Bureau of the Atlanta Police Department, which also handled child-abuse cases, consisted of four detectives and a secretary. Three of the detectives were women. The office was open from 8:00 A.M. to 8:00 P.M. Monday through Friday. You couldn't report a missing person on Saturday or Sunday; you had to wait until Monday morning. If the missing child was over seven years old, the bureau didn't start their search until a day after they got the report, to take into account the possibility that the child was a runaway. Camille knew for certain that Yusuf had not run away.

Because Yusuf was young, close to age seven, a detective from Missing Persons called late on Monday afternoon. She took more information and said that they would begin a search right away but that, with four detectives covering all of Atlanta, it was going to have to be a cursory one. Camille said she understood, but she was in no shape to understand anything, really. She had spent a sleepless night anticipating a phone call, a knock on the door, a car stopping outside the apartment house. Because she didn't have a phone, she was upstairs at her friend Sarah's apartment most of the night, chain-smoking and a nervous wreck. Her mind was working furiously and only coming up with horrible thoughts. That night set a pattern for the next eighteen days.

After a week of sleeping whenever and wherever exhaustion caught up with her and then waking up feeling guilty that she had not maintained her vigil, Camille felt that she could wait no longer. She had to get out and do something. She called the principal at the local high school, a man she had known through her community work, and he organized the school's ROTC members for a search. Two detectives from Missing Persons helped coordinate the teenagers, but that was the extent of the police participation. Camille thought that someone had kidnapped Yusuf and was holding him, though the searchers were looking for a body.

The police thought that Camille's ex-husband, John, Yusuf's father, had snatched Yusuf. He had visited the kids the Sunday of the disappearance. John had been at the house to give Jonathan a check to take to school; he and the three older kids were going on a school trip. Jonathan had walked him to the bus stop, but maybe he hadn't gotten on the bus. Camille and John had not been on the best of terms in the year since their divorce, but she thought it highly unlikely that John would kidnap Yusuf. She did feel that Yusuf would never have gotten in a car with a stranger unless he felt the stranger's authority superceded her own. Someone wearing what looked like a police uniform, a security guard for instance, might fit that bill. To the police, John, too, would come under that category, but Camille knew that Yusuf would have asked permission if John had offered to take him somewhere.

When the detectives went to John's house, they were accusatory almost from the beginning. John did not want to hear what the police were saying. Over the phone he had told Camille, when she had called to say that Yusuf was missing, that she had lost him and that she should go find him. He was just as curt with the police. He called for a patrol car and had the detectives from Missing Persons removed from his house. Camille was angry with John for his lack of support, but she also had sympathy for him given his brusque treatment by the detectives.

As a news story, Yusuf's disappearance was given little attention. But when Halloween came around ten days later, Camille thought that she could use television to her advantage. She went on a local station and made a plea to whomever had her son. She said that Halloween night would be a perfect time for the kidnapper to turn Yusuf loose, dress him up with a mask or costume, and give him a dime to call home. Camille said that she would not press charges and she meant it. She just wanted her little boy back.

Camille and Sarah waited up all Halloween night, even after the trick or treat noises in the street faded, but there was no phone call with a little voice on the other end of the line and there was no knock on the door. Sometime in the middle of that night, Camille realized that Yusuf was dead.

Five days after Halloween, Camille heard a radio report that the body of a young boy, presumed to be Yusuf Bell, had been found, badly decomposed, on Redwine Road. She became hysterical and was on the phone to the police immediately. They told her that the skeleton they had found was not Yusuf's, that it was the skeleton of an older, taller boy named Milton Harvey. Since Halloween, Camille's feelings had been a jumble. When she would try to picture Yusuf alive, she would begin to think of what he might be suffering. If they had found his body, she would at least have known that nobody could ever hurt him again. But without a body, she couldn't be sure that some crazy person wasn't out there torturing him. Her intuition led her to abandon hope, yet she didn't want to give up too soon.

On November 8, Sergeant Sturgess, the head of Missing Persons, came to the apartment house and found Camille and Cici in Sarah's apartment. The detective had tears in her eyes as she stood outside the screen door and told Camille that Yusuf's body had been found in a crawl space in an abandoned school in Mechanicsville. He had been strangled to death. She said that he had been dead four or five days, that he had not been sexually molested, and that, strangely enough, it looked like he had been well taken care of and was very clean. His clothes had been washed shortly before he was killed.

Camille took Cici downstairs to the apartment. She closed the door and shut the blinds and sat in a chair and stared. Sarah followed her after a few minutes, opened the blinds, and told her she shouldn't be alone. Camille and Cici went back upstairs, but the numbness wouldn't go away for weeks.

Camille did not have the money to bury Yusuf, so the first thing she had to do after learning of his death was to try to borrow some cash. She had worked at an employment agency until August of 1979, when she had become worried that Cici was seeing Kindercare as her mother. She had decided that she and the kids could live on the child support she was getting from John, and so she stayed home with her youngest child. Marie Fletcher, the woman in the housing project who had organized the first search, heard of Camille's plight and phoned Mary Mapp, a woman activist who used her citizens band radio network to organize various community functions. Mary Mapp put together a fund raiser and came up with sixteen hundred dollars for Yusuf's funeral. Camille borrowed some money and was given the rest by friends. She planned the whole funeral, but she never felt really involved. It all seemed to be happening to someone else.

Local news coverage of the funeral was heavy, with some television stations running long film clips of the packed church in Mechanicsville. Camille didn't mind the press being there; they were discreet, and she felt that her own attempts to publicize Yusuf's disappearance had prompted much of the attention. She granted some interviews with the press in which she cried and talked as best she could about her son, his disappearance, and the mystery surrounding his death. After the funeral, though, the reporters were soon gone.

A week after Yusuf was buried, Camille and her three children moved from their apartment to a nearby, city-run housing project, McDaniel-Glen Houses. She didn't know who had killed Yusuf and she feared for herself and her children. Before Yusuf's death, she had been thinking about moving to a bigger apartment, so she moved into a two-floor apartment at McDaniel-Glen.

The police had no leads in the case but had unofficially charged John with the killing. When Yusuf's body was found, they had taken him to the morgue, pulled Yusuf's body out, and said, "Here's your son; didn't you kill him?" John was furious, as was Camille. But since she didn't know who had murdered Yusuf, she suspected everyone. And she trusted the police to have good reasons for accusing John.

When John called to say he was coming to take the children out for the day, Camille told him he could only come to visit. He said he had a legal right to take them, but Camille wasn't about to budge. She got a court order to block the provision in the divorce that allowed John to take the kids occasionally. The kids themselves were scared of their father, at least Jonathan and Maria were. Camille is the kind of mother who talks many things over with her children as if they were adults. Jonathan reasoned on his own that if his father had killed Yusuf it must have been to get out of paying child support, and the only way to do that would be to kill all the kids, since the child support was not based on the number of kids but came in a lump sum. He had no intention of going out with his father. Camille couldn't believe that the police were right in suspecting John, but she was not about to test their theory.

November and December were horrible months for Camille. She was dazed and hurt, angry and fearful. And then there were Thanksgiving, Christmas, Jonathan's eleventh birthday, and Yusuf's birthday on December 30 to get through. It all just seemed so futile. She couldn't get her mind off that active nine-year-old—a Cub Scout who had been running for the treasurer of his class when he disappeared and who had dreamed of installing a computer in his room. There were always plenty of people for Camille to be with, but she wasn't really a part of any gathering she attended. She concentrated so much on the child who was gone that she often missed what was happening to the children who remained. Cici learned to move the button on the magnetic calendar every day, but Camille could only look at the calendar and see the square marked for Yusuf's birthday.

Jonathan, Maria, and Cici were as frightened as their mother. They had slept in separate beds, but now they all curled up in one bed at night. By morning they would all have moved in with Camille. Cici, who had seen Yusuf as an invincible older brother, wouldn't leave her mother's side and wouldn't think of going anywhere alone or even with her brother and sister. Jonathan and Maria hadn't seen Yusuf as invincible, but they knew that they were just as vulnerable to abduction and attack as Yusuf had been. The whole family passed a sad and fearful Christmas.

When his body was found, Yusuf's murder case was moved from Missing Persons to Homicide, and for several weeks Camille had frequent contact with the detective assigned to it. After Christmas, however, the phone calls from the police came less frequently, and then it became difficult for Camille just to get in touch with the detective. They kept saying that John had killed Yusuf, but they were making no move to arrest him. As far as Camille was concerned, they were no closer to solving the crime than they had ever been. She wondered whether they would ever be able to tell her what had happened.

But in the first few months of 1980, she found that chasing after a detective and worrying about her son's killer took a back seat to her own grief. Her father wanted her to move back to Philadelphia and live with him. Her mother had died and he was alone. He was a retired electrical engineer, a Republican, and he and Camille had had their differences over the years, especially when she had left the college she was attending in Tennessee to move to Atlanta and work for the decidedly leftist Southern Nonviolent Coordinating Committee (SNCC), where she had first met John. He thought she would be safer in Philadelphia. But Camille wasn't about to move to Philadelphia. She had always felt safe in Atlanta and had seen northern cities such as New York, Philadelphia, and Chicago as too dangerous for her children. Yusuf's murder had certainly disrupted her sense of security, but a flight north didn't seem to be the answer.

Camille's friend Sarah was helpful and supportive, but she could not fully understand what was happening to Camille in the winter and early spring of 1980. Camille hardly understood herself. She knew that in some ways she was becoming isolated. She is an open and intelligent woman with a good sense of humor, a secure woman who is able to laugh at herself as she works through a problem. She was certain that in the past other people had known this about her and that it had drawn them to her. But in her grief, things changed, and the people around her changed. Just mentioning Yusuf's name was enough to unsettle some people; she hardly ever heard his name spoken to her. Friends shielded her from news items about child murders because they felt she would have a tough time with such stories. She soon saw that she was surrounded by a veritable forest of "I-understand-and-I'm-so-sorry" people. When, toward the end of the spring, she felt that she was progressing through her grief, she could see that people around her weren't keeping posted on the changes because they didn't want to get that close.

The police had practically closed their investigation of Yusuf's murder and had repeatedly told Camille that they were certain John was the murderer, though they had no concrete proof. Besides the neighbor who had seen Yusuf with John that afternoon, there was no other evidence. Another neighbor thought she had seen Yusuf get into a blue car, but the woman was an alcoholic and no one was certain how accurate her observation was.

One day, about six months after Yusuf's disappearance, Camille decided to conduct a small investigation of her own. She went over every detail of the afternoon Yusuf had gone to the store. She wanted to see if the timing were such that John could have said good-bye to Jonathan and then walked around to pick up Yusuf. She asked Jonathan to show her the route he and his father had taken to the bus stop. When Jonathan ducked through a fence and started up Fulton Street instead of heading for the closest bus stop at Eugenia Street, Camille realized in a flash what had happened. Jonathan had walked John to the Fulton Street stop so that he could spend some of his money at the store. He was wearing cutoffs that day, and people were always mistaking him for Yusuf. The woman who saw John that afternoon must have seen him walking to the bus stop with Jonathan. No one had bothered to ask Jonathan which bus stop they had gone to.

When Camille brought this new information to the police, they did what amounted to a bureaucratic shrug. Camille had been relieved to know that the police were mistaken about John, but she had the feeling the police were annoyed by her call. Her information left the case wide open again.

In May of 1980, Mary Mapp called to say that she was putting together a fund-raiser for taxicab drivers who had been shot recently in holdups. She wanted to introduce Camille to two other women who would be there. Both women had children who had disappeared, one of whom had been found dead. Camille went and met Willie Mae Mathis, whose son Jefferey had been missing for three months, and Venus Taylor, the mother of Angel Lanier, a young girl who had been abducted and strangled to death.

Despite superficial differences (Venus, a small, shapely woman was raised in Chicago and Willie Mae, a large portly woman was a native Atlantan), when they talked they all found that their experiences with their children made for nearly instant, close friendships. They began to get together, to talk about the grief they had already come through, and to learn from each other what might be around the bend, how they might get on with their lives. The three women were all living with an unsolved crime, and none of them was willing to let the mystery lie. They felt that knowing who was responsible for their children's disappearances was crucial to their own healing.

This ad hoc support group made a world of difference to Camille.

She had always relished contact with other people, and this sharing came just as she thought much of her long-time support was falling away.

On May 19, the women got together and went to visit a friend of Willie Mae's, Evelyn Miller, whose husband's son, Eric Middlebrook, fourteen at the time, had disappeared the day before. They felt they had covered a lot of territory in their talks and could be of help to Evelyn. She found them helpful and joined their meetings.

Throughout the spring, whenever Camille would call the police and get no information, she would hang up and feel a combination of anger, frustration, and, oddly enough, guilt. She could see that something had been done to her, that her son had been murdered, and that the police had not been able to find the killer. But she could not shake the feeling that she had somehow done something to cause all that had happened.

In meeting with Willie Mae, Venus, and Evelyn, though, that feeling changed. Anger began to replace guilt when she saw that the other women had been treated much as she had. They had all lost children, and none of them were satisfied with the police investigation in their cases. Camille went from saying to herself, "What did I do to cause this?" to saying to the other women, "How dare they do this to us."

Venus and Willie Mae had heard about two bodies that were found out on Niskey Lake Road back in July 1979. They didn't know much more than that the bodies were those of young teenagers. They did a little research, and in a small news item on page 18A of the *Atlanta Journal Constitution* found mention of the bodies being discovered. Venus and Willie Mae hadn't heard about Milton Harvey, the boy whose body had been found on Redwine Road three days before Yusuf's was found. That made six similar unsolved crimes they knew of. The victims were all black, young but not little children, and they'd all been abducted from poor or low-income neighborhoods during daylight hours. They felt an obligation to warn parents about this possible pattern. The women decided to go to the mayor and have him alert the city when, on June 9, another black youngster, Christopher Richardson, disappeared.

They didn't get in to see the Mayor, Maynard Jackson, a black man in his second term who was well liked by the business community in downtown Atlanta. An aide heard the women, went to tell the mayor and came out with the word that the mayor didn't want to alarm the city. The women were surprised. They had seen themselves as citizens with a vital message and hadn't expected to be rebuffed in this way.

Had any of them been closer to politics or national affairs, though, they might not have been so surprised. Mayor Jackson, at the time, was sitting on a hot seat as far as crime was concerned, and their alarming news only increased the heat. While the women waited in an outer office for his response, the Mayor had to consider a number of crime-related topics that had nothing to do directly with young black children being snatched from the streets of his city. A year before, *Newsweek* had run a good-sized article about three American cities—Atlanta, Philadelphia, and Houston—and their response to rising crime rates. It was pointed out in the article that Atlanta had the highest per-capita crime rate in the country in 1978 and the largest annual crime increase of any U.S. city. The article noted that there had been a five-year hiring freeze in the police department due to a discrimination-in-hiring suit by black cops and a countersuit by white cops. Mayor Jackson was quoted as blaming inflation, unemployment, drug trafficking, and lack of gun controls as the reasons for the statistical jumps and was said to have chided the press for making too much of the story. In contrasting the reactions of the three cities to their rising crime rates, *Newsweek* made Atlanta and Mayor Jackson appear downright dyspeptic about their tarnished image. The "city too busy to hate," as Atlanta was called, appeared not too busy to tabulate possible lost income in that staple of Atlanta commerce, the convention business, if word got out that a crime wave was washing over all the new steel-and-glass buildings downtown.

Recently, the *Wall Street Journal* had picked up on a story about a conventioneer who had been shot in a routine holdup in downtown Atlanta and had warned its readers about the once-placid southern city. Mayor Jackson had had to do some fast talking.

There was just no way Jackson was going to go before the microphones and tell the city and the nation that black children were being killed and that the police didn't know who was doing it.

That day, when Camille left the mayor's office, she felt betrayed. In her days with SNCC, Camille had seen Maynard Jackson as a "brother," a fellow-traveler who was as concerned to obtain equal rights for blacks as she was. She could understand a white mayor thinking more of Atlanta's image than of the city's black youth, but she could not understand Maynard Jackson thinking like that.

Late in June, Latonya Wilson, a young black girl, was kidnapped from her bedroom at night and disappeared. About the same time Aaron Wyche, a ten-year-old black boy, was found beneath a railroad bridge. The police ruled the death an accident, but Aaron's parents contended that he had been afraid of heights and had most likely been taken up on the bridge and pushed off.

Camille and the women she had been meeting with heard about these deaths and made contact with the parents. They did some checking and found that the rate of unsolved child disappearances in Atlanta over the past year was double the normal rate. They decided that they had to do something more than sit in Mayor Jackson's outer office, so they went to see the Commissioner of Public Safety, Lee Patrick Brown, a scholarly black man with a national reputation for honesty and integrity. They didn't get in to see him either, but they did get his official word on their theory of a pattern of killings. He said that the police were treating the various cases as independent investigations and saw no connection between them.

A week later the women went over his head. They attended a meeting of the City Council's Public Safety Commission and put their evidence before that committee. They had more success there. They asked for and got a special police task force to look into the various killings and investigate them as if there were a connection between them. But the women were skeptical. The task force had only five members, and it was to report to Lee Brown. Camille didn't have a lot of confidence that Brown, who a week before had told her officially that there was no connection between the cases,

Camille Bell

would reverse his position and suddenly throw himself into the search for the childrens' killer or killers. She spoke to Brown at the meeting and he began his reply to her by saying, "Now Mrs. Bell" and treated her like a schoolgirl. She decided she and the women would have to do what they could to begin their own investigation.

Early in July, Anthony Carter, a nine-year-old black, disappeared and soon was found stabbed to death. Camille and the other women saw this as the eleventh related case—eight deaths and three disappearances—and they decided to go directly to the media. They called a crude press conference on the steps of City Hall and told the story they had been telling for a month. Camille and Venus spoke. Willie Mae thought it best she didn't go before the cameras because Jefferey was still missing. She did speak at one point, though. A reporter asked what the group they had formed was called, and nobody responded. They hadn't gotten to the point of giving themselves an official name. Then Willie Mae blurted out that they were the Committee to Stop Children's Murders.

On July 30, Earl Lee Terrell, a ten-year-old black, was thrown out of a city swimming pool for running on the pool apron. He sat on a bench outside the pool waiting for the kids he had come with. That was the last anyone ever saw of him. With the news of this latest disappearance, Camille realized that the Public Safety Commission had not even bothered to warn city agencies, especially recreational facilities, about the possibility of young black children being abducted. Had they done so, the lifeguards would never have disciplined Earl Terrell by putting him outside the pool fence.

By this time, Camille had taken a leadership role in the fledgling organization. In her SNCC days, she had been in the basement of the Atlanta office cranking the addressograph. But organizing the office the Committee to Stop Children's Murders was loaned in the Campbellton Plaza shopping mall, writing leaflets to be handed out to parents in black areas of the city, and chairing meetings came naturally to her. She, along with Willie Mae and Venus, was able to articulate the group's rising skepticism and anger. She became the committee's principal spokesperson.

In her SNCC days and up to Yusuf's murder, Camille had understood the reformation of government as a process of finding intelligent, uncorrupted, minority-sympathetic politicians to wrest power from the stupid, corrupt, bigoted ones who held office. In 1967, her vision of an ideal future might have looked like the Atlanta of 1979: a black mayor, a black Public Safety commissioner, a black police chief, and a number of black judges. But after Yusuf's murder, after the frustrations of having to force the city government to take action, she realized her earlier thinking was naive. As she came to see what the parents of the committee were up against, she began to understand that the government people get is the government they deserve, and that if people don't do anything for themselves, government leaders aren't going to rush in and do it for them. Mayor Jackson's administration, she felt, had been no more responsive to the committee of black mothers than a white administration would have been. She saw that she and the other mothers had no other recourse but to dig in and get to work.

On August 29, a thirteen-year-old black boy named Clifford Jones disappeared and was found the next day strangled to death. He was not an Atlanta resident. He lived in Cleveland and had been visiting relatives when he was abducted. News of his death was run in the *Cleveland Plain-Dealer* along with some sketchy information about similar murders in Atlanta over the past year. That news item was one of the first national reports that mentioned the possibility that a string of unsolved murders in Atlanta might be connected in some way. The national news media began to make inquiries, and the Atlanta Public Safety Commission felt the pressure. Soon after Clifford Jones's death, the task force investigating the murders was increased from five policemen to seventeen.

City officials were no longer trying to ignore either the possibility that the murders were connected or that the Atlanta Police Department might need outside help to solve the crimes.

The Committee to Stop Children's Murders was growing rapidly. After the press conference in July, the group got a lot of local press attention, much help from local individuals and organizations, and also its share of hangers-on and crackpots. Camille felt that the committee couldn't afford to turn anyone away without giving them a hearing, though. She and the other mothers (there were only a few fathers who worked with the committee) couldn't predict where a good, solid lead in the case might come from.

Camille had been helped by her first few months of contact with Willie Mae and Venus. The extremities of grief of the spring lessened. She found that she actually could go beyond the tears. She had worked through the initial stages of her grief and was ready to get on with her life. But her life in the late summer of 1980 was consumed with the work of the committee.

On September 14, a ten-year-old, Darron Glass, disappeared. A week after that disappearance Commissioner Brown invited a New Jersey psychic, who had claimed to have solved fourteen murders, to come to Atlanta. The woman, Dorothy Allison, was on tour at the time to promote her autobiography. She quickly took the spotlight with a prediction that the killer was a single black male. She said that she was certain he would be found soon. She visited Willie Mae and predicted that Jefferey would appear soon. Venus Taylor wasn't impressed. She told a news reporter, "She can sleep at night, but I can't."

That pretty much summed up the committee's feelings about the psychic from Nutley, New Jersey, whom some called the "Nut from Psychely." In bringing the psychic to Atlanta, the Police Department had implicitly admitted that it really didn't know what to do to solve the case. Commissioner Brown began to say that he and his police department were going to need outside help.

On October 9, another body was found that fit the pattern. Charles Stevens, age twelve, disappeared and was found suffocated to death the next day. There were now ten dead and four had disappeared, by the committee's count; but it wasn't until an unrelated event occurred four days later that the disappearances and murders began to get full, national media attention.

On October 13, there was an explosion at the Bowen Houses Day Care Center in the northwest part of Atlanta. Four children and one teacher, all black, were killed. There was suspicion at first that the explosion had been caused by a bomb.

Camille went to the scene of the explosion to see if there was something she could do for the parents of the victims. She and the other women of the committee had been to a number of funerals in the past few months, and they were experienced with the first effects of grief.

When she got to the Bowen Houses, she found that the press people who were there were getting more than just the story of the explosion. People in the neighborhood had read the leaflets the Committee to Stop Children's Murders had been handing out in the area, and when they first suspected that the explosion had been caused by a bomb, they began to suggest to the press that there might be a connection between the explosion and the murders of black children in Atlanta.

The national press people who had come to the Bowen Houses perked up at that suggestion. They had heard nothing of the Committee to Stop Children's Murders, or if they had they had not run the story. But the explosion and the murders, if linked, might just fit a national pattern of attacks on blacks that seemed, in the fall of 1980, to be emerging. Vernon Jordan, the black leader of the Urban League, had been shot in the back; black taxi drivers in Buffalo and ten black women in Boston had been murdered; and there had been sniper attacks on blacks in Salt Lake City and several other cities around the country.

Everyone from President Jimmy Carter to Maynard Jackson called for an investigation of the day care center explosion and implored people to keep their heads. The official conclusion of the investigation was that a boiler in the center had ruptured, causing the explosion; but now the national press began to include "the Atlanta murders" in their lists of attacks against blacks.

The next week, *Newsweek* had a page in their National Affairs section headlined: "The Fears of Black America." The photo on the page was of a mother holding her child outside the Bowen Houses Day Care Center after the explosion. In the article there was mention of the fact that the body of Alfred James Evans, one of the two bodies found in the summer of 1979 on Redwine Road, had just been identified and that he may have been the first in a series of disappearances and murders that the magazine said totaled fourteen. The implication that the murders might be racially motivated was apparent.

Camille soon found herself in the middle of a small movement that was growing with every phone call. The list of publications that called for interviews read like the *Readers Guide to Periodical Literature*. Requests for speakers came to the committee from all over the country. With all the new attention the committee was getting, relations with the Jackson administration became very strained. The task force, however, jumped quickly to twenty-four full-time policemen, and the pressure on both the mayor's office and the Police Department grew every day.

Shortly after the day care center explosion, Mayor Jackson hosted a meeting of prominent citizens at the Civic Center to discuss what could be done about the murders, what response the city could make. No one from the Committee to Stop Children's Murders was invited. Camille heard about the meeting through a television reporter.

Camille went to the Civic Center and, outside the building, had her first meeting with Mayor Jackson. She introduced herself, told him that she was worried by the city's attitude toward the murder of her son and the other murders and disappearances. Then she started to get worked up. Facing the man she felt had betrayed her and the other mothers, she let loose anger that had been building for months, ever since she had been rebuffed at his office. She called him a lousy mayor, a lousy person, and a lousy neighbor. He wasn't bothered by Camille's anger, or at least he didn't appear to be. He gave her a verbal pat on the head. "Oh, Mrs. Bell," he said, "you don't really believe that. You're just distraught." Camille was furious.

On October 18, Latonya Wilson's body was found strangled, and on November 1, Aaron Jackson disappeared and was found suffocated the next day.

The press was alert now and began to trumpet each new disappearance and discovery of a body. "The Atlanta Murders" and the mothers who had formed the committee were headline news. The November tenth issue of *People* magazine carried a two-page story about Camille that was both accurate and sensitive. She was almost too busy to read it, though. Camille and Venus were doing most of the speaking for the group, and that meant a lot of traveling. Camille considered the speaking important not only to their immediate concern but also to the wider goals they had been discussing for several months. The committee, in talking about the unsolved murders, could also address a nationwide problem of missing children (they didn't have any accurate figures, but, in making contacts with people around the country, they were beginning to see that the problem was not a small one) and promote what they called "child consciousness" in general. This was a combination of consciousness about child raising and education. Camille and members of the committee felt that it was important to use the podiums they were being given to raise questions and issues of concern to them that were only tangentially connected to the murders. After all, what could a college audience in Michigan do to help solve Yusuf's case?

The committee had been openly critical of the Police Department, even when the size of the task force was increased. The Fire Department had jumped in and conducted a door-to-door search for the killer. Now the police were being deluged with offers of help from all sorts of groups and individuals. The police were appearing to be less and less in control. They were not so much conducting the search as they were directing traffic of those who had come to help.

The police announced that the murderer was working on a twenty-five-day cycle and that meant he would strike again in late November. As the date approached, the police put more and more emphasis on the twenty-five-day cycle.

Camille did her own counting and concluded that the twenty-five-day cycle was nonsense. She became more convinced than ever that the committee had to conduct its own investigation. When a reporter from Philadelphia suggested to Camille that the committee use a professional investigator, Camille agreed but said they had no money to hire one. The reporter eventually introduced Camille to Don Laken, an investigator from Philadelphia who owned a kennel of search dogs. He volunteered to help with the investigation and soon moved to Atlanta. Under Camille's direction, he and several local investigators who volunteered their time began to comb the streets of Atlanta. Camille reasoned that the contacts the committee could make with people in the black neighborhoods from which the children were being taken would be much more fruitful than the gung-ho approach of the police and the swarms of volunteers who were starting to come to Atlanta.

Because the national media were making much of the possibility that the murders were racially motivated, Camille was asked frequently about her speculations on the identity of the murderer. She said the same thing practically every time: she didn't want to say anything about race, but she would hazard a guess that the person was an authority figure of some sort (she knew that most of the murdered children, like Yusuf, had been good kids who had been taught to obey and trust authority) who was known in the neighborhood. She told the *Journal Constitution* once that she could see the possibility of it being someone who had been rejected by a son or who had lost a son by divorce. And she once said that it might even be a religious cult of some sort. Many of the children, like Yusuf, had been washed before their murder, as if they had been prepared for a ritual sacrifice. But she really didn't have any firm idea of who might be behind all this. She did know, especially after her experience with John, that she did not trust the police.

When the twenty-fifth day came and went without a disappearance or death, Lee Brown announced publicly that the police were not convinced that the murders were related. But that statement had little effect on the hysteria that was building and being written about all over the country. In December, the FBI added twelve more agents to its Atlanta office and the task force went to thirty-five full-time policemen. Then the Police Department began to get federal aid for the investigation, and five "supercops," detectives from large cities who had reputations as particularly good crime-solvers, were loaned by their various police departments to help.

Camille was too busy to concern herself with much of this. She was in airports as much as she was home during December. She felt it was essential to use the attention Atlanta was getting both to keep up the investigation and to spread the word about the committee. She missed being in her community, though, and she missed the day-to-day contact with her children. Camille had been the person neighbors went to when they needed to have a phone bill straightened out or an official contacted. But now her friends saw her as too busy to be bothered with their little problems.

Jonathan, Maria, and Cici were being well taken care of. Sarah and other friends in Camille's old apartment building had always been like an extended family, and the kids hardly felt any disruption at all when they would go to spend time there. Cici couldn't understand why Camille was gone so much, but Jonathan and Maria did. Camille had told them that she would not visit Yusuf's grave until she could tell him that she had done all she could to find his murderer.

January provided no let-up. In the first week and a half of the month, a fourteen-year-old boy disappeared and two bodies of young boys were found seventy-five yards from where Milton Harvey had been found. One of the bodies was immediately identified as Christopher Richardson, and ten days later the other body was determined to be that of Earl Lee Terrell, the young boy who had disappeared from the city swimming pool.

On January 15, Camille spoke at a ceremony in honor of Martin Luther King's birthday. She shared the stage with Andrew Young and Coretta Scott King, and she called for a rededication to Martin Luther King's principles. A reporter for Rolling Stone magazine wrote about the ceremony and about Camille: "Nothing she said—as eloquent as it was—was as compelling as her very presence on the platform."

Camille and the other parents were becoming symbols. They were the "Atlanta mothers," and they were supposed to act out a role that was 75 percent grief and 25 percent anger. Camille, by this time, had gone through her crying times and, if asked to do so by some photographer, would just cut off the interview or photo session. The local reporters had been polite and discreet. Atlanta was their home and they had plenty of opportunities to cover the story of the missing children. But members of the national and international press were under extreme pressure to get their stories on film and get back home. Those stories had to have tears and anger and a racial angle. Camille realized that she and the committee had to work with these reporters and camera crews, but she had her limits. She would go as far as she could with the press and then she would just say no, stop the tape, and leave.

While the committee women were becoming symbols of one sort to the nation at large, they were becoming a symbol of another sort to the Atlanta city officials. Not only were they getting media attention, but they were grumbling openly in front of those cameras about the Police Department and the city administration. To the city officials they were stirring up already muddied waters, and every time they stirred the city looked worse. In the *People* magazine article about Camille, there had been a small picture of Major Jackson surrounded by a hundred thousand dollars in reward money that had been offered for information leading to the killer's arrest. Camille, in her photographs, looked strong and believable. The Mayor, dwarfed by the piles of money, looked fragile and helpless. That sort of thing did not go unnoticed at City Hall.

In fact, the members of the committee soon began to see that certain actions taken by the mayor and the City Council could be construed as subtle attempts to discredit the mothers, to make them look somehow guilty for what had happened. The curfew they imposed was one such attempt.

Back in October, the mayor had made appeals to parents to keep their children home Halloween night. The committee didn't want children to miss Halloween, so they organized a huge Halloween party in the parking lot of the mall in which their offices were located. Then the City Council set a curfew that banned children from the streets between 11:00 P.M. and 7:00 A.M. To the outside world this had several implications. First it showed that the city administration was really worried, and really doing something. Second, the curfew implied that the children who had been abducted had been running loose in the streets at all hours of the night and that their parents had to be told how to take care of their children.

Camille and members of the committee were incensed when they heard about the curfew and saw the play it got in the press. Nobody seemed to take note of the fact that only one of the children who had been killed or disappeared had been abducted at night. All the rest, like Yusuf, had been taken during daylight hours. And the police would occasionally drop some hints that the kids were street hustlers. Though a couple of them had been in some trouble with the law, to characterize them all as urchins set loose in poor neighborhoods by irresponsible parents was very far from the truth. But the news of the curfew implicitly made its point, and there was nothing the committee could do to counter it. The curfew was the hot story and not the women's objections to it.

The feud between Camille and Jackson came to a head when Mayor Jackson called a press conference, without notifying the committee, and announced that he was forming a committee of prominent citizens to solicit funds for the families of the victims.

Through a friend in city hall, the committee heard of the press conference and went and sat in the back of the room. Camille and the other women wanted absolutely no part of such a committee or the solicitations. In their travels around the country, the women had taken honorariums for their speaking engagements and had often asked their listeners to send money to the committee for the investigation and for the projects the committee was working on, such as a summer program for kids. But never had they asked for funds for the families. They thought such support could be harmful to families who might come to rely on the money. Some people had sent money to the committee for the families, and they had felt obligated to divide it among them. But they would never solicit such funds and they were angry that the mayor was trying to do so without consulting them. After the news conference was over, several of the women went to the front of the room and asked to be heard. They told their side of the story, but by then most of the national press had packed up. The local news media ran the committee's side of the story, but what went out to the world was that the families were soliciting funds for themselves.

This prompted editorials about the parents and the exploitation of their grief. A black state legislator and a leader of the Southern Christian Leadership Committee called a press conference on the steps of City Hall and denounced the parents for prostituting their children's deaths by soliciting donations. When a local television news reporter asked Camille about the allegations, Camille denied that they had ever solicited funds for the families. By the time that story hit the air, however, it came out sounding as if the committee was going to stop soliciting funds. Camille felt certain that Mayor Jackson's move had been a clever attempt to discredit the committee and to take some of the pressure off his office.

By February 1981, the story of the Atlanta murders was headline news worldwide. People everywhere were wearing green ribbons to show their support of the families. The committee had promoted wearing the ribbons but hadn't originated the idea. A woman on a Pennsylvania talk show, Georgia Dean, had suggested doing something similar to what was done for the Iranian hostages and said she thought green, symbolizing life, would be a good color. Camille heard of the suggestion and then passed it on. Soon it was hard to go down a street in America without seeing someone with a green loop of ribbon pinned to their clothes. Each new funeral, such as that of Terry Pue, fifteen, who was found strangled thirty-five miles from his Atlanta home on January 23, was deluged with press. Yusuf's funeral had been covered extensively but discreetly. Now parents sitting in pews or standing at gravesides could hear all sorts of camera and tape-recorder noises. A German camera crew used clappers right in a parent's face during one funeral service.

In March, Camille, Venus, and Willie Mae were invited to speak at a rally in Harlem for the "Atlanta children." By that time much of the media were focusing their attention on the fears raised by the Atlanta murders, especially the fear that the killings were racially motivated. The rally was to show support for the besieged black children.

It was preceded by a march that went through most of lower Harlem and ended at 135th Street. Some ten thousand people gathered on the street and held candles or flashlights. Camille stood up to speak and had a frightening feeling. She thought that if she raised her voice, told the crowd that her son had been killed in the Atlanta murders, and then exhorted all those people to go tear up New York City, they might just do so. Camille saw in an instant that she had to be extremely careful in what she said. Poor phrasing could set people off.

All this media attention brought with it plenty of unhelpful thrill-seekers or people with good intentions who were only going to get in the way. Camille, who was trying to keep order in the committee office, was well-organized, but often, while she was away speaking, things would get out of hand. Once she had to throw a reporter out of her office by long-distance telephone.

Camille was upset by the changes that came over some reporters. After the curfew was imposed and allegations were made about the families soliciting funds for themselves, many journalists, even local ones, who had written sympathetically about the victims' families now wrote with skepticism. Camille could understand one reporter writing one story and another reporter having a different opinion. But when a single reporter changed his or her story, she was baffled.

Camille received a lot of publicity. She was on all the major talk shows, did a tour of Westinghouse television stations, and was the focus of several major magazine articles about the Atlanta murders. She took a reporter from *Life* magazine to the school where they had found Yusuf. It was the first time she had gone there, and she cried outside the school. Life ran a picture of Camille crying, at the bottom of one page. Camille wasn't happy with that picture or the accuracy of the article, but because the piece was generally favorable to the mothers, she didn't feel she should protest.

In her speaking engagements Camille often had to contend with hecklers and angry questions about all the money the families were supposedly making off their children's deaths. She tried to handle these situations in two ways: she would mention all the controversial points before her questioners did, and she would try to give the committee's side of the story. If that failed and there were still hostile questions, she would reply to allegations about money, houses, and cars the families supposedly now owned by saying, "Give me the keys and tell me the address, please." She would continue, "I didn't ask to be here. If you can figure out a way to bring my son back, I'll go home."

In the midst of all the hoopla, Camille tried to keep the focus where she felt it belonged. Her war with the city administration had been out in the open since Mayor Jackson's press conference, and she never hesitated to point a finger at the police and city officials when she was interviewed. In February, she did just that, in very strong language, when she was interviewed by French television. She said that she could come to no other conclusion than that the mayor and the police were incompetent.

In March, Camille decided to move out of McDaniel-Glen Houses and back into her old private apartment house. Living in city housing, she was required to report all income and her job status. She didn't mind such inquiries, but she began to feel that the Housing Authority was prying rather than simply keeping track of her affairs. The week she was going to move she was in Annapolis, Maryland, on a speaking tour. Her friend Sarah packed all Camille's belongings and got the rooms ready for the move. But when Sarah returned the next day, half the furniture was missing, mattresses were on the floor and tramped upon, something sticky had been thrown around, the clothes she had packed were strewn about the room, and some plaques and awards that had been on the walls were gone. Sarah went upstairs to try to call Camille, and when she came back down there were two television film crews and several men in the apartment. As the crews filmed, one of the men said he was a Mr. Heider, the head of the Housing Authority, and asked Sarah what she was doing there. Sarah asked him what he was doing there. He said that he was evicting Camille and showing the television people the horrible conditions in which Camille raised her children. Sarah didn't back down. She said that if the television people ran footage of the apartment they would be sued for invasion of privacy. She said that she knew nothing of an eviction notice. When they had left, she called Camille. Camille didn't know what was going on, but she told Sarah to at least get her books and her washer and dryer out of the apartment.

The television reporters didn't run film of the inside of the apartment. They had shots of an old mattress outside of the building and used those while talking about the eviction. News of the eviction went out nationally, though, and created some problems for Mayor Jackson. He and Heider then had a public feud over the eviction. Jackson said that he disagreed with Heider about the eviction, that if Camille's apartment was as bad as he said it was then he should have found her children warm, safe housing. There was no way Camille could counter that or sue him. He, in a lawyerlike way, had simply implied that Camille was not taking care of her kids.

Mayor Jackson had every reason to be worried about the women of the committee. They had meant nothing but trouble for him. Had he and they been more congenial, the pressure on his office would not have been nearly so great. But with the press so accessible and the country generally sympathetic to their plight, the women, critical of the mayor and the city administration, were a distinct liability. Nine months of unsolved murders and disappearances in a city dependent on its image put an enormous amount of pressure on the police and the mayor to have the crimes solved.

In the second week in April, William Webster, the director of the FBI, made a statement at a news conference in Washington. Mr. Webster said that four of the twenty-three murders in Atlanta that were being investigated by the task force "were substantially solved" and were not related to the twelve to sixteen believed to have been done by one murderer. This took everyone in Atlanta by surprise. Mayor Jackson and Commissioner Brown protested, saying that they knew nothing about any of the murders having been solved. The committee knew no such thing either. The next day, Michael Twibell, an FBI agent in charge of the Athens, Georgia, office spoke to a civic group, endorsed Webster's statement, and went one step further. He said, "Some of those kids were killed by their parents" and offered as his theory of their motives that the children had been "nuisances." A storm of protest followed his speech once it had been picked up by the wire services. Brown and Jackson again protested, as did the committee. The members of the committee held a press conference on City Hall steps, and Camille read a telegram they had sent to Director Webster. In it they said that they weren't aware that FBI policy was coming out of central Georgia these days, but if it was and if there was evidence against some of the parents, then the FBI should make arrests immediately. If there was no evidence, the telegram went on, the committee expected an apology from the FBI within twenty-four hours.

The apology did not come, but a rather extraordinary semiapology came by mail shortly thereafter. The damage had been done, however. *Time* magazine had ended its story on the FBI statements (which it titled "A Break in the Investigation") by saying that its Atlanta chief did indeed find that three family members had been suspects. In the article it also said that "some of the twenty-three murdered were involved with adult homosexuals."

Though there appeared to be no collusion between the city administration and the FBI, the effect both of them had on the committee was the same. In the eyes of the casual observer, the reader of national newsweeklies, it appeared that the Atlanta murders were not necessarily connected, that perhaps some of the murders had been done by the parents themselves, and that the kids had been poor street kids ill-cared for by their parents.

There was little the committee could do to blunt such damaging press. Most of their rebuttals never made it past the local media. They were expected to be grief-stricken or angry at the unknown killer; when they stepped out of those roles, they were stepping out of the television lights and got little coverage. The suspicions cast by both the mayor and the FBI made them suspect to the reporters covering the murders and put them in the awkward position of having to defend themselves.

By the end of May, the investigation was at a standstill. The supercops were baffled and the Atlanta police had taken to staking-out areas around the city where they had found bodies in the past.

The list of murders that were under investigation by the task force was itself in for some scrutiny. Camille thought that some of the murders or disappearances on the list were only vaguely connected to the original ten or twelve murders. And she knew that there were some murders not being investigated by the task force that seemed to be more closely allied with the original murders than were some of those on the list. In January, the committee had fought with the police over the case of Terry Pue and finally had had his name added to the list. As summer approached in Atlanta, the cases that comprised what the entire country was calling the "Atlanta murders" were in fact a disputed series of possibly linked murders and disappearances.

One of the areas the police staked out was the Chattahoochee River. On the night of May 22, the police stopped a car as it drove over a bridge on the Chattahoochee. They questioned a young black man named Wayne Williams, searched his car, and, after several hours, let him drive on.

Two days after the bridge incident, the body of a twenty-seven-year-old man, Nathaniel Cater, was found downriver from the bridge where Wayne Williams had been stopped. Williams, a novice music producer and news photographer, was called in for questioning and then released. Two weeks later, there was speculation that the Atlanta district attorney, Lewis "Duke" Slaton, was going to charge Williams with the murder, but he said publicly that the case against Williams was too weak. It was then rumored that he met with Georgia governor William Busbee. Wayne Williams was soon charged with Nathaniel Cater's murder and the murder of Jimmy Ray Payne, twenty-two, who had also been found in the Chattahoochee.

The press, of course, shifted the entire focus of their reports to Wayne Williams. While he was being questioned before his arrest, Williams was so hounded by the press that he brought a lawsuit against the police for false accusations. Camille and members of the committee weren't making any public statements because they didn't know what evidence the police had, but they were, in private, saying that they couldn't believe the police had the right man.

In their investigation, the committee had heard Wayne Williams's name and had passed it on to the task force. But no one really believed he could be behind the killings. Camille could see that some other mothers suspected him, but she, after listening to the evidence against him, doubted very much that he had had anything to do with the murders, with any of them.

Wayne Williams was black, and so the much-speculated racial motive for the killings was dropped quickly. The only motive that made any sense to the press was one that might involve homosexuality. *Time* magazine, in reporting the arrest, raised the issue obliquely at the end of the article. Camille saw this as odd because in most of the twenty-three cases that were now being considered related there was absolutely no homosexual motive indicated. As in Yusuf's case, there had been some odd elements, such as the victim's clothes having been washed just before the murder, but there was no evidence that the murderer had molested the boys before killing them.

The police were basing their case against Williams on two major areas of evidence. First, there was the incident at the bridge. One policeman had heard water splash just before Williams drove across the bridge. The police theorized that Williams had thrown Nathaniel Cater's body into the river and had then run into the police roadblock. The other piece of evidence consisted of fibers found on the two bodies that matched fibers found on a blanket and a carpet in Williams's house.

This evidence came out slowly as the state prepared its case, indicted Williams, and then brought him to trial.

In the months before the trial, Camille became more and more convinced that Wayne Williams was innocent. There were other mothers who disagreed with her; some thought he was guilty of all the murders, others of only certain murders. But Camille, along with some of the mothers, saw Williams as as much a victim of the Atlanta murders as they were. She thought it preposterous for the police to claim that Williams had driven across a bridge, had hurled a body the same size as his own out the window of his car and over a bridge railing while in motion, and then had arrived at a police roadblock with his car empty of both the stench of a two-day-old body and the blanket in which the body had supposedly been wrapped, a blanket later found in his house. They thought that the fiber evidence was really no more than circumstantial. The rugs in the Williams house, from which the fibers supposedly came, were quite common, and the fiber mills for such rugs were upriver on the Chattahoochee. Bodies lying in the river could have picked up fibers floating downstream from the mills.

Before the trial, members of the Committee to Stop Children's Murders were not in a position to make statements about the arrest of Wayne Williams and for the most part they didn't. Wayne Williams's defense team, like the rest of the nation, assumed that the mothers believed the police had nabbed the right man.

Camille, however, was hoping someone on Williams's defense team would call and ask for help. She was looking for a way to make public her opposition to the arrest. When the trial was drawing near later in 1981, Camille went to Mary Welcome, Williams's lead lawyer, and volunteered to help in any way she could.

After two years of trying to find out who had killed her son, Camille realized how odd it would seem to some for her to volunteer to help the defense team of the man indicted for murders linked to Yusuf's. But to Camille there was no other choice. She did not believe Williams to be guilty of Yusuf's murder, and she could see that if he were convicted of the two murders he was charged with the investigation would most likely be closed immediately. In the months preceding the trial there had been indications to that effect. There had been no new additions to the list of murders and disappearances to be investigated by the task force, though the committee had learned of several that, before Williams's arrest, would certainly have been included. And shortly after Williams's arrest the task force offices became the headquarters for the whole homicide squad, though the task force still existed in name.

Camille refused to attend the trial. She referred to the proceedings as a "kangaroo court" and was especially displeased with the judge selected to hear the trial. He was a black man, Clarence Cooper, and reports said that he had been picked by a computer from all the available judges in Atlanta. But Camille knew that a computer had to be told what to look for. Judge Cooper was not the most experienced black judge available, in fact he was quite new to the job.

He had a lot of experience with the D.A.'s office, however, having worked under Lewis Slaton. Camille was not surprised when she heard that once during the trial Cooper had referred to Slaton as "boss."

The other reports Camille received from the courtroom were equally disturbing. Much was made of the possibility that Wayne Williams was a homosexual. The press found this an interesting angle and reported much of the trial testimony that touched on this point.

There were 197 witnesses in the three-month trial, which began early in 1982, and of those Camille had personal knowledge of a number of their original stories about the case and Wayne Williams. She was surprised on several occasions when the story someone had originally told her committee's investigators was changed by the time it came out in court.

For instance Darryl Davis, a fourteen-year-old, had come to the committee investigators and told them about two big men he had gotten into a car with who had made advances and given him money before he ran away from them. The investigators thought the information was important and passed Darryl on to the task force. When he testified in court, however, Darryl said he was certain that Wayne Williams was one of the men who had picked him up. To the committee Darryl had been certain that the two men were bigger than he was (about five-feet eight), but Wayne Williams was only five-foot seven and would hardly have appeared big to Darryl.

Camille was not surprised when Wayne Williams was convicted of both murders and given two life sentences. The death penalty had not been available in the case and Camille felt that made it easier for the jurors to bring in a guilty verdict. She also felt that pictures of kids with sweet-looking faces, like those of two victims—Patrick Balthazar and Lubie Geter—which were all over the newspapers, were in the minds of the jurors and contributed to the verdict. She didn't think a change of venue would have made much of a difference, either. There was no place in the country that hadn't been touched by the Atlanta murders.

As the verdict was returned, Camille went to the courthouse and gave her personal views on the trial to the media swarming outside on the steps. Some of what she said went out live and unedited on television. She said that she thought it was a shame that black judges and jurors had participated in the proceedings. "When they do it to us it's damnable, but when we do it to ourselves it's doubly damnable," she said.

After the trial the media packed up and went home, and the police closed the investigations of all the murders. When the police called to say that they were sending someone out to explain why Yusuf's case had been closed, Camille told them not to bother. Instead she went to police headquarters to talk to the new chief of police, Chief Redding. In the fall there had been a change in city government. Andrew Young was now mayor, Lee Brown had moved to Houston, and there had been several promotions in the police department. After Chief Redding gave his explanation, saying that the police were certain Wayne Williams had killed Yusuf, Camille let loose all her frustrations of the past half a year. She said that he was a liar and that he was too "sorry" to get out and solve the case. She left in a huff, knowing that the police were never going to make an effort to find out who killed her son.

In the nearly two years since she and Venus and Willie Mae had formed the Committee to Stop Children's Murders, Camille had come to understand much more about the serious danger to children in America. She had begun by thinking only poor and black children were the targets in society. But in going around the country to speak, she had met with parents of all races and classes whose children had disappeared. She found that no one really knew the number of children who disappeared each year, but the best estimate might be in the neighborhood of fifty thousand a year. There was a small city of children who had left home and never returned. Had fifty thousand redwoods died in one year, she thought, there would be an enormous outcry, but these children were missing and little was being done to find them. To her amazement, little was being done on a national level to coordinate the missing-child reports. Her conclusion was that there was a need for some sort of clearinghouse to which parents of missing children could turn to check their child's identity with those of children found throughout the country.

Other women in the committee shared Camille's conclusion. Most had moved from their immediate concerns to an understanding of a wider problem. They began to draw connections between obvious dangers such as unsafe streets and heroin use with less obvious dangers such as a poor education in a highly technological society.

But those concerns were, of course, less spectacular than their original ones, the ones that had attracted so much national attention. After Wayne Williams's arrest and trial, there was little hope that the earlier momentum of the organization could be maintained; operating funds were hard to find. The committee eventually organized under the name of Another Mother for Children, but the office had to be closed.

Camille's life changed radically after the trial. She was offered few forums in which to present her side of the Atlanta murders, and no national media came to ask her opinion. In the spring of 1982 she began to think that, not only was she being ignored, but that she might well be the target of an active campaign of harassment. Rocks were thrown against her apartment door, and she began staying up all night to watch the house. She would try to get sleep during the day, but the sleepless nights were beginning to wear her down. Two other mothers in the committee who had been vocal in their criticism of the Jackson administration, Venus Taylor and Annie Rogers, had sons slightly older than Jonathan who had recently been arrested on charges Camille thought were trumped up. When several neighbors mentioned that they had seen a man in the neighborhood who seemed to be tailing Jonathan, Camille decided it was time to leave Atlanta. Late in the spring she moved to Tallahassee, Florida, to live with friends there and to work in a women's health clinic.

Camille returned to Atlanta in the fall of 1982 for a week because investigators who had worked with the committee turned up a fifteen-year-old boy who said that he had witnessed the murder of one of the children on the task force list, Jo Jo Bell. Camille talked to the boy and tried to shake his story. He seemed to have details of the murder that had not been reported and could be checked by the police. He cried when Camille told him that he could be arrested for having withheld the information about the murder. He said he didn't care, that people on the street were saying that he was about to be killed anyway. He'd rather be in jail than dead. Camille left Atlanta believing his story but frustrated. The investigators, not trusting the Atlanta police, had taken their information to the Georgia Bureau of Investigation and the news media. Neither did anything with the testimony, and the young boy was not put in protective custody. Camille didn't have any idea whether or not the murderer named by the boy had anything to do with Yusuf's murder, but she could see clearly that as far as the police were concerned the Atlanta murders were closed cases.

In the three years since Yusuf had disappeared much had changed in Camille's life. Yusuf's disappearance and murder had, of course, been responsible for part of those changes. But perhaps just as much change had been caused by the fact that Yusuf's murder was still unsolved. Camille had come to see herself as someone who could, when injured, back off and not fight; but when she saw someone else being injured, she had to jump to the defense. When she had thought Yusuf's was an isolated murder she had backed off. With the formation of the committee, though, she had jumped into the fray. In her speaking around the country she had come in contact with many more people who had been injured. Wayne Williams's conviction solved nothing for her. Even as she left Atlanta she knew that she was not backing off and probably never would again.